RETHINKING CLASS

**LITERARY STUDIES AND
SOCIAL FORMATIONS**

For Joan Scott —
With admiration,
Wai Chee

D1115867

The Social Foundations of Aesthetic Forms Series
Jonathan Arac, Editor

The Social Foundations of Aesthetic Forms
A series of
COLUMBIA UNIVERSITY PRESS
Jonathan Arac, Editor

RETHINKING CLASS

LITERARY STUDIES AND
SOCIAL FORMATIONS

*Edited by Wai Chee Dimock
and Michael T. Gilmore*

COLUMBIA UNIVERSITY PRESS
NEW YORK

Columbia University Press

New York   Chichester, West Sussex

Library of Congress Cataloging-in-Publication Data

Rethinking Class   :   Literary studies and social formations / edited by
  Wai Chee Dimock and Michael T. Gilmore.
      p.   cm. — (The Social foundations of aesthetic forms)
  Includes bibliographical references and index.
  ISBN 0–231–07600–2
  ISBN 0–231–07601–0 (pbk.)
  1. Social classes in literature.   2. Marxist criticism.
3. Literature and society.   I. Dimock, Wai-Chee.
II. Gilmore, Michael T.   III. Series: Social foundations of
aesthetic forms series.
PN56.S64R48   1994
809'.93355—dc20   94–16980
                                                          CIP

Richard Brodhead, "Regionalism and the Upper Class" from *Cultures of Letters: Scenes of Reading and Writing in Nineteenth-Century America* by Richard Brodhead. Copyright (c) 1993 by Richard Brodhead. Reprinted by permission of University of Chicago Press.

Eric Lott, "White Kids and No Kids at All: Languages of Race in Antebellum U.S. Working-Class Culture" from *Love and Theft: Blackface Minstrelsy and the American Working Class* by Eric Lott. Copyright (c) 1993 by Eric Lott. Reprinted by permission of Oxford University Press, Inc.

Anne Janowitz, "Class and Literature: The Case of Romantic Chartism" from Stephen Copley, ed., *The Picturesque.* Copyright (c) 1993 by Anne Janowitz. Reprinted by permission of Cambridge University Press.

Printed in the United States of America

c 10 9 8 7 6 5 4 3 2 1
p 10 9 8 7 6 5 4 3 2 1

CONTENTS

ABOUT THE
CONTRIBUTORS

Richard H. Brodhead is Professor of English and Dean of the College at Yale University. His books include *The School of Hawthorne* (1986) and, most recently, *Cultures of Letters* (1993).

Wai Chee Dimock, Associate Professor of English at Brandeis University, is the author of *Empire for Liberty* (1989). Her new book, *Cognition and Justice,* is forthcoming.

Michael T. Gilmore, who teaches at Brandeis University, has written *American Romanticism and the Marketplace* (1985). He is a contributor to the *Cambridge History of American Literature* (1994).

John Guillory is Professor of English at the Johns Hopkins University. He is the author of *Poetic Authority* (1983) and *Cultural Capital* (1993).

Anne Janowitz is Associate Professor of English at Rutgers University. She is the author of *England's Ruins* (1990).

Amy Schrager Lang teaches in the Graduate Institute of the Liberal Arts at Emory University. She is the author of *Prophetic Woman* (1987).

Eric Lott is the author of *Love and Theft* (1993). He teaches American Studies at the University of Virginia.

Mary Poovey is Professor of English at the Johns Hopkins University. Among her books are *The Proper Lady and the Woman Writer* (1984) and *Uneven Developments* (1988).

RETHINKING CLASS

LITERARY STUDIES AND
SOCIAL FORMATIONS

INTRODUCTION

Wai Chee Dimock and Michael T. Gilmore

This collection of essays is an attempt to acknowledge, to fret over, and, if such a thing is possible, to enlarge upon the tremendous difficulties now facing the concept of class. For many, the imminent demise of Marxism, evidenced by the collapse of the Soviet Union and of Eurocommunism, would seem to mark the demise as well of "class" as a category of analysis. How can we continue to use the word with any sense of political efficacy, when its instrumental expression—"class struggle"—has ceased to be a vital historical force? And how can we continue to use the word with any sense of analytic authority, when the privileged subject of that analysis—the "working class"—has thus far shown no sign of being a privileged locus of agency, so that the vocabulary of class has come to seem no more than a flat description, a matter of taxonomy, shorn of the animating coloration of will and necessity, incipience and dialectic?

These questions are the irritant as well as the inspiration for the papers collected here. Mindful of the unprecedented crisis now facing Marxism, most of the contributors have approached class not as a self-evident concept, and not necessarily as a category of Marxist analysis, but rather as a conceptual hurdle of its own, a site of explanatory impasse, inviting us to rethink the premises of Marxism itself. Toward that end, some of us have tried to historicize class, foregrounding not only its cognitive environment but also its contextual associates, the company it kept at its moment of emergence. It is a concept with a genetic history of its own, we argue, a concept that came into being within a particular universe of discourse, under the exigencies of some particular circumstances, and carrying with it attendant premises and preoccupations, accents and ellipses. Class, in other words, is not (or at least not merely) a privileged analytic category here; it is itself an analyzable artifact, itself to be scrutinized, contextualized, critiqued for its commissions and omissions. In reminding ourselves of the historical provenance of the concept—in restoring to it a genealogy and a habitat— we hope, at the same time, to open up some space for ourselves, some critical distance from which we can take stock of a powerful idea without submitting completely to its inscribed epistemology. Our attempts at class analysis are therefore neither predicated on nor reducible to some universal determinant, neither predicated on nor reducible to the notion of a privileged historical subject. As we dispense with the security of a foundationalist epistemology, we look toward a hermeneutic that is not entirely arbitrary for being suspenseful, and not entirely pessimistic for being without guarantees, since the lack of certainty is not only the occasion for analysis but the occasion for hope.

What results, then, is a variety of explanatory methods more modest and more flexible than those traditionally called Marxist. The modesty comes from our sense that the boundaries of class are unstable, that the experience of it is uneven, that it is necessary but not sufficient for the constitution of human identities. And the flexibility comes from our desire to build on these limitations, to use the analytic inadequacy of "class" as a rallying point, a significant juncture from which to rethink concepts such as "identity," "explanation," and "determination." We are interested, that is, in the category of class less as an instance of "reality" than as an instance of the "made-real," less as an empiricial description of social groups than as a theoretical enterprise, an attempt to attach a cause and give a name to "something which in fact happens (and can be shown to have happened) in human relationships."[1]

Class, Anthony Giddens has argued (in a Weberian supplement to Marx), can be understood as a mediate relation between the economic and the noneconomic, as a mode of structuration, a set of constitutive relays linking economic identities with social identities.[2] Understood as such, as a relationally derived construct rather than a self-executing entity, the operations of class necessarily involve an entire spectrum of interdependent terms, whose mutually defining character is progressively obscured as social identities become "real"—become solid, integral, and perhaps even acquirable—to the point where they appear entirely objective and self-evident. What we have done, in some sense, is to disturb these objectivized realities, to reconstruct from their seemingly empirical surfaces some hypothetical generative process, and to speculate on the complex relations elided by identities grown unitary and transparent.

Our analytic universe is therefore one of acknowledged opacity. It is also one of contingent attribution. As objective identities give way to differential relations, and as integral terms give way to terms that are mutually (and sometimes multiply) defining, questions of cause and effect, of figure and ground, also become matters of interpretation, matters of uncertain conjecture. Class, some of us argue in this context, might turn out to be as much an effect as it is a cause, as much a second-degree register as it is a determinative ground. Whether it is indeed the deep structure—the controlling foundation of social identities and cultural forms—or whether it is something of an epiphenomenon itself, is an issue that remains unsettled in this volume, and that we have no wish to settle. If this weakens the explanatory power accorded class in orthodox Marxism, what is gained is a broader spectrum of permissible questions (not to mention imaginable conclusions). We are compelled, that is, to entertain a range of interactive relations—class and culture, class and race, class and gender—without making causality a one-directional phenomenon, and without attributing to the first term a determinative weight.

The possibility of a Marxism stripped of its absolutist claims and made assimilable to other structures of thought was proleptically contemplated by the Polish political theorist, Leszek Kolakowski, almost twenty-five years ago. Which part of Marxist thinking, he asked, can outlive the inescapable fading of communism as a political and economic system? (In 1968, the year Soviet forces crushed the Prague uprising, Kolakowski's question sounded as improbable as the revival of Marx seems today.) Kolakowski argues that as institutional Marxism collapses, Marxism as an autonomous doctrine would likewise disintegrate. It would endure, however, as a kind of intellectual accent or disposition, its legacy residing not so much in its unified position as in its continuing ability to energize certain areas of inquiry, to propel certain kinds of questions into the heuristic foreground.[3] Kolakowski's prophecy has in fact come to pass in the disciplines of philosophy, sociology, and history, where a reconceived and (to some degree) de-autonomized Marxism is very much alive and well. In particular, the difficulties facing the concept of class have generated the liveliest conversations. Questions of ideology and subjectivity, language and culture, autonomy and determination, gender and the family, have all been debated in this context, making class the most capacious as well as the most incendiary of topics.

Louis Althusser, with his disdain for teleology, and his almost comic incredulity directed at "the proletariat as the site and missionary of the human essence," has been a formidable critic, not only of that aspect of Marx he calls "historicist humanism," but also of an entire epistemology predicated on the idea of "historical necessity," even though he professes continual allegiance to "determination in the last instance by the economic."[4] He has thus inaugurated a major trend in contemporary sociology, a Marxism subtilized and recharged, which, especially in the work of Nicos Poulantzas, has labored to loosen up the deterministic character of class by appealing to such mitigating concepts as historical "conjunctures."[5] In a different setting,[6] however, Althusser might also be said to have precipitated a major crisis on the left, described by Ernesto Laclau and Chantal Mouffe in the opening pages of *Hegemony and Socialist Strategy*:

> What is now in crisis is a whole conception of socialism which rests upon the ontological centrality of the working class, upon the role of

the Revolution, with a capital "r," as the founding moment in the transition from one type of society to another, and upon the illusory prospect of a perfectly unitary and homogeneous collective will that will render pointless the moment of politics. The plural and multifarious character of contemporary social struggles has finally dissolved the last foundation for that political imaginary. Peopled with "universal" subjects and conceptually built around History in the singular, it has postulated "society" as an intelligible structure that could be intellectually mastered on the basis of certain class positions and reconstituted, as a rational, transparent order, through a founding act of a political character. Today, the left is witnessing the final act of the dissolution of that Jacobin imaginary.[7]

For Laclau and Mouffe, the epistemological ruins of Marxism are the grounds for an alternative democratic theory. Reworking Althusser's concept of overdetermination, they come up with what amounts to an *under*determined theory of "hegemony," with its conception of identity as at once unsaturated and overflowing, and its conception of the social as at once nonunitary and incomplete. Rejecting the idea of a working class propelled by objective interests inherent in their class position, Laclau and Mouffe argue instead for a nonessentialist political subjectivity, predicated on the noncoincidence between economic position and subject effect, and a contingent democratic politics, predicated on the nonexistence of absolute ends.

The cautions and precautions brought to bear on the concept of class by sociologists and political philosophers have shown up among historians as a shift in practice. Here, the evolution of class-oriented scholarship might be traced in roughly three stages since the 1960s. The first wave involved a departure from older institutional narratives of organized labor. Identified in England with Eric Hobsbawm and E. P. Thompson, and in the United States with David Montgomery and Herbert Gutman, among others, this first generation of revisionary historians give us a working class rendered surprisingly unfamiliar, primarily through their interest in areas of experience not previously considered class-specific or class-motivated. Turning away from trade unions, the traditional focus for labor historians, they concentrate instead on activities at once less rationalized and less obviously geared toward economic ends. They write about plebeian politics, spontaneous protests, outlaws and bandits, the persistence of preindustrial customs, religious beliefs, leisure and pastime. Still, it can be argued that, even though their work chips away at the primacy of the economic on the one hand, they remain committed, on the other hand, to a kind of class essentialism, an implicit belief that shared forms of life—whether cultural or political—stem from an anterior economic determination.[8]

A second wave of class-oriented historiography arose in the late 1970s and early 1980s to qualify and challenge this assumption. Two influential books reflecting this sea change are Sean Wilentz's *Chants Democratic: New York City and the Rise of the American Working Class, 1788–1850* (1984), and Gareth Stedman Jones's *Languages of Class: Studies in English Working Class History, 1832–1982* (1983). Wilentz urges historians to abandon the search for an American class consciousness comparable in its economic determinations to its European counterparts. He calls attention, instead, to an ideology of labor in America that was primarily political, rather than economic, one that expressed its opposition to capital in the vocabulary of radical republicanism. Stedman Jones, meanwhile, pushes matters even further by mounting a frontal attack on orthodox Marxist assumptions. Noting that Marx devised his theory of class from the English case, he disputes both the typicality of that example (Britain lacked the complications of race and ethnicity), and the assumption that discourse and politics are expressions of a prior economic reality. The English Chartists held a different, indeed an opposite view, and Stedman Jones insists on taking them seriously. He concludes that their grasp of their economic condition was determined by their politics, not the other way around. Like Wilentz's American workers, the Chartists spoke in the idiom of radicalism, but this language was hardly unique to nineteenth-century artisans. Radicalism had supplied "the vocabulary of grievance for a succession of political and social groups," including Country Tories in the late seventeenth century and American revolutionaries in the eighteenth.[9] Radicals saw the unequal distribution of political power as the cause of class privilege, and the Chartists thus staked their hopes on a political instrumentality—universal suffrage—to redress their economic grievances.

Clearly revisionary in their specific arguments, Wilentz and Jones remain attached to a general sense of the working class as a locus of shared interests, and as a more or less integral (not to say privileged) historical subject. It is this assumption that is implicitly qualified by a third trend in historiography, one very much in evidence by the late 1980s. Turning to the middle class as an equally legitimate object of study, this new social history also transforms, in the same gesture, the very terms of class analysis. Two major studies, one American, one English, dramatize the point: Mary P. Ryan's *Cradle of the Middle Class: The Family in Oneida County, New York, 1790–1865* (1981) and Leonore Davidoff and Catherine Hall's *Family Fortunes: Men and Women of the English Middle Class, 1780–1850* (1987). As the home joins the factory as the primary site of class formation—as the "cradle" within which the middle class performs its tasks of self-definition, self-improvement, and social reproduction—domesticity emerges as the vehicle as well as the tenor of class identity, and gender becomes as crucial to the making of classes as economic determinations. For literary critics such as Nancy Armstrong, what this entails is nothing less than an inversion of Marxist causality. In *Desire and Domestic Fiction* (1987), she argues that it was domestic novels, rather than modes of production, that structured middle-class development, and that it was the bourgeois woman, rather than the enterpreneurial man, that emerged as the first modern individual, commanding love and attention through her personal virtues, rather than through the aristocratic edicts of status and birth.

Gender, true to the urgings of Joan Wallach Scott, has indeed become a central category of historical analysis.[10] In the structural and relational space that it opens up, differentiation loses its naturalness, and identities become nothing if not problematic. In the context of class analysis, this brings into play not only an enlarged *area* of inquiry, but also a more refined *grid* of inquiry. And so, along with the rediscovery of the middle class, the working class too has been subjected to a scrutiny more nuanced, more intricately featured, and more respectful of internal differences. In important studies such as Thomas Dublin's *Women at Work: The Transformation of Work and Community in Lowell, Massachusetts, 1826–1860* (1979) and Christine Stansell's *City of Women: Sex and Class in New*

York, 1789–1860 (1987), the singular character of the working class is broken down into a pattern of gendered asymmetries, not only in the specific experience of industrialization and urbanization, but also, more generally, in the constitution (and possible transformation) of social identities. If this weakens the putative unity of class interests, what it puts in its place is the complex agency of class as a differential field: a field unevenly structured, with varying relays between the economic and the social, and therefore also with multiple points of action, and multiple registers of experiential effect. Dublin's and Stansell's upbeat conclusions about the conditional benefits for urbanized and industrialized women suggest the extent to which "history" and "necessity" might be imagined to be mutually contesting categories, and the extent to which indeterminacy and agency might count as epistemological allies.

Our volume is very much an offspring of these currents of thought, and tries, in turn, to make satisfying arguments out of a provoking conditionality. In the first section, "Historicizing Class," we dispute the analytic absolutism of class by contextualizing it, by framing it within a family of discourse, both antecendent to and contemporaneous with its moment of inception. Mary Poovey relates the concept to a history of classificatory thinking, a history that includes not only Karl Marx but also William Petty and Adam Smith, dominated not only by an emerging economic rationality but also by its complex borrowings from a Hobbesian political rationality and an "empirical" natural philosophy. Out of this genealogy (of which classical political economy and Marxist analysis are the twin heirs), the concept of class arises—at once a unit and an aggregate, at once a theoretically motivated construct and an objectively descriptive category—an epistemological confusion that continues to plague us today, and that, Poovey argues, partly accounts for the failure of Marxism to theorize about women. Wai Chee Dimock, linking Marxist materialism more generally to the Enlightenment, critiques what she calls its "metonymic" rationality, at work in its evidentiary logic and its inductive generalizations. Class for Marx is ultimately a generalized effect, she argues, generalized from the material integrity of the bodily subject. The concept is thus especially problematic in situations where "materiality," "generalizability" and "integrity" cannot be taken for granted. Using stories by Herman Melville and Rebecca Harding Davis, and letters and memoirs of women workers, she gives special emphasis to gender as a mediating relay, and challenges the explanatory adequacy of class by celebrating the limits of its generalizations.

In the second part, "The Cultures of Class," we test out some of the propositions set forth in part I, by breaking down the integrity of class into various internal differentials and various genetic histories. In a complex analysis of our contemporary situation, John Guillory takes the case of the "intellectuals" as an especially salient example of what *not* to assume about categoric identities. Noting our current obsession with the "political intellectual" (a figure condemned on the right and applauded on the left), he calls attention to a complex web of questions that fail to be addressed by such an automatic association (and equation) of those two terms. Rejecting this blanket attribution, Guillory argues that a rigorous conception of the intellectual can be developed only by looking at the division of labor between various cultural domains (between, say, the humanities and journalism, once kindred, now at odds), and only by sorting out the nonunitary articulations within a single category. This relational analysis, further developed by Richard H. Brodhead in the next essay, unsettles the categoric identity not only of a social group but also of a literary genre. In his provocative discussion of regionalism, Brodhead disputes our traditional view of it as a self-contained vernacular, and as a vernacular strictly analyzable in literary terms. He argues, to the contrary, that this apparently *literary* phenomenon must be seen also as a *social* process, as a web of relations activated by the cultural exertions of a self-conscious upper class. Regionalism came into being, he suggests, not only in differential relation to "high art," but also in companion relation to the vacation habits newly fashionable in the late nineteenth century, both being obligatory markers for a class anxious to be so constituted. For Brodhead, then, it is through the analytic agency of class that literature can be examined as a relational field. But class, too, in turn, can be subject to the same relational analysis, as Eric Lott shows in the next essay. In this exuberant account of working-class culture, an important supplement to Wilentz's, Lott argues that class consciousness was articulated partly through representations (and appropriations) of blackness. Class was *staged* through race, he suggests, blackface was a shorthand for class identity. And, as "the stale patter and bad puns and achieved grotesquerie kept sliding from racial burlesque into class affiliation," we are faced with a cultural field in which class and race can never again remain discrete terms.

In part III, "Class and Literary Analysis," we ask in what manner and to what effect might we invoke class as a literary category. Michael T. Gilmore takes up this challenge by focusing on the instabilities of the "middle class" as a way to think about the instabilities of a literary text, in this case, *The Scarlet Letter*. Hawthorne's personal politics notwithstanding, the novel is far from being a coherent transcript of class sympathies, for the "middle class" encoded here turns out to be not at all coherent. In an argument parallel to Lott's, Gilmore argues that class is complexly staged—staged through gender, on this occasion—to such an extent that it "threatens to come apart even as it comes into being," thus rendering problematic any assumptions about the integrity of the text. Working from the same premise, Anne Janowitz, in a passionate defense of Romanticism, argues against the genre-determinism that equates the lyric form with a universalized bourgeois subjectivity. She invokes class, then, as the possibility of contestation within a seemingly homogenized poetic medium. Making her case with Chartist poetry, she presents Romanticism itself as a nonintegral phenomenon, and urges us to "recover from the terrain of Burkean reaction the progressive and utopian aspects of tradition and community." In the concluding essay, Amy Schrager Lang returns to our initial (and polemical) point about the inadequacy of class as a category of analysis, an inadequacy she explores rather than laments. She is impressed, in fact, less by the pragmatic instrumentality of class than by its rhetorical substitutability. She speaks of it not as an autonomous category but only as a syntax—one among others— that makes up the language of social identity. Focusing on Elizabeth Stuart Phelps's *The Silent Partner*, she shows how the language of class is ceaselessly displaced, and how the operations of the novel cannot be understood apart from that displacement. With that thought, and with a renewed sense that there is really nothing obvious about class, no last word, no possibility that it will ever be adequate to what it purports to describe, but also no way to get rid of it, we hope we have managed to make the concept continually problematic and problematically indispensable.

NOTES

1. E. P. Thompson, Preface to *The Making of the English Working Class* (New York: Vintage, 1966), 9.

2. Anthony Giddens, *The Class Structure of the Advanced Societies*, 2d ed. (London: Hutchinson, 1980), 105.

3. Leszek Kolakowski, "Permanent vs. Transitory Aspects of Marxism," in *Towards a Marxist Humanism: Essays on the Left Today*, trans. Jane Zielonko Peel (New York: Grove Press, 1968), 173–87.

4. Louis Althusser, *For Marx* (London: New Left Books, 1977); Louis Althusser and Etienne Balibar, *Reading Capital* (London: New Left Books, 1970).

5. Nicos Poulantzas, *Political Power and Social Classes* (London: New Left Books, 1973); Nicos Poulantzas, *Classes in Contemporary Capitalism* (London: New Left Books, 1975).

6. For a well-known attack on Althusser, see E. P. Thompson, *The Poverty of Theory* (New York: Monthly Review Press, 1978).

7. Ernesto Laclau and Chantal Mouffe, *Hegemony and Socialist Strategy: Towards a Radical Democratic Politics* (London: Verso, 1985), 2.

8. Eric Hobsbawn, *Labouring Men* (London: Weidenfeld and Nicolson, 1964); E. P. Thompson, *The Making of the English Working Class* (New York: Vintage, 1966); David Montgomery, *Beyond Equality: Labor and the Radical Republicans, 1862–1872* (New York: Knopf, 1967); Herbert Gutman, *Work, Culture, and Society in Industrializing America: Essays in American Working-Class and Social History* (New York: Knopf, 1976).

9. Gareth Stedman Jones, *The Languages of Class: Studies in English Working-Class History, 1832–1982* (New York: Cambridge University Press, 1983), 102.

10. Joan Wallach Scott, "Gender: A Useful Category of Historical Analysis," *American Historical Review* 81 (1986):1053–75.

I HISTORICIZING CLASS

1 THE SOCIAL CONSTITUTION OF "CLASS"

TOWARD A HISTORY OF CLASSIFICATORY THINKING

Mary Poovey

In this essay, I offer some observations about two phases in the history of classificatory thinking as a means of illuminating the discursive matrix that preexisted and made possible the Marxist category of class.[1] Because the two episodes I examine here predate Marx and the formation of the capitalist-industrial society with which the Marxist usage of "class" is historically associated,[2] I may seem to be taking a position in the debate about what the term *class* describes—about whether it refers to an objective set of material conditions (or relations) that can be observed in every modern society, or to a mode of understanding or articulating one's place in a social hierarchy, which only became available in the nineteenth century.[3] Rather than engaging in this controversy, however, I am actually suggesting that we set aside the reflection model upon which this debate is based in favor of a paradigm that emphasizes the social constitution of the terms in which the debate has been conducted. This will lead us away from questions about what "class" describes and toward an investigation of the history of classificatory thinking and the assumptions frequently carried over in subsequent deployments of class analysis.

"Classificatory thinking" is an awkward phrase, and I use it only for lack of a better. By "classificatory thinking" I mean to designate an epistemology that was gradually consolidated in the late seventeenth century and elaborated during the course of the next two centuries alongside, and in a complex relationship to, the development of the material conditions we generally associate with "class." Classificatory thinking combined two modes of understanding the natural and social worlds. The first, which dates back to Aristotle and finds its characteristic modern form in taxonomy, makes sense of the discrete particulars of the world by grouping them into categories (or classes) that foreground and isolate a single feature or group of features as definitive. The second, whose origin is probably equally ancient, conceptualizes "value" in terms of features that can be quantified, then commodified.[4] When these two modes of understanding were brought together under the particular conditions of seventeenth-century England, they provided the terms for some of the characteristic concepts of modern Western societies—including the notions that quantity is more important than quality and that some kinds of activities are more "productive" (hence both more valuable and significant) than others.

As this description suggests, classificatory thinking is related to the notion of instrumental rationality, by which writers like Weber and Horkheimer have characterized modernity. In this essay, however, I want to maintain a distinction between classificatory thinking and instrumental rationality in order to achieve a greater level of historical specificity than is sometimes produced. In the articulations of classificatory thinking I discuss here, which involve theories of economic behavior, "rationality" is an issue, but the meaning it most often carries is not quite Horkheimer's idea of a scientific rationality enlisted in the service of a fully developed capitalism. Instead, the model of rationality I examine hovers somewhere between the purely theoretical (and for *that* reason orderly and self-consistent) schema associated in the seventeenth century with Hobbes, and the (theoretically) descriptive schema, associated with Bacon, that claimed to derive its order from the orderly world it simply describes. As we will see, the tension between theory and description is one of the characteristic features of the mode of thinking with which I am concerned.[5] This tension was so prominent, especially in the late seventeenth century, both because neither capitalism nor science had yet to achieve their modern forms and because information about these formations was still rudimentary and unsystematic. As a consequence, it was not always clear whether the knowledge produced about financial transactions and natural phenomenon was speculative or descriptive. This situation was further complicated by the fact that, as the extent and kind of information available about the world changed, so too did the relative prestige granted to theory and empiricism.

In order to describe the epistemological developments of this period, then, it seems helpful to distinguish among kinds of rationality.[6] I will call the form of rationality associated in the seventeenth century with theory and with Hobbes political rationality, and the kind of rationality associated with Bacon and the emergent notion of objectivity scientific rationality. My focus here is on a kind of rationality that borrowed from each of these but that coincided with neither. Economic rationality retained vestiges of political rationality at the same time that it repeated many of the claims of experimental science (or natural philosophy). Whereas political rationality was articulated as an attempt to secure the power of a sovereign government and scientific rationality was codified in order to delineate a realm outside of politics, economic rationality was formulated to make sense of the relationship central to the emergent civil society of the late seventeenth century—that between individual productivity and national prosperity. To do so, early theorists of economic rationality adopted some of the claims advanced by theorists of political rationality but abandoned the latter's emphasis on sovereignty; at the same time, they borrowed the claims about "disinterest" and objectivity that natural philosophers made without duplicating the experimental procedures that came to characterize science. As nascent economists like William Petty moved toward more fully articulated theories of individual productivity, like those formulated by Adam Smith, in other words, they invoked the claims advanced by natural philosophers in order to lend prestige to a political theory that purported simply to describe a realm of behavior that was outside of politics but within nature.

What I am decribing in this essay, then, is a phase in the development of instrumental rationality as well as a phase in the development of class analysis. More precisely, my contention is that the classificatory thinking that developed in England in the seventeenth century was *not* intended simply to describe the material conditions of English society (as a discourse modeled more specifically after scientific rationality might have done) but also to contribute to discussions about how any ruler could govern in the wake of the radical challenge to sovereignty posed by the events of the 1640s. As such, early classificatory thinking was a polemical alternative to the paradigm by which social divisions were most frequently conceptualized in this period, a paradigm that emphasized religious and political affiliations. In order to legitimize their interpretive intervention, however, these same theorists invoked the language of scientific rationality; they claimed to represent social groups by criteria that were "rational" because they could be quantified *in specific contrast* to other descriptions that emphasized features considered "irrational" because so fraught with passionate investments as to provoke controversy and civil unrest.

I am not suggesting that the new interpretive paradigm was simply interpretive or completely unrelated to the massive reorganization of material conditions and social relations encapsulated by the phrase "the rise of capitalism." Indeed, I am arguing that the same social conditions that facilitated the formation of the groups Marx called "classes" also underwrote the emergence of classificatory thinking. By the end of this essay, moreover, it should be clear that the classificatory epistemology whose early manifestations were a proto-, then a fully articulated, economic rationality also produced, by the end of the eighteenth century, two distinct forms of self-commentary or analysis. One of these, which is epitomized by Ricardian political economy, I will call the ideological form, since it effaced altogether the constitutive role of theory and took the observations offered by economists as objective, scientific descriptions of natural phenomenon.[7] The other, which culminated in the work of Karl Marx, I will call the critical or analytical form, because it focused on the vestiges of political rationality that persisted in economic rationality. Thus, political economists presented the "classes" that Petty knew to be the effects of his interpretive intervention as the natural units of production in a "modern" society, and critical analysts (Marxists) took the formation of "classes"—if not classificatory terminology itself—as the object that required analysis.

The single origin of what were eventually articulated as two distinct modes of analysis also left its mark on another effect of classificatory thinking, which has long bedeviled critics intent upon using the second form without mobilizing the first. In general terms, this effect was produced by the persistence, in both political economy and Marxist critique of the same unexamined overlap between theory (or interpretation) and description that characterized their common ancestor. The tension that persisted between theory and description means that each mode of analysis excluded (and often continues to exclude) some element of the universe it purported to describe because this phenomenon does not conform to the theoretical assumptions that govern the analysis. For both political economy and Marxist analysis, one component that could not be accommodated by the theory that passed as description was female labor. Because women were assumed to belong to nature, their labor seemed to defy rational organization and analysis. Yet because these modes of analysis also depicted women's labor as central—indeed, as constitutive of what produces "value" in every sense—that which each theory excluded also functioned as the ground of its possibility.[8]

The two phases of classificatory thinking that I examine in this essay include William Petty's various attempts to address the "problem" of Ireland in the second half of the seventeenth century and Adam Smith's reworking of moral philosophy between 1759 and 1776. I hope it will be clear from what follows that I am not claiming a simplistic causal relationship between Petty's ideas and those of Adam Smith and that I am not suggesting that these two writers made the only significant contributions to classificatory thinking before Marx.[9] Instead, I suggest that Petty and Smith constitute symptomatic figures in this history—the first because he shows how rudimentary classificatory thinking initially (and repeatedly) vied with other interpretations of social differentiation; the second because he demonstrates how, even after it was codified in the putatively "scientific" discourse of political economy, classificatory thinking reproduced *as inequalities* the social differentiations it purported simply to describe.

THE MAPPING OF IRELAND AND THE
CREATION OF POLITICAL ARITHMETIC

In 1654, William Petty, professor of music at Gresham College and physician to Cromwell's victorious New Model Army in Ireland, petitioned to take over the mammoth project of surveying the confiscated land of the newly conquered country.[10] This project, which was already under way, had to be completed expeditiously because Cromwell wanted to disband his fractious troops but could not do so until the land that had been promised the soldiers was divided into equitable lots. William Petty received permission to take over what had become known as the Down Survey because he promised to map the army's portion of the confiscated land in thirteen months. Against all odds, and with only a slight extension, Petty completed the Down Survey in 1655.[11]

Petty's mapping of Ireland, which can be read as an early attempt to implement classificatory thinking, highlights two features that continued to characterize this epistemology. The first is the disavowed but nonetheless pronounced political nature of classificatory thinking: from the seventeenth century, classificatory thinking was implicated in a series of highly politicized practices that included (but was not limited to) the brutal subjugation of one population by another. The second, related feature is the overlap—and tension—between an underlying theoretical schema and a language that emphasized the rational and "objective" nature of the procedures. This language simultaneously masked the political agenda legitimized by the theory and generated, alongside the theory's ordering principles, an impression of totality and objectivity. This impression could never be rendered completely convincing, however, precisely because of the interpretive element in what was presented as pure description. In the Down Survey, this constitutive gap within classificatory thinking shows up in Petty's inability to carry out both parts of his assignment successfully. That is, Petty succeeded in creating a descriptive map of Ireland, but as soon as he imposed upon this description the interpretive system necessary to commodify the land, he provoked exactly the kind of controversy he aimed to foreclose.

The tension between description and theory is evident in every facet of the Down Survey. On the one hand, Petty's method aimed to produce the most exact description possible. Setting aside the conventional approach of the estate surveyor, Petty trained common soldiers each to carry out a single part of the surveying process or to make a single part of an instrument.[12] He sent these soldiers, along with their supervisors and recorders, into every part of the confiscated areas, so that all the details were obtained by exact, on-the-spot measurement with the most sophisticated equipment available. On the other hand, however, this procedure not only embodied but also imposed a theory of political rationality upon Ireland, for one goal of Petty's cartography was to create a series of uniform representations that would enable the English government to tax the Irish in a rational manner. Some such standardization was necessary for taxation because, prior to 1654, the subdivision of some areas into ploughlands, others into tates, bullibos, or bullibellas, had made tax assessment and collection in Ireland nearly impossible.[13]

Petty's assignment embodied elements of political rationality not only because his maps imposed an improved and more equitable system for English taxation, but also because the Down Survey was explicitly intended as an instrument of religious and political repression. As such, it was designed to strengthen the protestant English government at the expense of the Catholic Old English.[14] Because the redrawing of the estate boundaries was essential to Cromwell's punishment of the rebellious Catholics and because the reassignment of land was crucial to the financing of the war, Petty was also asked to assign monetary values to the confiscated land so that it could be transferred to the soldiers. To accomplish this part of his task, Petty assigned cadastral boundaries not simply in relation to the natural features of the landscape but also according to the distinction between "profitable" and "unprofitable" kinds of land. Inevitably, imposing this distinction onto his descriptive project created problems for those who tried to carry it out. As surveyors sought some basis for greater accuracy in their assessments, the simple opposition between "profitable" and "unprofitable" proliferated subsidiary categories. "Profitable" became "arable, meadow, and pasture," and "unprofitable" became "wood, bog, and mountaines." This subdivision simultaneously demonstrated that "profitable" was not simply a category of measurement based on extent and scarcity and exposed the project's governing assumptions about the proper relationship between Ireland and England. To call a "wood" or a "mountaine" "unprofitable," after all, was to ignore the fact that the abundant timber and ore were potentially two of Ireland's most salable resources. By the same token, to call only "arable, meadow, and pasture" land "profitable" was to assume that some commitment on the part of profiteers to residence and to agriculture (whether tillage or pasturage) was necessary if Ireland was to constitute a permanent, self-supporting, and tractable English colony.

Predictably, once the land was subjected to this interpretive schema, disputes also flared about the meaning of Petty's central terms. The tension that results from superimposing theoretical concepts onto a descriptive and quantitative project are clear in the "patheticall" report submitted by two of Petty's surveyors, who had been charged with incompetence by disgruntled soldiers. "We can very well justifie quantities," lamented surveyors Smith and Humphreys, "but as for the quality of land wee had noe rule to walke by, only as aforesaid, but did according to the best of our judgements, and the best information wee could get." "Either must the Act admitt of some interpretation of the words profitable and unprofitable," the harassed surveyors concluded, "or else there is very little unprofitable land in Ireland, if any; for that is only barren that beares nothing, or that only unprofitable which is good for nothing" (*Down*, 97, 98).

What Smith and Humphrey's report reveals is that the interpretive schema by which Petty tried to appropriate land for the English government's use imposed a theory about value and desire that superceded the ostensible goal of objective description. According to this theory, what makes land "valuable" is its capacity to produce (a certain kind of) exchangeable products; what renders these products "valuable" is the fact that other people want them; and what makes other people want these products is a model of desire that renders the craving for (some) products "rational" while other kinds of desire are marginalized or dismissed. The normalization inherent in each step of this logic is signaled by the use of money as the single, universal equivalent that signifies value and (eventually) becomes itself an object of (rational) desire. In this circular logic, in other words, only when value is constituted in terms of possession of some finite and desirable resource will all individuals want the same thing; and only when other kinds of desire are dismissed as "irrational" will one finite resource be considered the only source of value. That the kind of value implied by commodification also enhanced the control of the English government over the Irish people reinforced the notion that this was the "natural" meaning of value. Even though commodification was naturalized (for some), however, not all of its effects were as rational as the classificatory scheme that underwrote it. Desire for the land whose commodification as "property" gave it a single kind of value generated envy, not only because greed does not know the same limits as do natural resources but also because the very rewriting by which all subjects were constituted as desiring the same thing necessarily made them rivals. William Petty learned this the hard way—when he found himself repeatedly charged with profiting unfairly from his surveying work.

The most serious of these complaints was a charge of treason, which was brought against Petty by Sir Jerome Sankey in 1659. The case came to trial in Parliament in April of that year, but the proceedings were interrupted before the end of the month because England itself had descended into irrationality: in the confusion surrounding Richard Cromwell's fall, Parliament was dissolved and the nation nearly succumbed to anarchy. In April 1660 a semblance of order was achieved when the monarchy was restored, but, not surprisingly, some issues left unresolved in 1659 remained so. Among these was the charge against Petty, which was simply never brought before Parliament again. Far from being grateful for a fortuitous reprieve, however, Petty was upset because he had been deprived of what he considered his due: a chance to defend his survey publicly as a fair and rational solution to the problem of the Irish. In order to address the problem of irrationality once more, then, Petty composed two defenses of the survey. In both the *History of the Down Survey* and the more vituperative "Reflections Upon Some Persons and Things in Ireland," Petty pleaded for a return to a rational system of law anchored in a principle of just financial compensation. "I desire all now in power," he declaimed, "especially such who, as I had, have the dispensing of benefits to multitudes, by way of antidote to themselves, to procure a fair hearing of Sir Hierome's articles, as also of my services and sufferings in Ireland, that I or my adversaries may be repaired or punished according to our respective demerits."[15]

Even if Petty's written defenses were inadequate substitutes for the juridical procedure he desired, his accounts of his efforts in Ireland were logical extensions of the mapping project itself, both because they sought to impose order where "irrationality" had once reigned and because they displaced one history of Ireland—that which the Celts or even the Old English might have told—with another—the history of Petty in Ireland. Like the imposition upon Ireland of English place names and assumptions about value and property, Petty's defenses constitute polemical interpretations designed to enhance the power of those institutions that strengthened the English government. In this sense, the defenses are examples of what Michel de Certeau calls "writing that conquers": they erased one version of Ireland's history so as to secure the sovereignty of the conqueror by emphasizing the rationality of the victory.[16] Thus, Petty's defenses helped displace the civil contests that could not be rationalized with a contest that epitomized the version of rationality Petty had in mind because it emphasized something that could be quantified—labor and money. Petty's defenses, in other words, represented the history of struggles over and in Ireland as the story of a man who received just compensation for doing his job only to be challenged by others who "envy [his] wages." Even though such greed was understandable, even according to Petty's interpretation, his detractors soon tested the limits of Petty's belief that wanting more was rational. When Petty's detractors accused *him* of distorting their actions to get more land for themselves, Petty was reduced to representing their accusations as fantastic and to characterizing their descriptions of him as signs of the mania they suffered. To those who contested his cartographic evaluations, Petty explains in his *History*,

> the Dr himself . . . came to bee esteemed the . . . evil angell of the nation. . . . Hee became the Robin Goodfellow and Oberon of the countrey; for, as hitherfore domestique servants in the countrey did sett on foot the opinion of Robin Goodfellow and the ffaries, that when themselves had stolen junkets, they might accuse Robin Goodfellow for itt . . . in the same manner severall of the agents of the army, when they could not give a good accompt to those that

entrusted them, to say Dr Petty was the cause of the miscarriage was a ready and credible excuse. (*Down*, 209)

Although Petty was never able to silence his accusers or to settle all of the contests over the Down Survey, he soon redoubled his effort to strengthen the sovereignty of the English government. After the Restoration, Petty composed a series of economic treatises designed to apply his version of political rationality to government. Petty's desire to counter the obscure alliances and machinations by which political decisions were made led him to adopt another version of the form of rationality that was increasingly associated with natural philosophy and with Baconian empiricism in particular. In the introduction to his *Political Arithmetick*, Petty set out his claims for this mode of representation:

> The Method I [employ] is not yet very usual; for instead of using only comparative and superlative Words, and intellectual Arguments, I have taken the course (as a Specimen of the Political Arithmetick I have long aimed at) to express my self in Terms of *Number*, *Weight*, or *Measure*; to use only Arguments of Sense, and to consider only such Causes, as have visible Foundations in Nature; leaving those that depend upon the mutable Minds, Opinions, Appetites, and Passions of particular Men, to the Consideration of others. (*Economic Writings*, I:244).

The "visible Foundations in Nature" to which Petty appealed were offered as a counter both to politics, which had become even more impenetrable and unpredictable under Charles II,[17] and to the ornamental rhetoric with which politics, scholastic disputes, and religious controversies were associated. Even though Petty advocated the Baconian method of political arithmetic because he hoped to base political decisions on something that seemed indisputable because visible and quantifiable, what he ultimately sought to quantify was an abstraction—the conceptual entity that we have come to call the "economy."[18] In a process I can only sketch here, Petty reified and elaborated this abstraction in such a way as to make the idea of an autonomous fiscal realm address both the problematic relation that Ireland continued to bear to England and the problems of England's own political turmoil. On the one hand, conceptualizing an "economy" as the feature that characterized and constituted the "value" of a "nation" depicted the proper relationship between Ireland and England as a financial relationship, whose "health" could be measured by entities that could be translated into the quantifiable, universal equivalent of money and whose robustness would benefit—and further consolidate the alliance between—the two countries. On the other hand, imagining an "economy" as something that was composed of but transcended all the discrete particulars that could be counted enabled Petty to evade the problems otherwise created by the fact that technologies capable of gathering and storing comprehensive information did not exist. At the same time, this imaginary entity confirmed the impression, also promoted by experimental natural philosophy, that "objectivity" distinguishes the unbiased, "disinterested" observer's report of things as they are from the "irrational," because "interested" accounts offered by contemporaries who wanted to advocate one position or another.

I will return in the next section to the concept of "disinterestedness." For now, it is important to stress the element of political rationality that persists in Petty's ostensibly arithmetic and descriptive analysis. Petty's political arithmetic was specifically designed to enhance the monarch's security against competing claims. To ensure the control of the king, Petty argued, it was important to devise some system by which the monarch could know the resources of his own people. Such knowledge, in theory at least, would ensure civil peace because it would spare individuals the "vexation" and envy that Petty represents as the primary causes of England's civil war. "Ignorance of the Number, Trade, and Wealth of the people, is often the reason why the said people are needlessly troubled, *viz.* with the double charge and vexation of two, or many Levies, when one might have served. . . . Besides, for not knowing the Wealth of the people, the Prince knows not what they can bear; and for not knowing the Trade, he can make no Judgment of the proper season when to demand his Exhibitions" (*Economic Writings* I:34). If obtaining reliable descriptions of production will underwrite fair taxation (and civil order), then accurate tax records will generate more knowledge about the people and promote more cost-effective government policies. Thus Petty claims that better government tax records will decrease the number of lawsuits and therefore the number of lawyers in the country; improved bills of mortality will enable the government to regulate the number of medical men; better bank records will indicate how many merchants and retailers are necessary. All of these measures are designed to eliminate what Petty considers the "unproductive" elements of the fiscal system—those individuals who take money from the nation without producing any goods. Among these, Petty also numbered the politicians whose intrigues were leeching the "productive" lifeblood of the country. Petty explains: "Upon these grounds [accurate records] I presume a large proportion of these also might be retrenched, who properly and originally earn nothing from the Publick, being onely a kinde of Gamesters, that play with one another for the labours of the poor; yielding of themselves no fruit at all, otherwise then as veins and arteries, to distribute forth and back the blood and nutritive juyces of the Body Politick, namely, the product of Husbandry and Manufacture" (*Economic Writings* I:28).

We can begin to see here how Petty is pushing the political rationality associated with Hobbes toward a nascent economic rationality, in which the individual's contribution to national productivity will be foregrounded.[19] If unproductive "Gamesters" can be "retrenched" by a centralized apparatus for gathering and managing information, then the "economy" as a whole can be rendered more rational—hence, according to Petty, more productive. Enhancing economic rationality, however, requires more than eliminating unnecessary politicians and lawyers. Indeed, it also requires more than keeping accurate records and ensuring equitable taxation. According to Petty, enhancing economic productivity entails concentrating and maximizing the nation's most important fiscal resource, its people. In his proposals for managing human resources, Petty reveals that his political arithmetic was not merely a more accurate system for describing what exists. Despite his attempts to distance political arithmetic from "interested" theories, this mode of analysis was like the Down Survey in imposing upon existing conditions a (politicized and interpretive) program that forcefully manipulated the lives of the individuals it purported to describe. In order to facilitate the king's efforts to gather information and collect taxes, Petty argued, the population had to be concentrated in a relatively small geographical area. Such concentration would also decrease the costs of government service, bureaucracy, and the transportation of goods. In order to increase the sovereign's power, he continued, the population should be made to increase more rapidly, for a larger population would provide more workers to cultivate the land, develop manufactures, and pay taxes. Although they had clear implications for England as well, Petty presented his ideas about the population in relation to Ireland, for the problems of sparse population and costly government oversight were greatest in this country. Petty's plan, as it was worked out in the *Political Anatomy of Ireland* and then in the unfinished *A Treatise of Ireland*, promised to solve all of Ireland's and England's problems at once. It would overcome the differences between the two peoples by bringing them into the same economic unit; concentrate a tractable and productive population in England; and maximize the resources, both agricultural and human, of fertile Ireland. In its initial version, this plan entailed forcibly transporting 200,000 Irish individuals to England. As Petty's scheme became more elaborate, the number grew, until it reached one million by 1687.

In order to make his plan seem both palatable and feasible, Petty rewrote the Irish population. Just as he had displaced Gaelic history with his maps and his accounts of his own labor, so he displaced the distinctions by which the Irish had traditionally been divided with a new system of classification. The distinctive feature of this classificatory scheme, which constitutes Petty's closest approach to what would be formulated in the nineteenth century as a system of classes, is that the single characteristic it isolates and makes definitive is the individual's relationship to economic productivity.

> We shall consider the Present Inhabitants of Ireland, not as old Irish, or such as lived there about 516 Years ago, when the English first medled in that Matter; Nor as those that have been added since, and who went into Ireland between the first Invasion and the Change of Religion; Nor as the English who went thither between the said Change, and the Year 1641, or between 1641 and 1660; Much less, into Protestants and Papists, and such who speak English, and such who despise it.
>
> But rather consider them
> 1. As such as live upon the King's Pay.

2. As owners of Lands and Freeholds.
3. As Tenants and Lessees to the Lands of others.
4. As Workmen and Labourers. (*Economic Writings* II:561–62)

Rewriting the Irish in terms of their relation to the (agricultural) mode of production enables Petty to present his solution as a series of rational (because quantifiable) calculations. Because every individual is now defined exclusively by his relation to production, every individual can be measured according to the same universal equivalent by which the "productivity" of land is quantified. The enabling condition of the universal equivalent, as we have already seen, is the reduction of the variety of human desires to a single desire for the same thing. According to this revision, religious preference, culture, language, and political affiliation are reduced to versions of what Petty calls "Perverseness of Humor." After this revision, every Irish individual can be represented as wanting to be (like) the normal Englishman. Petty's transportation scheme both recognizes and brings to its logical conclusion this conceptual revision. Moving the Irish to England will presumably complete the project of obliterating "all old Animosities," which was initiated by Petty's mapping and continued by political arithmetic, because the transformed Irish will be glad to be "ingrafted and incorporated into a Nation more Rich, Populous, Splendid, and Renowned." "More pleasant and profitable Imployments" and the "greater Variety of agreeable Objects and Exercises" will convince the Irish to labor for what will then be their country, just as the political arithmetic by which national prosperity is measured and made known will encourage the English to work harder for the richer nation that an expanded population will produce (*Economic Writings* II:578).

By substituting one set of classificatory terms for another, Petty transforms all men—Irish and English alike—into instances of what Adam Smith will call *homo economicus*. In so doing, of course, Petty was drawing upon both the importance that capital played in a trading nation and the proprietary conceptualization of the land, which was already available in England.[20] My point is neither that Petty conjured from thin air the idea of subsuming other differentiations into a classificatory scheme based on quantifiable productivity nor that the representation set out most starkly in the *Treatise of Ireland* misrepresented existing social relations. Instead, I am suggesting that such a rationalized—and rationalizing—system of representation that emphasizes the quantifiability and commodification of men and objects was only one of the available modes of conceptualizing society. Other government officials—among them John Locke—seemed at least as concerned with representational paradigms that addressed questions about legitimacy as those that foregrounded quantification or economic productivity.[21] Read as a contribution to debates about legitimacy and authority, Petty's formulation seems to take the long way round, but read in the context of the role that Ireland played in exacerbating and encapsulating the problems raised in these debates, Petty's use of Baconian empiricism to authorize commodification and to mask the role that Petty's own assumptions played in his work can be seen as a real alternative to what he considered the more obviously theoretical "intellectual Arguments" deployed by disputacious English philosophers.

As he elaborated the various facets of his project, Petty exposed another paradox of classificatory thinking that persisted in its later incarnations. This paradox was an effect of Petty's effort both to efface the kind of differentiations that had promoted controversy and intrigue in the first place and to incorporate into the image of the social body all versions of human productivity. On the one hand, Petty's classificatory system effaced the differences among (and within) individuals, so that one person was interchangeable for another, every individual desired the same thing, and the value of a person could be written in monetary terms. On the other hand, however, Petty's model of national productivity required the maximization of all resources, and *this* mandated the recognition of at least one form of difference whose mode of productivity resisted the kind of rationality associated with quantification. This was the difference of sex.

In most of his writing, Petty simply effaces sexed difference along with religion, ethnicity, and language. Every time Petty calculates the "value of a Person," for example, he simply assumes that the normative "person" is an adult, laboring male.[22] While the effacement of sex supports Petty's effort to devise a rational, because quantitative, system of representation, however, it does not support the end that this representational system was developed to serve. For, according to the mercantilist philosophy that Petty advocated, population growth—what Petty called the "multiplication of Mankind"—was crucial both to economic productivity and to national security. Because human reproduction most visibly depends on the female body, Petty's attempts to bring this form of production into his rationalized model all focused on women. Once more, these schemes were all developed specifically in relation to Irish women, both because the Irish woman—like Ireland itself—was considered an "animal" fit for experimentation[23] and because the problem of (scant) population was most acute in this war-ravaged country. Many of Petty's writings on the population problem have disappeared, but in an unfinished essay that survives, he details how female productivity could be increased in Ireland if only the government would apply to women the rational and punitive measures by which the Down Survey (theoretically) managed the land. According to this plan, "teeming" women would be penalized if they did not give birth once every three years; marriage contracts would be dissolved if conception did not occur within six months of the union; women over forty-five would be prohibited from "using" men unless younger women were "provided"; and monetary incentives would be offered to women who gave birth to three children in three years or to ten, fifteen, or twenty children altogether.[24]

Petty's plan to rationalize human breeding constitutes the logical conclusion of that process of abstraction by which both the "economy" and the "person" were conceptualized in the first place, for this scheme reduces individual women to instances of the same, each of which is defined by the single function that gives her monetary "value." When applied to reproduction, however, this logic generates a constitutive contradiction. For, at the same time that classificatory thinking erases difference in order to render every individual an instance of the same, value-producing entity, it also retains (sexed) difference as the origin of the human beings who ultimately produce value through their labor. This logic also assigns a contradictory position to women. On the one hand, a woman only becomes a "person" amenable to this representational scheme when she is abstracted, so as to be reduced to the function that gives her value. On the other hand, however, because the process of abstraction to which both she and her male counterpart submit is intended to rationalize productivity, reducing the woman to her reproductive function also excludes her from the representational model this abstraction serves. Despite his suggestions for rationalizing breeding, that is, Petty's comments about reproduction suggest that even he considered the reproductive female body to be like nature itself—irrational and therefore ungovernable.

Unlike the Down Survey, Petty's plan to rationalize female productivity was never implemented, not only because the transportation scheme that would have converted Ireland into a giant dairy and baby farm was too controversial, but also because James II's appetite for profit never completely conquered his passion for political and religious intrigue. But if Petty's fantasy about maximizing human reproduction did not capture contemporaries' imaginations, many of the classificatory procedures he set out in his economic writings were institutionalized in the decades after his death. The improved systems of record keeping, tax collection, and fiscal management that accompanied, facilitated, and were further enhanced by the establishment of the Bank of England, the Stock Exchange, and the national debt were not, of course, developed primarily to "solve" the Irish problem. Nor were they specifically intended to counteract the divisiveness occasioned by political and religious sectarianism. In retrospect, it may seem ironic that the rationalized scheme of classificatory logic by which one minor government functionary sought to enhance the monarch's authority and the nation's wealth provided the terms by which a civil society capable of challenging that authority could emerge in the early eighteenth century. In the long run of history, however, such unintended effects often prove more consequential than the best laid plans of the most rational men.

FROM POLITICAL ARITHMETIC TO POLITICAL ECONOMY

In many respects, Adam Smith's *Wealth of Nations* belongs to a different conceptual universe than Petty's writings on Ireland and the economy. Not only was Smith not concerned with Ireland or religious controversy, but he neither supported mercantilist policy nor believed that the economic transactions of a nation could be known or regulated by a sovereign government.[25] Writing in the context of a complex and ramified civil society, in which many of the Restoration monarchy's functions had been assumed by private organizations, Smith was interested not in explaining how the monarch's power could be increased but in describing how individual prosperity could augment national security. In Smith's work, the political rationality that lingers in Petty's formulations has been replaced by a fully articulated economic rationality. In keeping with this, Smith's emphasis shifts from the aggregate "person" and issues of government regulation to the psychologized individual and issues of "freedom" and "choice."[26] In Smith's account, atomistic, self-interested individuals constitute the norm; these individuals form societies and initiate exchanges only because no man can survive alone, and, even then, each man serves his own interests by appealing to the self-interest of another. "Man has almost constant occasion for the help of his brethren," Smith writes, "and it is in vain for him to expect it from their benevolence only. He will be more likely to prevail if he can interest their self-love in his favour, and shew them that it is for their own advantage to do for him what he requires of them."[27]

Despite the obvious differences between Petty's ideas and Adam Smith's, however, the work of the latter both resembles Petty's work in important ways and contributed significantly to the projects Petty initiated. Smith's claim to ground his account of a society of self-interested individuals in a theory of (universalized) human psychology extends and relocates the authoritarian model of government that Petty formulated by recasting it as a form of *self*-government that can be both described and monitored by the educated individual. Similarly, Smith's discussions of money as the universal equivalent provide a theoretical basis for Petty's attempts to calculate the value of a "person" at the same time that Smith's labor theory of value lends the appearance of arithmetical exactness to such calculations. Finally, Smith's claim that monetary exchanges are politically neutral because free individuals meet in the market as structural equivalents elevates Petty's effort to displace the particular political controversies of the late seventeenth century into a general principle of market society; it does so by discounting all potentially contestatory encounters among individuals who are manifestly not equal as the unfortunate side effects of a natural system of exchange. Thus, the fact that Smith reached different conclusions from Petty about specific issues—most notably, the role of the monarch and the importance of free trade—should not obscure the extent to which both contributed to what eventually became an identifiable cultural logic.[28]

As my summaries of these continuities should make clear, the tension between theory and description that characterized Petty's writings also appears in Adam Smith's work. By the middle of the eighteenth century, however, the political component inherent in this fusion had generally been masked by the elaboration of a concept associated most frequently with natural philosophy. By borrowing the concept of "disinterestedness" from natural philosphers (and, secondarily, from aesthetic theorists), Smith was able to depoliticize theory at the same time that he was able to present his conclusions about the economy as objective observations about a natural realm. Even as it lent prestige to economic analysis, however, the theory of disinterestedness also wrote inequality into the very production of knowledge. The most striking manifestation of the "interested" nature of disinterestedness also constitutes Smith's most important contribution to classificatory thinking—the notion that the laboring poor constitute a special kind of aggregate (or "class").

Just as Petty developed specific aspects of his argument in relation to contemporary events and controversies, so Adam Smith's work contributed to the effort to legitimize and comprehend civil society that preoccupied eighteenth-century British philosophers and statesmen. The most important articulation of this enterprise focused on the relationship between wealth or commerce and what contemporaries called virtue.[29] In part, this relationship cried out for philosophical analysis because the challenge that new commercial fortunes posed to land as the traditional basis of political and social power also threatened to render traditional expressions of virtue obsolete. In part, this relationship demanded attention because long-standing suspicions about the morality of commercial enterprises had been reactivated in the early eighteenth century by critics like Bernard Mandeville and by the vicissitudes of the rambunctious market, best (or most disastrously) exemplified by the collapse of a heavily subscribed but vastly overrated trading company, known as the South Sea Bubble. While all of Smith's writing can be read in the context of this cultural reassessment, his two most important contributions to the defense of civil society are the *Theory of Moral Sentiments* (1759) and *The Wealth of Nations* (1776).[30]

Smith's defense of civil society constitutes an explication of economic rationality. Essentially, this defense consists of two arguments. The first, which Smith developed in his University of Glascow lectures on ethics, elaborates a psychological infrastructure that equates self-interested (and, implicitly, commercial) activities with social virtue. The second, set out in *The Wealth of Nations*, provides historical and descriptive accounts of various modes of production that link social "progress" to laissez-faire market transactions. In each argument, Smith anchors his bid for authority in the paradoxical fusion of description and theory that characterizes classificatory thinking. We see this first in Smith's explanation of how an individual comes to know—so as to judge—himself.

> When I endeavour to examine my own conduct, when I endeavour to pass sentence upon it, and either to approve or condemn it, it is evident that, in all such cases, I divide myself, as it were, into two persons; and that I, the examiner and the judge, represent a different character from that other I, the person whose conduct is examined into and judged of. The first is the spectator, whose sentiments with regard to my own conduct I endeavour to enter into, by placing myself in his situation, and by considering how it would appear to me, when seen from that particular point of view. The second is the agent, the person whom I properly call myself, and of whose conduct, under the character of a spectator, I was endeavouring to form some opinion.[31]

When Smith divides himself into two, he simultaneously establishes the grounds for his claim that he provides an authentic account of himself and creates a nonsubjective basis for judging that self. The authenticity of Smith's self-evidence comes from the priority he assigns to "immediate experience," which, presumably, can yield descriptions as accurate as the images produced by Smith's favorite metaphor—the mirror.[32] On the basis of accurate observations, Smith's moral individual can know what behaviors are most likely to receive social approbation; he can know, in other words, what constitutes virtue.

As Smith explains his theory of a specular self, one problem emerges. Smith is forced to acknowledge that the other people who form the social looking glass do not always judge with the same clarity and impartiality that his model requires. As a result, Smith begins to supplement what apparently originated as a description of a social transaction with an account of an imaginary encounter whose dynamics come not from Smith's observations but from his theory.

> We are pleased to think that we have rendered ourselves the natural objects of approbation, though no approbation should ever actually be bestowed upon us: and we are mortified to reflect that we have justly merited the blame of those we live with, though that sentiment should never actually be exerted against us. The man who is conscious to himself that he has exactly observed those measures of conduct which experience informs him are generally agreeable, reflects with satisfaction on the propriety of his own behaviour. . . . He anticipates the applause and admiration which . . . would be bestowed upon him; and he applauds and admires himself by sympathy with sentiments, which do not indeed actually take place, but which the ignorance of the public alone hinders from taking place, which he knows are the natural and ordinary effects of such conduct, which his imagination strongly connects with it, and which he has acquired a habit of conceiving as something that naturally and in propriety ought to follow from it. (*MS*, III, ii, 115–16)

This logic—whereby authority accrues to an empirical observation whose insufficiency must be supplemented by theoretical assertions—also characterizes *The Wealth of Nations*. In a telling passage early in that text, Smith sets out his basic procedure. What he wants to do, Smith explains, is to compare the "real values" of a single commodity under different circumstances. Since records of what might facilitate such a comparison do not exist, however, empiricism must be supplemented with "approximation."

> In such a work as this . . . it may sometimes be of use to compare the different real values of a particular commodity at different times and places, or the different degrees of power over the labour of other people which it may, upon different occasions, have given to those who possessed it. We must in this case compare, not so much the different quantities of silver for which it was commonly sold, as the dif-

ferent quantities of labour which those different quantities of silver could have purchased. But the current prices of labour at distant times and places can scarce ever be known with any degree of exactness. Those of corn, though they have in few places been regularly recorded, are in general better known and have been more frequently taken notice of by historians and other writers. We must generally, therefore, content ourselves with them, not as being always exactly in the same proportion as the current prices of labour, but as being the nearest approximation which can commonly be had to that proportion. (*WN*, 38)

The impossibility with which this example confronts Smith is only incidentally a function of poor record keeping. Even under "improved" conditions, what looks like poor record keeping actually signals the overwhelming quantity of natural objects and the potentially limitless variety of categories by which one might represent them. Partly because the natural world presents the observer with an overwhelming number of discrete particulars, then, the philosopher must generalize at every level.

The priority of generalization over description is also partly a function of the fact that the natural world Smith seems to want to describe can only be presented as corresponding to his theory *of* "nature" if his descriptions highlight some features and marginalize or omit others. The extent to which Smith's descriptions follow from, rather than informing, his theory is clearest in his comparative accounts. Smith is able to present laissez-faire as more "natural" than mercantilism, for example, only because he assumes both that "the uniform, constant, and uninterrupted effort of every man to better his condition" takes the form of economic rather than other kinds of activity and that "improvement" can best be measured by prosperity, not by some more qualitative criteria.

The uniform, constant, and uninterrupted effort of every man to better his condition, the principle from which public and national, as well as private opulence, is originally derived, is frequently powerful enough to maintain the natural progress of things toward improvement, in spite both of the extravagance of government, and of the gravest errors of administration. Like the unknown principle of animal life, it frequently restores health and vigour to the constitution, in spite, not only of the disease, but of the absurd prescriptions of the doctor. (*WN*, 326)

The interdependent web of assertions articulated in this passage depends, in turn, upon another set of theoretical positions, including the assumptions that human nature is everywhere the same (every man is a version of *homo economicus*) and that economic transactions are governed by an innately moral, providential, and manipulative "invisible hand." The latter can be read as a further abstraction of the "impartial spectator" by which Smith naturalizes the morality of the specular self. In another sense, however, the "hand" can be seen to obviate the need for social *and* self-approval. It discourages reflection and introspection, because, by definition, it undermines the best laid plans of every self-interested individual. "By directing . . . industry in such a manner as its produce may be of the greatest value, [the individual] intends only his own gain, and he is in this, as in many other cases, led by an invisible hand to promote an end which was no part of his intention" (*WN*, 423).

The simile of the invisible hand makes up for the failure of actual behavior to replicate Smith's theory by generalizing the morality his theory requires to the economic system as a whole. This generalization is nonrational and anti-individualist in the sense that it does not matter whether individuals are capable of reason, sympathy, or judgment, much less of self-sacrifice or virtue. It therefore admits to the society that the "hand" directs everyone who wants what Smith says it is natural to want. "Virtue," therefore, is rendered equivalent to (a certain kind of) desire. And since (this kind of) desire leads "naturally" to exchange, commerce becomes the manifestation of virtue, just as (unthinking) virtue becomes the motor of commerce. So comprehensive is Smith's system that the "hand" even disciplines reproduction. "The demand for men," Smith coolly observes, "like that for any other commodity, necessarily regulates the production of men" (*WN*, 80).

There are moments in *The Wealth of Nations* when Smith's collapse of description into theory implicitly challenges the authority he is trying to establish.[33] For the most part, however, Smith was able to ignore the possibility that theoretical assertions might be considered partial or interested because he had available to him a theoretical position that had only begun to be developed when Petty wrote. By examining briefly the historical development of the concept of disinterestedness, we can begin to see both why Smith's elaboration of the classificatory system Petty sketched was considered persuasive by his contemporaries and how Smith's theory of economic individualism also—and incidentally—produced a rudimentary theory of unequal social classes.

The concept of disinterestedness was initially articulated by those seventeenth-century experimental natural philosophers who wanted to distinguish between the controversial theories produced by political radicals and a kind of knowledge that was reliable because impartial.[34] By agreeing not to meddle with matters of church and state, experimental philosophers like Robert Boyle tried to exempt the knowledge they produced about the natural world from the more obviously "interested" claims of those who fomented civil unrest.[35] In order to maintain this distinction, Robert Boyle insisted that disinterested knowledge was produced according to certain investigative procedures and under specific social conditions, which were epitomized by the laboratory. According to Boyle, the laboratory was not a "private" place where knowledge was generated in seclusion. Instead, it was a "public" space where knowledge was produced for and in front of a group of like-minded witnesses who understood the rules by which experiments were conducted.[36] The universality of such "public" knowledge was guaranteed both by the presence of eyewitnesses and by the fact that the experiment could be repeated in other places by other men, who were considered virtual witnesses of the event.

During the first half of the eighteenth century, the conditions under which scientific knowledge was produced gradually changed, but, if anything, the notion that this knowledge was disinterested was reinforced. As the rituals of public performance, carried out most notably in the Royal Society, were gradually replaced by dispersed laboratory experiments, scientific instruments like electric globes were increasingly understood to register the "truths" of these experiments automatically, without the intervention—much less the interest—of the scientist. Many experiments, however, particularly those that involved the human body, still required some reliable reporting of phenomenon that could not be provided by an instrument; in these experiments, the self-evidence of the scientist was generally taken to be authoritative. Paradoxically, then, as mechanical instruments shored up the concept of disinterest (in the sense of disembodied), the disinterest of the scientist who experimented on his own body was also reinforced—not primarily because he had voluntarily given up politics, but in analogy to the impartiality of the instruments he used.[37]

The concept of disinterest was also elaborated in the first decades of the eighteenth century in relation to a completely different sphere of activity—aesthetic appreciation. In his *Characteristics*, Anthony Ashley Cooper, Third Earl of Shaftesbury, distinguished between the two modes by which a gentleman related to the world. One mode was "public" in the sense that it was engaged, active, and focused on the social consequences of behavior. The other was "private" in the sense that it was contemplative and concerned neither with consequences nor with actions.[38] In keeping with the prevalent theory of civic humanism, the first mode was epitomized by the public service of parliamentary representation; the second was best expressed in aesthetic contemplation. Both modes were, in theory at least, linked to gentlemanly virtue. Indeed, in a formulation that Smith would echo, Shaftesbury proclaimed that private virtue was providentially linked to public good: "the wisdom of what rules, and is first and chief in Nature, has made it to be acccording to the private interest and good of every one to work towards the general good."[39]

In the first half of the eighteenth century, as economic activity became increasingly ramified and important to British security, apologists for the new commercialism imported the notion of disinterest to lend prestige to their own activities. In the realm of the market, however, the concept of disinterestedness could only retain its connotations of objectivity, nonpartisanship, and virtue if it could be distinguished from the self-serving activity that Bernard Mandeville had designated "vice." Joseph Addison helped secure this distinction by elaborating Shaftesbury's concept of "taste" and by carrying over into his descriptions of "polite" behavior Shaftesbury's distinction between contemplation and acquisition. In the process, Addison represented contemplation as a form of metaphorical possession. "The Man of a Polite Imagination," Addison explained, feels "a greater Satisfaction in the Prospect of Fields and Meadows, than another does in the Possession. It gives him, indeed, a kind of Property in everything he sees, and makes the most rude, uncultivated Parts of Nature administer to his Pleasures."[40] As we have already seen, Adam Smith completes this transposition by containing the potential "vice" of self-serving greed within a providential scheme of innumerable acts of self-interest supervised by an invisible hand.

The level of abstraction created by Addison's metaphorical revision of possession and repeated in Smith's image of the invisible hand points to another bias that economic rationality adopted from the aesthetic elaboration of disinterestedness. As apologists for the new commercial world sought authority for their attempts to explain why acquisition was virtuous, they mobilized an assumption inherent in the traditional distinction between gentlemanly pursuits and all other kinds of labor. According to this distinction, gentlemen, who did not pursue a single occupation or work with their hands, were able to achieve a greater distance from the things of the world, while workers—whether professional, artisanal, or manual— were necessarily immersed in the specific details of their labor. Thus, abstract or theoretical knowledge was considered superior to concrete knowledge; in this regard, the latter was held to be "interested" not because it involved politics but because it emphasized the immediacy of possession, consumption, or use.[41] Theoretical observations, by contrast, were considered disinterested because they signaled a man's disengagement from utilitarian considerations. Because it required the capacity to see objects in terms of their formal properties or relationships or as common members in a representative category, the ability to generate theory was a sign of a man's gentlemanly education, just as a liberal education produced this capacity in gentlemen.

The continuity between the eighteenth-century concept of disinterestedness and assumptions about social inequality should now be clear. This connection characterized both the natural-philosophical and the aesthetic articulations of the concept, although it was more explicitly theorized in the latter. Whereas the elitism within the community of natural philosophers seemed as much a function of practical considerations as of principle, the elitism of aesthetic disinterestedness was explicit from the beginning. The "manners" that Shaftesbury discussed were exclusively and explicitly those of gentlemen—men whose capacity to exercise public virtue was understood to be directly correlated to their ownership of land.[42] The theory formulated to justify limiting political participation to the landed elite emphasized both the permanence of the land (and thus its coextensivity with "Great Britain") and the immunity enjoyed by those who did not have to work to the "interests" of a particular occupational group. Because gentlemen were free of both occupational ties and the necessities that bound laborers to the materiality of the world, they were arguably uniquely able to identify and advance the welfare of society as a whole. Anyone who was not a gentleman could be said to belong to that capacious category, "the vulgar," which was defined not solely by income or birth but also by the mode of apprehension produced by having to work. "The vulgar look no further than to the scenes of culture," explained James Harris in his *Philological Inquiries* (1780–81), "because all their views merely terminate in utility." They are "merged in sense from their earlier infancy, never once dreaming anything to be worthy of pursuit, but what either pampers their appetite, or fills their purse"; they "imagine nothing to be real, but what may be touched or tasted."[43]

The elitism that was explicit in Shaftesbury's discussion of aesthetics and implicit in the practice of natural philosophy also characterized those Scottish societies developed in the eighteenth century to produce new philosophical and natural knowledge. In accounts of their own work offered by groups like the Philosophical Society (founded 1737) and the Select Society (1754), moreover, we see even more clearly how the elitist theory of disinterested knowledge was articulated in relation to a paradoxical definition of the "public." Because the activities of societies like the Select depended upon patronage for funding, their more intellectual members (like Smith) represented their theories as truths available to the general public rather than as esoteric or specialized knowledge comprehensible only by experts.[44] The "public," of course, included only those (men) with wealth and social status or with connections sufficient to attract the notice of a patron.[45]

Despite the fact that the "public" was an exclusive rather than an inclusive category, its members were understood to be and act as individuals. Indeed, the universalism that characterizes both the philosophy of the Scottish Enlightenment and the version of economic rationality set out by Adam Smith is consistently offset by the assertion that "human nature" is embodied in multitudes of discrete individuals. The individualism that theorists insisted upon in this segment of the population was not held to characterize everyone, however. Instead, what Smith (and others) called "the great body of the people" was represented as an undifferentiated mass, not an assembly of individuals. John Barrell suggests that the aggregation and objectification of the "people" is in part at least a function of the tendency of "disinterested" observers to produce and value abstract knowledge over concrete particulars. This epistemological relationship creates, on the one side, an elite observer who is impartial, integrated, and capable of speaking about—and for—other men; and, on the other, an abstract and aggregate object, whose members are paradoxically so immersed in the details of their immediate pursuits that they can be reduced to a single generalization—although they can speak for no one, including themselves. The philosophical narrator of *The Wealth of Nations*, Barrell remarks,

> is . . . accredited with an impartiality, an integral subjectivity (manifested in the pronoun "we"), and a disinterestedness, which enable him to perceive the real history of society as the real and unchanging coherence of continuously subdivided activities and interests; and he is imagined as articulating that perception in terms which, because they cannot be identified as the terms of any specific occupation, elude the constraints of specific discourse as entirely as they elude determination by an economy of exchange. Knowledge becomes a disinterested knowledge of what the public is, and of what is good for the public, and it becomes the property of a particular *social*, and not simply of a particular occupational class. Ignorance too becomes the property of a particular class, the class which is the object of knowledge, and so the object of the discourse.[46]

Such objectification and aggregation is evident throughout *The Wealth of Nations*. Even when he seems to describe an individual poor man, Smith's use of generalizing abstractions renders the object of his analysis a type of reified, stupified labor.

> The torpor of his mind renders him, not only incapable of relishing or bearing a part in any rational conversation, but of conceiving any generous, noble, or tender sentiment, and consequently of forming any just judgment concerning many even of the ordinary duties of private life. Of the great and extensive interests of his country he is altogether incapable of judging; and unless very particular pains have been taken to render him otherwise, he is equally incapable of defending his country in war. (*WN*, 734–35)

Such incapacities, according to Smith, authorize the government to interfere with the poor on a scale he nowhere else countenances. "The public can impose upon almost the whole body of the people the necessity of acquiring those most essential parts of education," he explains, because an "ignorant and stupid" people threatens society with "the most dreadful disorders" (*WN*, 738, 740). The asymmetry of the two collective nouns is striking. Whereas the "public" consists of individuals like Smith himself, who can and should be free, the "body of the people" is a group that cannot be trusted to act as individuals. This "body" does not consist of trustworthy individuals because the same division of labor that ensures freedom for some and the prosperity of the whole has also deprived the many of the very capacities that Smith says elsewhere make men "human"— reason, sentiments, and the ability to judge.

In *The Wealth of Nations*, Smith does not develop this aspect of his argument. Indeed, in his discussion of state-sponsored education, he suggests that as members of the laboring poor are educated they will become more like the individuals who populate the rest of Smith's society: they will become "more decent and orderly . . . more respectable, and more likely to obtain the respect of their lawful superiors" (*WN*, 740). If individual members of "the people" may acquire the attributes of "human nature" through education, however, the division of labor will always produce a "great body of the people" that is internally differentiated only by the tasks its members perform and whose constitution *as* a "body" underwrites for others the "freedom" they "naturally" enjoy.

In the epistemological relation I have been describing, the disinterestedness of the elite, individualized spokesman for the "public" both depends on and produces another subject position, whose representatives are interested and undifferentiated and not possessed of humanizing virtues. The latter constitutes a rudimentary version of what Marx would call the "working class." As an aggregate whose social position was given both by its opposition to an individualized disinterestedness and by the quantifiable abstraction "labor," the consciousness that this group would eventually achieve was consciousness of itself as a social *group* whose progress could be measured by its relative share of the national wealth. If the self-consciousness of the working class depended in part upon the classificatory logic I have been describing, however, the "humanity" that made members of the elite "public" individuals depended upon something in addition to the stupidity of the "people." According to the logic by which Smith converts Petty's external coercion into the psychologized faculties of sensibility and desire, the individualized subject seems to be self-sufficient as well as self-observant and self-regulating. As we have already seen, however, Smith's specular model of the subject complicates this self-sufficiency, and the insufficiency of the social world—its failure consistently to affirm the judgments of the impartial spectator— deprives the specular self of the reinforcement it needs to be virtuous. During the second half of the century, in a process I can only sketch briefly, the reproduction of virtue that ought to occur as an effect of living in a virtuous world came increasingly to be designated the work of another segment of the population. The group was also constituted as relatively undifferentiated, but because women were defined not by their quantifiable (waged) labor but by the role nature assigned them, they seemed to be excluded from the social order whose virtue they were believed to ensure.

I have already alluded to the paradoxical notion of an exclusionary "public" that developed alongside the natural philosophers' articulation of disinterested knowledge. We have also begun to see how Shaftesbury's elaboration of disinterest in relation to gentlemanly behavior reinforced the elevated status of disinterest and strengthened the opposition between a superior kind of knowledge (theory) and a devalued mode of apprehension associated with an objectified aggregate. What remains to be specified now is the epistemological history of the other half of the opposition to which "public" belongs. As John Barrell has argued, "public" and "private" were differentiated in the early eighteenth century primarily in relation to landed gentlemen: as a vestigial remainder of feudal responsibilities, "public" activities were epitomized by a gentleman's parliamentary service; his "private" activities included contemplative pursuits as well as more hedonistic indulgences like gambling and hunting. As part of the elaboration of civil society and the new importance acquired by commercial wealth, however, the opposition between public and private also received new elaboration. As writers like Addison and Steele devised rationales for ennobling the taste of well-to-do capitalists and manufacturers, and as Shaftesbury's disciples elaborated new modes of virtue that were compatible with civil society, the notion of public and private spheres was gradually abstracted from the activities of the highest social rank and generalized to both behaviors and material spaces in the commercial world. In the process, "private" began to encompass both domestic activities and the psychological feelings assumed to flourish in the home, and "public" was aligned with all kinds of waged work outside the home, as well as with political and military activities.

Even though a full-fledged psychology of feelings was not articulated until the last decades of the eighteenth century, we can already see some of the implications of this redefinition in Smith's *Theory of Moral Sentiments*. Although Smith is less explicit on this point, we can also begin to see the extent to which this epistemological and spatial opposition had become a gendered opposition by the second half of the century. In his brief comments on women's education, Smith associates women with the "private" realm of family and home and designates as their "purpose" actions that will improve those qualities and behaviors believed capable of improving the behaviors of others.[47]

> There are no public institutions for the education of women, and there is accordingly nothing useless, absurd, or fantastical in the common course of their education. They are taught what their parents or guardians judge it necessary or useful for them to learn; and they are taught nothing else. Every part of their education tends evidently to some useful purpose; either to improve the natural attractions of their person, or to form their mind to reserve, to modesty, to chastity, and to oeconomy; to render them both likely to become the mistresses of a family, and to behave properly when they have become such. (*WN*, 734)

By the last decades of the eighteenth century, the association of women with both domesticity and virtue was fast becoming a cultural commonplace. In theory at least, women were guardians of the home, nurturers of children, and exiles from the workplace; as such, they functioned as supplements to the impartial spectator with which Smith had superintended the interior space of the moral man. In this sense, as in others, women were assigned responsibility for reproducing not only literal human beings but also the very qualities that Smith thought necessary to "humanity" itself. Women were increasingly thought to provide this service for all men, moreover, not just for those whose impartial spectator was momentarily distracted by the allure of personal gain.

The place that women as a group were assigned by the same classificatory logic that aggregated a working "class" eluded most analysts in the late eighteenth and early nineteenth centuries, whether they were (proto) Marxists or political economists. This is true because both groups of theorists—albeit for different reasons—tended to repeat the eighteenth-century assumption that women's subject position is assigned by nature, not by the social division of labor that characterizes modern society. As early as the 1790s, however, the contradiction between these definitional systems was visible to some. As theorists of the French Revolution introduced a vocabulary of rights into discussions of human nature, a few critics, like Mary Wollstonecraft, realized the sexual asymmetry that classificatory logic entailed.[48] Defined by nature, women were excluded from assessments of value even as their labor was considered of inestimable worth; rendered a group by the common properties of their bodies, women were excluded from the narrative of individual and national progress they helped sustain. According to Adam Smith and all the political economists and Marxists who have written in his wake, no amount of education or virtue can lift a woman from nature to freedom.

By 1826, when Lord Grey, doyen of the Whigs, lamented that class interests had displaced party interests as the driving passion of the day,[49] classificatory thinking had clearly assumed the two distinct modes to which I have referred. The discourse of political economy elaborated Smith's assumptions that (some) individuals were by nature free and that economic inequality and the aggregation of the masses were inevitable conditions (and effects) of national progress. The discourse to which Marx would soon give his name, by contrast, elaborated another of Smith's conclusions—that the economic group whose waged and divided labor made it an aggregate rather than a collection of individual men might become conscious of its disadvantages and work together for revolutionary change. Even the brief history of classificatory thinking I have offered here should help explain how these two theories could coexist. Once a theory that equates value with quantity and figures it in relation to both a finite pool of resources and a single kind of desire is supplemented by another theory that uses inequality to organize the competition that results, then models of both individual effort and class identity seem defensible.

Despite the continuing coexistence of these theoretical positions, the ironies and omissions that classificatory thinking has bequeathed its descendants should not be lost on modern critics. Petty would no doubt have shuddered if he had lived to see his design to strengthen the monarchy used to bolster the bureaucratic and organizational apparatuses of civil society, and Smith would no doubt have rued the class conflict that his incidental aggregation of a "social body" fomented. Explaining—and exposing—such ironies have become the staples of the two modes of analysis I have identified. Because both remain within classificatory logic in an important sense, however, neither political economy nor Marxist critique has been able to theorize women's place in the society to which classificatory thinking belongs. This is hardly surprising, of course, for, in a very real sense, women have never been included in the classificatory scheme by which quantification has rendered the rest of modern society comprehensible.

NOTES

1. For a discussion of classificatory procedures in general and in the nineteenth century in particular, see Elaine Hadley, "The Melodramatic Mode," Ph.D. dissertation, Johns Hopkins University, 1991.

2. By this, I mean both that the nineteenth century—and nineteenth-century

Britain in particular—is generally considered the moment at which the concept of class in the modern usage became available and that this and subsequent periods have received most—although not all—of modern Marxists' attention. For a brief discussion of the two uses of *class*, see Michael McKeon, *The Origins of the English Novel, 1600–1740* (Baltimore: Johns Hopkins University Press, 1987), pp. 163–64. For an argument that "class" as a concept is historically specific *and* a description of an objective set of conditions, see E. P. Thompson, "Eighteenth-Century Society: Class Struggle without Class?" *Social History* 3(2) (1978):147–50. For a discussion of the various uses of the word *class* in the eighteenth century, see Penelope J. Corfield, "Class by Name and Number in Eighteenth-Century Britain," in Penelope J. Corfield, ed., *Language, History and Class* (Oxford: Basil Blackwell, 1991), 101–30.

3. Recent contributions to this debate include Ellen Meiksins Woods, *The Retreat from Class: A New "True" Socialism* (London: Verso, 1986), which argues for the descriptive position; and Ernesto Laclau and Chantel Mouffe, *Hegemony and Socialist Strategy: Toward a Radical Democratic Politics*, trans. Winston Moore and Paul Cammack (London: Verso, 1985), which argues a variant of the representational thesis.

4. The formulation closest to the epistemological configuration I have designated "classificatory thinking" is Foucault's "governmentality." As subsequent notes will acknowledge, I am indebted to many of the essays in *The Foucault Effect*. Nevertheless, "governmentality" stresses the end to which what I call classificatory thinking was put instead of the tensions written into the discourse as its practitioners attempted to advance that end. See Colin Gordon, "Governmental Rationality: An Introduction" and Michel Foucault, "Governmentality," both in Graham Burchell, Colin Gordon, and Peter Miller, eds., *The Foucault Effect: Studies in Governmentality* (Chicago: University of Chicago Press, 1991), 1–52, 87–104.

The aspect of classificatory thinking to which I have devoted the least attention here is its reliance on taxonomy. For further discussions of this representational and epistemological mode, see Michel Foucault, *The Order of Things: An Archaeology of the Human Sciences* (New York: Vintage, 1973), 125–65; and Harriet Ritvo, "New Presbyter or Old Priest? Reconsidering Zoological Taxonomy in Britain, 1750–1840," *History of the Human Sciences* 3(2) (1990):259–76. Foucault also speculates on the conjunction of the two features I have associated with classificatory thinking in *The Order of Things*, see 179, 203, 206.

For a discussion of early uses of the second facet of classificatory thinking, see Peter Spufford, *Money and its Use in Medieval Europe* (Cambridge: Cambridge University Press, 1988), esp. part I.

5. The tension between theory and description continues to persist in both modern economics and modern science, but the latter in particular has embraced a paradigm of objectivity that masks the more "interested" dimensions of theory. One of my concerns in this essay is to trace the history of the process by which economics tried to adopt this scientific stance.

6. I am grateful to John Guillory for helpful discussions about the distinctions that follow and for his extensive comments on earlier drafts of this essay.

7. The historical development of classificatory thinking is intimately linked to the consolidation of the concept of "objectivity," a process in which the Royal Society (of which Petty was a member) played a major part. For important discussions of this relat-

ed development in the history of science, see Lorraine Daston, "Marvelous Facts and Miraculous Evidence in Early Modern Europe," *Critical Inquiry* 18(1) (Autumn 1991):93–124; Simon Schaffer, "Self Evidence," *Critical Inquiry* 18(2) (Winter 1992):327–62; and the essays in the four issues of *Annals of Scholarship* entitled "Rethinking Objectivity": 8(3 and 4) (Fall 1992) and 9(1 and 2) (Winter 1993).

8. Thus we have the oft-lamented "unhappy marriage" of Marxism and feminism in which, to paraphrase Blackstone, "there is one, and that one is class." The classic formulation of the conflict between Marxism and feminism is Heidi Hartmann, "The Unhappy Marriage of Marxism and Feminism: Towards a More Progressive Union," in Lydia Sargent, ed., *Women and Revolution: A Discussion of the Unhappy Marriage of Marxism and Feminism* (Boston: South End Press, 1981), 1–41. See also Azizah Al-Hibri, "Capitalism is an Advanced Stage of Patriarchy: But Marxism is not Feminism," in Sargent, ed., *Women and Revolution*, 165–94; Nancy Hartsock, *Money, Sex, and Power: Toward a Feminist Historical Materialism* (New York: Longman, 1983); and Barbara Foley, "Marxism in the Poststructuralist Moment: Some Notes on the Problem of Revising Marx," *Cultural Critique* 15 (Spring 1990):30–37.

9. For a compatible but more systematic treatment of the history of economics—although not understood as classificatory thinking—see William Letwin, *The Origins of Scientific Economics: English Economic Thought 1660–1776* (New York: Methuen, 1963). Even more relevant to my thesis are the essays in *The Foucault Effect*.

10. Biographies of Petty include Charles Henry Hull, "Petty's Life," in *The Economic Writings of Sir William Petty* (Cambridge: Cambridge University Press, 1899), I:xiii-xxxiii; Lord Edmond Fitzmaurice, *Life of Sir William Petty, Chiefly From Private Documents Hitherto Unpublished* (London: John Murray, 1895); E. Strauss, *Sir William Petty: Portrait of a Genius* (London: Bodley Head, 1954); and Alessandro Roncaglia, *Petty: The Origins of Political Economy* (Armonk, N.Y.: M. E. Sharpe, 1977), 3–18.

11. The name "Down Survey" originated in the fact that the figures were written down. Petty's history of this survey is entitled *The History of the Survey of Ireland, Commonly Called the Down Survey*, ed. Thomas Aiskew Larcom (Dublin: Irish Archaeological Society, 1851; rpt. New York: Augustus M. Kelley, 1967). This text is cited hereafter as *Down*.

12. One of the most interesting documents in the *History of the Down Survey* is "A Briefe Accompt of the Most Materiall Passages Relatinge to the Survey Managed by Doctor Petty in Ireland, Anno 1655 and 1656." This account relates how "the said Petty, consideringe the vastnesse of the worke, thought of dividinge both the art of makeinge instruments, as alsoe that of usinge them into many partes, viz., one man made onlye measuring chaines, viz., a wire maker; another magneticall needles, with theire pins, viz., a watchmaker; another turned the boxes out of wood, and the heads of the stands on which the instrument playes, viz., a turnor; another, the stands or leggs, a pipe maker; another all the brasse worke, viz., a founder; another workman, of a more versatile head and hand, touches the needles, adjusts the sights and cards, and adaptates every peece to each other" (*Down*, xiv).

13. Petty complains of this confusion in his *Political Anatomy* (*Economic Writings* I:373). In 1824 the authors of the Spring Rice Report were still complaining about the same problem. See "Appendix A" in J. H. Andrews, *A Paper Landscape: The Ordnance Survey in Nineteenth-Century Ireland* (Oxford: Clarendon Press, 1975), 301.

14. Useful histories of this period include Nicholas Canny, *From Reformation to Resistance: Ireland 1534–1660* (Dublin: Helicon, 1987), chapter one; and T. W. Moody, F. X. Martin, and F. J. Byrne, eds., *A New History of Ireland*, vol. III: *Early Modern Ireland, 1534–1691* (Oxford: Clarendon, 1976), chapter two.

15. From "Reflections," (quoted in *Down*, 347).

16. Here is de Certeau on Theodor Galle's engraving of America as a female body: "The conqueror will write the body of the other and trace there his own history. From her he will make a historied body—a blazon—of his labors and phantasms. . . . What is really initiated here is a colonization of the body by the discourse of power. This is *writing that conquers.* It will use the New World as if it were a blank, 'savage' page on which Western desire will be written" (quoted in Louis Montrose, "The Work of Gender in the Discourse of Discovery," *Representations* 33 [Winter 1991]:6).

The "body" that is appropriated in the case of Ireland is not feminized to the same extent that the New World was for Galle and Sir Walter Raleigh because the country was not "virgin" in the same way that the Americas were. The long history of the English in Ireland worked against representations that would present the country as "blank" or passive and considerably complicated the kind of colonizing gestures that the English could make.

17. One contemporary historian has characterized the politics of this period as follows:

> Deceit and double-dealing on the part of kings, ministers and politicians, cynicism on the part of the people, produced an appalling debasement of politics. Nothing was taken on trust or at its stated face-value. Self-interest, hypocrisy and corruption were taken for granted. Politicians, like revellers in a carnival, were assumed to be wearing masks in order to conceal their true features, and to aid them in the seduction of their victims. Indeed, Charles's most effective political attribute was his skill in the art of dissimulation; like Cardinal Richelieu, he was a master at concealing his own feelings and views, while penetrating the thoughts and intentions of others. It was no accident that the word "sham" was coined during this period, when there was a succession of sensational revelations—of the number of catholics in high places in 1673, during the Popish Plot in 1678–9, the whig Rye House Plot of 1683, and perhaps the most monstrously successful lie in the whole of English history, the story that James passed off as a newborn prince of Wales a suppositious child, who was smuggled into the queen's bed in the celebrated warming pan. (J. R. Jones, *Country and Court, England, 1658–1714* [Cambridge, Mass.: Harvard University Press, 1978], 2–3)

For another interpretation of Petty's political arithmetic as a solution to political problems, see Peter Buck, "Seventeenth-Century Political Arithmetic: Civil Strife and Vital Statistics," *Isis* 68 (1977):67–84.

18. Two modern studies examine Petty's role in the creation of the idea of an economy. See Letwin, *Origins of Scientific Economics*, 114–46; and Roncaglia, *Petty*, especially chapter 2. See also Foucault, "Governmentality," and Graham Burchell, "Peculiar Interests: Civil Society and Governing 'The System of Natural Liberty,' " in *The Foucault Effect*, 87–104 and 119–50. I develop my argument at greater length in *Fig-*

ures of Arithmetic, Figures of Speech (Chicago: University of Chicago Press, forthcoming), chapter 2.

19. Hobbes also defines men in terms of their value, but when he moves from quantitative to qualitative terms he moves away from economic rationality and back toward political rationality. Here is Hobbes:

> The *Value*, or WORTH of a man, is of all other things, his Price; that is to say, so much as would be given for the use of his Power: and therefore is not absolute; but a thing dependant on the need and judgement of another. . . . The manifestation of the Value we set on one another, is that which is commonly called Honouring, and Dishonouring. To Value a man at a high rate, is to *Honour* him; at a low rate, is to *Dishonour* him. . . . The publique worth of a man, which is the Value set on him by the Common-wealth, is that which men commonly call DIGNITY. (*Leviathan*, ed. C. B. Macpherson [1651; Harmondsworth: Penguin, 1968], 151–52)

On this point, see McKeon, *Origins of the English Novel,* 163. I am indebted to John Guillory for pointing out this passage to me.

20. David McNally estimates that three-fourths of all enclosures had occurred by 1700. See *Political Economy and the Rise of Capitalism: A Reinterpretation* (Berkeley: University of California Press, 1988), 10, 25.

21. See J. G. A. Pocock, "Authority and Property: The Question of Liberal Origins," in *Virtue, Commerce, and History: Essays on Political Thought and History, Chiefly in the Eighteenth Century* (Cambridge: Cambridge University Press, 1985), esp. 56.

22. Those few times he does differentiate within this abstraction, as in the following passage from the *Political Arithmetick*, he subordinates the difference of sex to some other diacritical mark, in this case the difference of age.

> Suppose the People of *England* be Six Millions in number, that their expence at 7 *l. per* Head be forty two Millions: suppose also that the Rent of the Lands be eight Millions, and the profit of all the Personal Estate be Eight Millions more; it must needs follow, that the Labour of the People must have supplied the remaining Twenty Six Millions, the which multiplied by Twenty (the Mass of Mankind being worth Twenty Years purchase as well as Land) makes Five Hundred and Twenty Millions, as the value of the whole People: which number divided by Six Millions, makes above 80 *l.* Sterling, to be valued of each Head of Man, Woman, and Child, and of adult Persons twice as much; from whence we may learn to compute the loss we have sustained by the Plague, by the Slaughter of Men in War, and by the sending them abroad into the Service of Foreign Princes. (*Economic Writings* I:267)

23. In the "Author's Preface" to *The Political Anatomy of Ireland*, Petty explains his choice of subjects: "as Students in Medicine, practice their inquiries upon cheap and common *Animals*, and such whose actions they are best acquainted with, and where there is the least confusion and perplexure of Parts; I have chosen *Ireland* as such a *Political Animal*, who is scarce Twenty years old; where the *Intrigue* of *State* is not very complicate, and with which I have been conversant from an *Embrion*; and in which, if I have done amiss, the fault may be easily mended by another" (*Economic Writings* I:129).

24. See "Of Marriages &c." in Marquise of Lansdowne, ed., *The Petty Papers: Some Unpublished Writings of Sir William Petty* (London: Constable and Co., 1927),

II:50–51. While Petty apparently wrote and intended to publish an entire treatise on population growth, the *Essay Concerning the Multiplication of Mankind* has never been found, and the only documents on this subject that survive seem to be appendices to this lost tract or else brief project outlines. See *Petty Papers* II:47–49.

25. See Burchell, "Peculiar Interests," 126–33.

26. As in my discussion of Petty, I use the masculine pronoun advisedly throughout my treatment of Smith. It should become clear by the end of this section that Smith's "generic" human is gendered male.

27. Adam Smith, *The Wealth of Nations* (1776; New York: Random House, Modern Library, 1937), 14. Hereafter cited as *WN* in the text.

28. The "laws" that Smith claimed to have discovered in human society can be summarized as follows: 1) because all individuals are instances of the same, the universal desire of all individuals is for personal advantage or gain; therefore, 2) money, as a universal equivalent, can be substituted for any other object of desire as the medium by which advantage can be gained; 3) because individuals meet each other in the market as structural equivalents, monetary exchanges are politically neutral; therefore, 4) free trade is conducive to personal liberty; and 5) because free trade is conducive to personal liberty and therefore to exertion, free trade is conducive to national prosperity. The first four of these formulations are derived from William M. Reddy, *Money and Liberty in Modern Europe: A Critique of Historical Understanding* (Cambridge: Cambridge University Press, 1987), 87. The fifth formulation exemplifies the logic of the aggregate in Smith's thinking, which Reddy does not discuss extensively.

29. The most influential analyst of this debate is J. G. A. Pocock. See *The Machiavellian Moment: Florentine Political Thought and the Atlantic Republican Tradition* (Princeton: Princeton University Press, 1975), especially chapters 13 and 14; "The Mobility of Property and the Rise of Eighteenth-Century Sociology," in *Virtue, Commerce, and History*, 103–24. See also Istvan Hont and Michael Ignatieff, eds., *Wealth and Virtue: The Shaping of Political Economy in the Scottish Enlightenment* (Cambridge: Cambridge University Press, 1983).

30. By presenting these two texts as contributors to a discussion about civil society, I elide the famous "Adam Smith problem." For discussions of this old chestnut, see Ralph Anspach, "The Implications of *The Theory of Moral Sentiments* for Adam Smith's Economic Thought," *History of Political Economy* 4(1) (1972):176–206; T. W. Hutchinson, "The Bicentenary of Adam Smith," *Economic Journal* 86 (September 1976):481–92; Albert O. Hirschman, *The Passions and the Interests: Political Arguments for Capitalism before its Triumph* (Princeton: Princeton University Press, 1977), 108–10; Jerry Evensky, "The Two Voices of Adam Smith: Moral Philosopher and Social Critic," *History of Political Economy* 19(3) (1987):447–68; and Nathan Rosenberg, "Adam Smith and the Stock of Moral Capital," *History of Political Economy* 22(1) (1990):1–17.

31. Adam Smith, *The Theory of Moral Sentiments*, ed. D. D. Raphael and A. L. Macfie (Indianapolis: Liberty Classics, 1982), part III, chap. i, p. 113. Hereafter cited as *MS* in the text. It is customary to cite this text by part, chapter, and page number.

32. Here is just one example of Smith's metaphorical use of the mirror:

Were it possible that a human creature could grow up to manhood in some solitary place, without any communication with his own species, he could no more think of his own character, of the propriety or demerit of his own sentiments and conduct, of the beauty or deformity of his own mind, than of the beauty or deformity of his own face. All these are objects which he cannot easily see, which naturally he does not look at, and with regard to which he is provided with no mirror which can present them to his view. Bring him into society, and he is immediately provided with the mirror which he wanted before. (*MS*, III, i, 111)

33. Smith comes closest to acknowledging the interested nature of both theory and description in his discussion of Columbus. In this extended narrative, Smith recounts how Columbus, having mistaken St. Domingo for the wealthy countries described by Marco Polo, tried to convince Ferdinand and Isabella that the Americas were worth the monarchs' attention. Because the actual resources of the West Indies bore no relationship to the "wealth, cultivation and populousness" that Marco Polo had described, Columbus had to misrepresent what he actually found so that St. Domingo's scant gold resources would seem like traces of a hidden but "inexhaustible" wealth. From his description, it is not clear whether Smith thinks that the explorer deliberately misled his rulers or was himself misled by his own self-confidence. In either case, the effect of Columbus's storytelling and of the pathetic parade of "riches" he assembled is clear. "In consequence of the representations of Columbus," Smith writes, "the council of Castile determined to take possession of countries of which the inhabitants were plainly incapable of defending themselves" (*WN*, 528). "The natives were . . . stript of all that they had" in six or eight years, gold mines were sunk into the earth, and, when they failed to yield sufficient ore, the mines and the now impoverished people were abandoned. Smith suggests that the temptation to which Columbus succumbed was to confuse description with theory. Columbus saw in St. Domingo what he would have seen had he been where he thought he was—or, phrased differently, he represented what he actually saw in terms derived not from empirical reality but from what he believed about himself: that his "daring project of sailing to the East Indies by the West" would succeed (*WN*, 526). In this sense, Smith's story about Columbus hints at the narcissism—the interest—inherent in both description and theory.

34. See James R. Jacob and Margaret C. Jacob, "The Anglican Origins of Modern Science: The Metaphysical Foundations of the Whig Constitution," *Isis* 71(257) (1980):251–67.

35. See Steven Shapin and Simon Schaffer, *Leviathan and the Air-Pump: Hobbes, Boyle, and the Experimental Life* (Princeton: Princeton University Press, 1985), 337.

36. The best study of seventeenth-century laboratory culture is Shapin and Schaffer, *Leviathan and the Air-Pump*, especially chapter 8. Shapin and Schaffer point out that Thomas Hobbes also associated philosophical knowledge with a notion of disinterest that was intimately tied to his notion of the "public":

Hobbes's philosophy had to be public in the sense that it must not become the preserve of interested professionals. The special interests of professional groups had acted historically to corrupt knowledge. Geometry had escaped this appropriation only because, as a contingent historical matter, its theorems and findings had not been seen to have a bearing on such interests: "Because men care not, in that subject, what be truth, as a thing that crosses no man's ambition, profit or lust." (333–34)

Because of the anathema that Hobbes's supposed atheism generated, however, his articulation of disinterest was less explicitly influential than was the notion of "objectivity" developed by members of the Royal Society.

37. See Simon Schaffer, "Self Evidence," *Critical Inquiry* 18(2) (Winter 1992):327–62. The concept of disinterest is obviously related to the complex development of two other concepts, "objectivity" and "facts." For a discussion of these notions, see Lorraine Daston, "Marvelous Facts and Miraculous Evidence in Early Modern Europe," *Critical Inquiry* 18(1) (Autumn 1991):93–124; and Daston, "The Factual Sensibility," *Isis* 79(298) (September 1988):452–67.

38. For helpful discussions of disinterest, see John Barrell, " 'The Dangerous Goddess': Masculinity, Prestige, and the Aesthetic in Early Eighteenth-Century Britain," in *The Birth of Pandora and the Division of Knowledge* (Philadelphia: University of Pennslyvania Press, 1992), 63–88; Jerome Stolnitz, "On the Origins of 'Aesthetic Disinterestedness,' " *Journal of Aesthetics and Art Criticism* 20(2) (1961):131–43; and Martha Woodmansee, "The Interests in Disinterestedness: Karl Philipp Moritz and the Emergence of the Theory of Aesthetic Autonomy in Eighteenth-Century Germany," *Modern Language Quarterly* 45(1) (March 1984):22–47.

39. Shaftesbury, *Characteristics of Men, Manners, Opinions, Times*, ed. John M. Robertson (1711; Indianapolis: Bobbs-Merrill, 1964), 338. Helpful discussions of Shaftesbury include Howard Caygill, *Art of Judgment* (Oxford: Basil Blackwell, 1989), 44–50; and Robert Markley, "Sentimentality as Performance: Shaftesbury, Sterne, and the Theatrics of Virtue," in Felicity Nussbaum and Laura Brown, eds., *The New Eighteenth Century: Theory, Politics, English Literature* (New York: Methuen, 1987), 210–30.

40. *Spectator* 411 (June 21, 1712), in *The Spectator*, ed. Gregory Smith (London: Dent, 1970; Everyman Library), 3:278.

41. See John Barrell, "The Public Prospect and the Private View: The Politics of Taste in Eighteenth-Century Britain," in *The Birth of Pandora*, 42, 45.

42. Ibid., 51.

43. Quoted in ibid., 47.

44. See Steven Shapin, "Property, Patronage, and the Politics of Science: The Founding of the Royal Society of Edinburgh," *British Journal of the History of Science* 7 (1974):1, 8.

45. For a discussion of the membership of the Select Society, see Roger L. Emerson, "The Social Composition of Enlightened Scotland: The Select Society of Edinburgh, 1754–1764," *Studies on Voltaire and the Eighteenth Century* 114 (1973): 291–329.

46. John Barrell, "Visualising the Division of Labour: William Pyne's *Microcosm*," in *The Birth of Pandora*, 91–92. For a discussion of Smith's insistence that no government can produce a totalizing view of society, see Foucault, "Governmentality," in *The Foucault Effect*.

47. For a discussion of Adam Smith's treatment of women, see Jane Rendall, "Virtue and Commerce: Women in the Making of Adam Smith's Political Economy," in Ellen Kennedy and Susan Mendus, eds., *Women in Western Political Philosophy: Kant to Nietzsche* (New York: St. Martin's, 1987), 44–77.

48. For an analysis of Wollstonecraft's critique of Smith, see my "Aesthetics and

Political Economy in the Eighteenth Century: The Place of Gender in the Social Constitution of Knowledge," in George Levine and Carolyn Williams, eds., *Ideology and Aesthetics* (New Brunswick: Rutgers University Press, 1994).

49. See Peter Mandler, *Aristocratic Government in the Age of Reform: Whigs and Liberals 1830–1852* (Oxford: Clarendon Press, 1990), 31.

2 CLASS, GENDER, AND A HISTORY OF METONYMY

Wai Chee Dimock

In a suitably graphic moment in "The American Scholar," Emerson thrusts before the reader a catalog of bodily parts, amputated and randomly assorted, "strut[ting] about" like "so many walking monsters—a good finger, a neck, a stomach, an elbow, but never a man." With this grotesque image he castigates a phenomenon he finds equally grotesque—a phenomenon amounting to a kind of metonymic perversion, a substitution of part for whole—brought about, in this case, by the division of labor in modern society. Every task is "so distributed to multitudes, . . . so minutely subdivided and peddled out," Emerson complains, that human beings too have become mere fractions of what they might have been.[1] Speaking of human fractions, Emerson's neighbor, Thoreau, is even more emphatic: "It is not the tailor alone who is the ninth part of a man; it is as much the preacher, and the merchant, and the farmer. Where is this division of labor to end? and what object does it finally serve?"[2]

Writing in the 1830s and 1840s, some sixty years after Adam Smith's celebrated (and celebrating) account of the division of labor,[3] Emerson and Thoreau were visibly tempered in their enthusiasm. Smith had been thrilled by the projected gains, his most famous example being the worker who, once upon a time, had been capable of making "perhaps not one pin in a day," but who, under modern management, "might be considered as making four thousand eight hundred pins in a day."[4] Emerson and Thoreau, on the other hand, saw such industrial gains only as a human loss, only as a substitutive violence, whereby the "ninth part of a man" was made to stand for the man who, they assumed, was once upon a time fully himself, organic and integral. "A man in the view of political economy is a pair of hands," Emerson had written in an earlier lecture.[5] This image of modernization as a metonymic horror—an inversion between part and whole—was very much a staple of social critique on both sides of the Atlantic. It was the burden of Ruskin's pointed rebuke to Adam Smith, in *The Stones of Venice* (1853), when he complained about laborers being "divided into mere segments of Men—broken into small fragments and crumbs of life; so that all the little piece of intelligence that is left in a man is not enough to make a pin, or a nail, but exhausts itself in making the point of a pin or the head of a nail."[6] And it was the burden, as well, of Marx's critique of industrial capitalism. Capitalism, Marx wrote, institutes a regimen of "partial function" and "fractional work"; it "rivet[s] each labourer to a single fractional detail," and runs a "productive mechanism whose parts are human beings."[7] In so doing, it

> converts the labourer into a crippled monstrosity, . . . just as in the States of La Plata they butcher a whole beast for the sake of his hide or his tallow. . . . Not only is the detail work distributed to the different individuals, but the individual himself is made the automatic motor of a fractional operation, and the absurd fable of Menenius Agrippa, which makes man a mere fragment of his own body, becomes realised.[8]

METONYMY AND MATERIALISM

Central, then, to the critique of modernization was a rhetoric of part and whole, a rhetoric I here call "metonymic," not so much in the sense of Roman Jakobson[9] as in the sense of Kenneth Burke, and, more recently, in the sense now current among cognitive linguists, especially George Lakoff. For Burke, metonymy is the trope that instantiates "some incorporeal or intangible state in terms of the corporeal or tangible"; it is thus a form of reduction, involving the telescoping of an immaterial order within a material embodiment.[10] Lakoff, meanwhile, links metonymy to what he calls the "prototype effect" in human thought: the tacit derivation of a broader, more integral category—presupposed as an ideal case—from a term understood to be its representation or partialization.[11] Metonymy involves, in other words, a kind of cross-mapping, a cognitive traffic between two ontological orders, the immaterial here being invested in (and encapsulated by) the material in a generalizable relation: a relation of representative adequacy or logical inferability. Seen in this light, metonymy would seem to be a cognitive form especially open to cultural conditioning, since the notions of the "representative" or the "generalizable" invariably carry with them a silent set of normative assumptions. Inferring a putative whole from an actualized part, it operates not only by instantiation but also by projection, not only by a play of salient details but also by a play of latent horizons. In this particular example, the bodily parts adduced by Emerson and Thoreau, Marx and Ruskin, would seem to be intimations, however monstrous, of a normative principle of wholeness, shadowed by its very loss.

This essay is concerned with just this "shadow" effect—this logic of metonymic entailment—opening outward from a salient part to a generalized whole. As a mental operation that dwells on the partial only to summon into being some plenary term, at once its ideal type and its inferential extension, metonymy is crucial both to the making of entities, the categorization of autonomous units, and to the making of epistemologies, the projection of a cognitive universe, the fullness and adequacy of which are guaranteed by the fullness and adequacy of its generalizations, by a representative relation between part and whole. My interest, however, is not to develop a general account of metonymy but to examine a particular moment in its long (and presumably various) history. What concerns me is a quite specific conception of part and whole, the intersection between a theory of entities and a principle of epistemology. The assumption here, of course, is that what counts as a part, what counts as a whole, and what counts as a universe must be seen not as timeless constants but as contextual variables. What is striking to me, then, is that Marx (like Emerson, Thoreau, and Ruskin) should choose to condemn what he saw as the "fractional work" of capitalism by invoking the ideal of an unfractionalized whole—a whole encapsulated by its physical body, here called "the individual himself"—whose much-publicized dismemberment he lamented, but whose original (and eventual) integrity he apparently never questioned.

The nineteenth-century concept of a "whole," including Marx's and perhaps most especially Marx's, was thus very much a materialist concept, in the sense that it was predicated on, anchored to, and imaged after the boundedness and integrity of a physical body. What this made possible was a new confidence about the mappability of the world, a new confidence about the inferable relation between the material and the immaterial, a relation I here call "metonymic." Here, too, I depart from Hayden White, who, in identifying metonymy as a central trope in Marx, has emphasized its opposition to the metaphoric (and thus atomizing) relation imposed by capitalist exchange.[12] And yet, it might be argued, as well, that, in its very opposition to atomization—in its very drive toward integrity—metonymy might turn out to be stipulating an exchange of its own, based on the adequation between the material and the immaterial. It was through metonymy, for example, that the idea of the person was here equated with the physical fact of the person, making the bodily subject virtually coextensive with the self as an epistemological category. Charles Taylor has referred to this coextension as the "strong localization" of the self, a phenomenon he links not only to modern individualism but also to modern materialism, the paradoxical union of which, he argues, would usher in the equally paradoxical spectacle of a "radical subjectivity" consorting with a "radical objectivity." Under this new dispensation, this collapse of the immaterial into the material, "we come to think that we 'have' selves as we have heads."[13] It was this categoric confusion—this confusion of "selves" with "heads"—that prompted these nineteenth-century writers to make the bodily subject a founding unit, an empirical whole, integral not only in physical space but also in the nonphysical space of a polity, an economy, and a morality.

Here, then, was one version of nineteenth-century materialism, one that, oddly enough, is almost never mentioned in conjunction with the "materialism" associated with Marx, and summed up by his much-quoted preface to the *Critique of Political Economy* ("The totality of these relations of production constitutes the economic structure of society, the real foundation, on which arises a legal and political superstructure and to which correspond definite forms of social consciousness").[14] Seen as a form of economism, materialism has been the target of numerous critiques. Rather than rehearsing those familiar arguments, I want to give the term a different definitional scope, and situate it within a different order of vulnerability. Taking materialism to be, above all, an epistemology, I want to align it with the practice of metonymy, and critique not so much its thematic dependence on the economic as its procedural dependence on generalizations, especially generalizations from part to whole, from the tangible to the intangible. It is through this critique of metonymy that I want to examine Marx's dream of an unfractionalized body as an adequate representation of "the individual himself," or his dream of an integral explanatory universe based on the mappability of the economic onto the legal, the political, and the social.

Marx was not alone, I should add, in being intelligible within this tradition. We, too, are intelligible within it, for the legacy of metonymy is still with us today, still current in the debates in contemporary political theory, between, say, Michael Sandel and John Rawls, about the physical and epistemological boundaries of the self.[15] It is current as well, I would further argue, in the institution of literary criticism, in our shared practice, as critics, to read the text as a "body" with contents, as if its epistemological moment could be encapsulated as a locatable identity. Metonymy dies hard, it would seem. And yet, its longevity notwithstanding, it is worth pointing out that this cognitive form has not always been in ascendancy, and that, historically, the material and the immaterial have been otherwise correlated, and wholes otherwise embodied.

THE BODY IN NONPHYSICAL SPACE

In Book V of the *Nicomachean Ethics*, for example, the imagined whole turned out to have something other than a human body, and answered to something other than a personal name. It was the *community* that counted as an integral unit for Aristotle, the community that represented the ideal of some fundamental and plenary wholeness. Not surprisingly, it was also the ideal of the community—rather than the body of the individual—that struck Aristotle as being in danger, and being in need of fortification, against the fragmenting effects of the division of labor. Since there was no natural bond between the builder and the shoemaker, and between the shoemaker and the farmer, Aristotle worried that "a community or association between them would be impossible." Indeed, if it were not for that fortunate necessity, the necessity of "reciprocal exchange," which reunited those separated by the division of labor, binding them together "as if they were one single unit," the always precarious whole called the community might otherwise "not hold together."[16]

I have highlighted the degree to which the bodily subject was not deemed an endangered whole (or a unit of concern) for Aristotle, not only to supply a foil to Marx but also to bring into focus an alternate epistemological tradition. For all his defense of concrete particulars, Aristotle was nonetheless not willing to equate the bodily subject with an epistemological whole—not willing to imagine the immaterial as coextensive with, exhausted by, or generalizable from a material unit—and, in this regard at least, he was firmly within the tradition of ontic logos, a tradition prevalent in Greek antiquity and summed up, most memorably, by Plato's theory of forms.[17] This subtle but crucial space of ontological difference—a space left open (and left opaque) by the explanatory inadequacy of the material world—would persist for the next two thousand years, with obvious changes but also with significant continuities. It was kept alive, not least of all, by Christian theology, under whose auspices the explanatory inadequacy of the material world would become not only a point of contention but also a cause for celebration.

In the eleventh and twelfth centuries, in particular, a major doctrinal battle would erupt over the enigmatic materiality of the "body" of Christ. The problem with this term, as exasperated commentators noticed from the outset, was that it had "multiple" meanings—at least three, in fact—referring simultaneously to "the body of Christ in human form, the body of Christ in the Sacrament, and

the body of Christ in the church."[18] The apostle Paul hardly clari-
fied matters when he offered the following explanation: "The bread
which we break, is it not the communion of the body of Christ? For
we being many are one bread and one body, for we are all partakers
of that one bread."[19] Augustine, in turn puzzling over this supposed
gloss, thought that "the communion of the body of Christ" meant
"the unity of the body and blood of Christ," which he interpreted as
"the society of his body and members, which is the holy church in
those who have been predestined and called."[20] The holy church as
the "body of Christ" was indeed a central tenet of medieval theology, but it was also a central enigma, as imperfectly apprehended by
human reason as it was imperfectly registered by the physical senses,
a "body" in no way coextensive with the corporeal reaches of its
members. The efficacy of the Church, its power to secure salvation
for all through its power of communal mediation, was founded on
this very noncoincidence, this ineffable (but not unimaginable)
margin of discrepancy, between the two kinds of bodies. For it was
only in the midst of—and yet in its nonequivalence to—the mortality of the human body that one could properly appreciate the
immortality of the corporate Church: a body in nonphysical space,
invisible, intangible, available to sensory apprehension and indeed
sensory adulation, but hardly reducible to its terms.

The enigma of the corporate Church—the sense that it was somehow not just a body, somehow more than a body, though it was
nonetheless a body—attested not only to the commingling of the
material and the immaterial in medieval theology but also to the
complex lack of adequation between these two orders of reality. As
much as anything else, the corporate Church was marked by its cognitive slipperiness, its refusal to conform to the bounds of the senses. Even so, it was less of an enigma, and less of a knotty theological
problem, than the problematic materiality revolving around the
other meaning of the "body of Christ," having to do with the character of the sacramental host in the Eucharist. Almost to a man,
Christian exegetes rejected the cheap excuse that the "body" might
be no more than a figure of speech. Almost to a man, they agreed
that body was material, a "real presence," and that, in the act of con-
secration, the bread actually stopped being bread and was "converted into the nature and substance of the flesh" of Christ.[21] What was

unclear, however, was how this "conversion" came about. In what sense could the bread and wine be said to be the body and blood of Christ, and what relation did this eucharistic "body" bear to the historical body of Christ, the body received from the womb of the Virgin Mary and sacrificed on the cross? In the eleventh and twelfth centuries, these theological fine points would flare up into debates of the most gargantuan proportions.

Berengar of Tours, author of *De sacra coena* [*On the Holy Supper*], one of the chief antagonists in this controversy, argued that the eucharistic body could not possibly be that historical body, because otherwise it would "have been in existence already for a thousand years and more." Even if one could stomach the idea of eating some thousand-year-old meat, Berengar thought it unlikely that the body of Christ in heaven would be daily cut up, and "a particle" daily "sent down to the altar."[22] And, in any case, what did it mean to "eat" this Christic flesh? Guitmond of Aversa, an opponent of Beranger's, but like him also driven by an overactive imagination, began to worry about a mouse nibbling on the consecrated host. Would that animal be eating the "body of Christ"?[23] Clearly, these were questions not everyone would like to entertain. Berengar was condemned by a succession of councils and synods (fourteen in all). In 1059, he was forced under duress, in Rome, to recant his position and to affirm that "the bread and wine are the true body and blood of our Lord Jesus Christ," even to the point where that body might be "ground by the teeth of the faithful."[24] This did not quite end the controversy, however, which went on for another hundred and fifty years, until finally, in 1215, the Fourth Lateran Council established the doctrine of transubstantiation (the actual presence of the body and blood of Christ "under the outward appearances of bread and wine"),[25] a doctrine that successfully withstood even the pressure of the Reformation, being reaffirmed by the Council of Trent in 1551.

The debate about the eucharistic body reflected, to a large degree, the complex relation between "reason" and "sense" in medieval theology, and the frequent lack of agreement between the two.[26] As Galileo would say (in a different context), the Christian theologians were "able to make reason so conquer sense that, in defiance of the latter, the former became the mistress."[27] And so, even though the "holy mystery of the Lord's body" was not exactly comprehensible as a *sensory* phenomenon, the theologians were nonetheless able to argue for its *rational* defensibility.[28] The "rationality" at work here, then, would seem to be of a distinct, and distinctly premodern, stripe, predicated not on the evidentiary adequacy of the senses, and not on a postulate of generalizability from the material to the immaterial. Within the terms of our discussion, we might say that such a rationality was profoundly antimetonymic. The material and the immaterial commingled, that is, only in enigmatic apposition, and not at all in explanatory adequation: it would be folly to start out from the actual bread and wine and generalize about the "body of Chirst." Acceding, then, to the explanatory limits of the material world, the Christian theologians acceded as well to an order of reality not absolutely transparent to and only imperfectly registered by the senses.

This premodern rationality, with its constitutive opaqueness, was discernible not only in Christian theology but also in that most sober and unmystical of domains, jurisprudence, where, as Ernest H. Kantorowicz has shown, the legal fiction of the "King's Two Bodies" was to prevail for hundreds of years, providing one of the most important threads of continuity from the Middle Ages through Tudor and Stuart England, and reappearing, as late as 1765, in Blackstone's *Commentaries on the Laws of England.* For Kantorowicz, this was a supreme instance of the transposition of religion into politics, in the constitution of the state as a *corpus mysticum.*[29] In any case, the King, too, like Christ, had a "body" that amounted to a kind of ontolgoical enigma, an enigma that nevertheless did nothing to prevent the most determined as well as most virtuoso sort of legal reasoning, displayed, on this occasion, by the learned judges in the celebrated case of the Duchy of Lancaster (1562). The King, they reasoned, had a Body natural as well as a Body politic:

> So that he has a body natural, adorned and invested with the Estate and Dignity royal; and he has not a Body natural distinct and divided by itself from the Office and Dignity royal, but a Body natural and a Body politic together indivisible; and these two Bodies are incorporated in one Person, and one Body and not divers, that is the Body corporate in the Body natural, *et e contra* the Body natural in the Body corporate. So that the Body natural, by this conjunction of the Body politic to it (which Body politic contains the Office, Gov-

ernment, and Majesty royal), is magnified, and by the said Consolidation hath in it the Body politic.[30]

The syllogism, self-announced as it was, was not strictly speaking
sensible—if one defines "sense," that is, by the reckoning of the
physical senses. Like the Christian theologians, the learned judges
here seemed to be doing some fancy footwork with arithmetic, and
with physical concepts such as spatial location and extension. Bacon,
confident New Physicist that he was, and supremely intolerant of
such mysteries, complained that this was "a confusion of tongues
[having] their foundations in subtlety and imagination of man's wit,
and not in the ground of nature."[31] This complaint was repeated in
the twentieth century by Frederic Maitland, the great jurist and legal
historian, in an essay called "The Crown as Corporation," in which
he said he would "not know where to look in the whole series of our
law books for so marvelous a display of metaphysical—or we might
say metaphysiological—nonsense."[32]

THE EVIDENCE OF THE SENSES

Maitland is right, of course. Or he is right, at least, within a particular cognitive universe, in which the "metaphysical" and the "metaphysiological" have come to mean the "nonsensical," and in which
"sense" itself has come increasingly to be equated with that order of
comprehension registered by the physical senses. This conflation of
sense with sensation—a phenomenon traceable to the seventeenth
century, to the new emphasis put on the physical and mechanical
properties of the mind—would, in the succeeding centuries, profoundly transform the relation not only between body and mind
but, in the same measure, between the mind and the world. Henceforth the mind would increasingly engage the world only in its material intelligibility, only through the evidence furnished by the physical senses, on the assumption that such empirical data would
unlock mysteries elsewhere operative. Enlightenment rationality—
linked, most directly, to seculariazation, and, more obliquely, to
Protestantism—might be seen critically, then, as an alternate form of
mystification: the mystification of empirical reason itself into what
Bacon called "the ground of nature." Its materialism was thus very

much a foundationalist epistemology, grounded in the materiality of the body—or rather, in the materiality of the world as registered by the materiality of the body—a materiality that was then adduced as an account of the mind as well as an account of the world.[33] In sharp contrast, then, to the enigmatic apposition of the material and the immaterial in medieval theology, a relation of explanatory adequacy would now come to prevail, subordinating the immaterial to the material as a logical entailment, or perhaps even, as Michael McKeon suggests, as an "analogy."[34] Within the terms of our discussion, we might also call Enlightenment rationality an instance (and an especially long-lasting instance) of metonymic thought, predicated on the integral relation between two ontological orders: between body and mind, between thought and world, between the visible and tangible order of empirical facts, and the intangible and invisible order of immaterial suppositions.

To press home the distinction between the modern and the premodern rationality that I have tried to outline, we might point to one particular area of contrast, having to do with the postulate of "generalizability," and with the cognitive spaces underwritten by that concept. Unacceptable (and indeed inconceivable) to premodern rationality as an adequate relation between the material and immaterial realms, this postulate has become, since the Enlightenment, nothing other than the founding tenet of modern rationality.[35] Unlike medieval cognitive practice, which assigned to the senses no evidentiary primacy and to the material realm no explanatory adequation, Enlightenment rationality came into being not only through the elevation of the senses into evidentiary ground but also through the elevation of physical evidence into generalizable evidence, so that sense and reason, materiality and reality would all be strung together now—in logical entailment, if not altogether in absolute agreement. Material generalizability thus imposed on the world a new texture, thinning it out into a "sensible" order. No longer opaque, no longer an admixture of the material and the immaterial, it would henceforth acquire a uniform comprehensibility, submitting without fail to empirical tests and material explanations. The physicalization of sense, in short, went hand in hand with the attribution to the world of a kind of anticipated (and therefore compulsory) transparency. We usually associate these imperial

claims of reason with modern science, but such claims would seem
to have been shared by a much broader spectrum of Enlightenment
epistemologies, especially its materialist variant, which, embracing a
physicalized world as its evidentiary ground, would effectively invert
the Cartesian mind/body dualism into an *explanatory* dualism, in
which the material would be separated from the immaterial only to
serve as its epistemological foundation, the foundation upon which
the immaterial might be reincorporated as a secondary effect.[36]

This Enlightenment materialism of physical evidence and transparent explanation was very much the philosophical tradition
inhabited by Marx.[37] To be sure, he was witnessing its darkening
moment, the moment when, as Foucault suggests, the field of
knowledge was increasingly troubled by a new sense of "obscure verticality," of "great hidden forces" invisibly controlling the "visible
order."[38] Still, this darkening world would seem only to have
inspired (and not deferred) Marx, propelling him toward material
explanations of antithetical clarity, if equal verticality. His critique of
the commodity form (punctuated by the word "mystery" as a kind
of incantatory accusation) was driven very much by an explanatory
passion, by a desire to make sense of the world, to deliver it from its
intolerable opacities through an attribution of cause. For him, the
idea of an immaterial order—ungrounded in, inexplicable by, and
nongeneralizable from material facts—was nothing if not an intellectual affront. And, as his grudging tribute to Bacon, Hobbes, and
Locke made amply clear, not the least of the attractions of materialism was its epistemological certitude. Praising Bacon, for example,
for the "rational method [he applied] to the data provided by the
senses," and for his "teaching [that] the senses are infallible and are
the source of all knowledge," Marx acknowledged that "materialism
is the son of Great Britain by birth."[39] And, as if further to under-
score that kinship, he here had recourse to the same argument—and
indeed the same vocabulary—that Sir Frederic Maitland would use
fifty years later, noting with some vehemence that "an *incorporeal
substance* is just as much a nonsense as an *incorporeal body. Body,
being, substance* are one and the same real idea."[40] It was this equation of "body" with "being"—and the casual relegation of the incorporeal to the realm of "nonsense"—that made for the explanatory
texture of Marxist materialism, an evidentiary model predicated not

only, as we all know, on the primacy of the economic but, just as cru-
cially, on a conception of man as a *"corporeal,* living, real, sensuous,
objective being."[41] As an entity both material and immaterial (and
Marx would insist on the lack of distinction between the two), the
bodily subject furnished the very foundation for an epistemology in
which the physical world was always the ground of knowledge. The
bodily subject was the locus of metonymy in Marx, we might say, the
point of cross-mapping between two ontological orders, and the
point where he could derive his generalizations from matter to spirit, from part to whole, from a phenomenon visible and tangible to a
phenomenon invisible and intangible.

But to say that is also to suggest a certain tropism, a certain grav-
itational pull, between Marxist materialism and nineteenth-century
individualism. For within an evidentiary universe of the physical
senses, it was only the corporeal subject—only the individual as
actualized by his body—that could ever be demonstrable as "real."
As Marx said, "Since only what is material is perceptible, knowable,
nothing is known of the existence of God. I am sure only of my own
existence."[42] Only the bodily subject could ever stand, empirically
and incontestably, as a founding unit of Marxist epistemology. And
since the relation between the material and the immaterial was now
one of explanatory adequation (rather than, previously, one of enigmatic apposition), it was the bodily subject that must now stand as
the ground of generalizations, the ground out of which bodily
shapes might be derived for otherwise nonphysical bodies: "bodies"
such as society, or such as class.

To give the paradox an even sharper edge, we might say that
Marxist communism was, almost by necessity, an inferential derivation from Marxist individualism, the "collective" here being derived
always from a prior notion of the bodily subject. The suggestion is
not as outrageous as it might seem. It was not entirely fortuitous,
after all, that Marx should be found, on at least one occasion, in the
company of Emerson and Thoreau. And Alasdair MacIntyre has
suggested, some time ago, that Marxism is a nineteenth-century philosophy "as much because of what it has inherited from liberal individualism as because of its departures from liberalism."[43] That
inheritance, I would argue, is less substantive than cognitive. The
bodily subject is central to Marxist thought, in other words, not as a

matter of thematics but as a matter of epistemology. As the material foundation of a materialist philosophy, it provides the necessary grounding for Marxism, the necessary evidentiary register, allowing it to make sense of the world by reflexively incorporating the world, generalizing from body to person, from person to class, and from class to history.

BODILY GENERALIZATIONS

Still, the notion of a "Marxist individualism" might seem something of an oxymoron, since Marx (unlike Emerson and Thoreau, for example) was on record as having rejected the individual as a legitimate category of thought. He had begun the *Grundrisse*, for example, with the acid remark that "the individual and isolated hunter and fisherman, with whom Smith and Ricardo begin, belongs among the unimaginative conceits of the eighteenth-century Robinsonades." "The more deeply we go back into history," he said, "the more does the individual, and hence also the producing individual, appear as dependent, as belonging to a greater whole."[44]

When Marx went on, however, to imagine this "greater whole," when he tried to offer a historical survey of "community" as a counterpoint to the individual, the terms with which he did so turned out to be surprisingly individualistic, derived from the attributes of the bodily form. Thus, the "first form" of community as he envisioned it (an "initial, naturally arisen, spontaneous" development), also happened to be a "comprehensive unity." And, since this "unity is the real proprietor and the real presupposition of communal property, it follows that this unity can appear as a particular entity above the many real particular communities," so much so that it "exists ultimately as a *person.*"[45] Similarly, in classical antiquity, the "second form" of human association, even though the community was no longer "the substance" integrating its members into "purely natural component parts," Marx noted with satisfaction that the city-state was still a "*political body,*" still a "presence," a "whole," indeed "a kind of independent organism."[46]

As Marx's organic language suggests, the collective for him— whether as historical reconstruction or (as I will argue) as dialectical forecast—turned out to resemble nothing so much as a body, a body personified and objectified, and imaged forth as a natural fact. And since this immaterial "body" now stood to the natural body not in a relation of discrepancy (as the medieval Church once did) but in a relation of analogy, we might speak of the collective in Marx as the effect of a metonymic entailment. It was this metonymic entailment that made the natural body not only constitutive of but fully *representative* of the immaterial body, of which it was both a participating member and an emblematic index. The immaterial body, in other words, took on all those attributes—the empirical objectivity as well as the physical integrity—which presumably characterized the natural body. The logic of metonymy, in this sense, dispensed with the need to theorize about the community, for it was already accounted for, its defining features already immanent and generalizable from those of a physical given. And so it turned out that, in Marx, an immaterial entity was imaged after the materiality of the corporeal subject, an entity objectified even as it was naturalized.

This metonymic entailment—from the material to the immaterial, from physical bodies to nonphysical collectivities—underwrote Marx's conception of "species life" in his celebrated account of alienated labor. Proceeding from the corporeal integrity of the individual (an integrity not only bounded against but also projected upon "Nature, man's inorganic body"), Marx defined "species life" as the generalization of this phenomenon of self-boundedness and self-projection (and defined alienated labor, conversely, as the breakdown of this generalizability of "species from man," the breakdown of this emblematic representation of the universally human in the individually human).[47] Marx's conception of "species life," in short, depended on metonymy for its conceptual passage from a material body to a collective body, from the particular to the general. And, in a sense, metonymy might be said to be the cognitive medium, not only of Marxist materialism but of the entire Marxist dialectic, as it was articulated, for example, in the introduction to the *Grundrisse*. There, Marx turned his own procedural difficulties into a theoretical meditation, confessing both to his use of "simple abstractions" (such as labor) on the one hand, and to his desire, on the other hand, to see those simple abstractions as the necessary accretions of "an already given, concrete, living whole." He insisted that simple abstractions had no independent existence, that they must either "express the dominant relations of a less developed whole, or else those subordinate relations of a more developed whole."[48] The relation between part and whole was thus properly dialectical. And yet, we might notice as well, that the "whole" posited here as ontologically prior was nonetheless inferentially *derived*: derived as a metonymic effect, we might say, a generalized shadow, a kind of all-purpose organic container for simple abstractions, its living parts.

It is within this entanglement of metonymy and materialist dialectic that I want to examine Marx's conception of "class." Like other instances of the Marxist "whole," the concept of class also came into being as a shadow effect, extrapolated from (though posited as a container for) some material given. For Marx, then, class was a collective "body" in an altogether literal sense of the word: a body with an integrity all its own, with features objective and empirical,[49] with a historical "life" the way an individual might be imagined to have a biological life. Marx's image of the "working class," I suggest, was not so much that of a *class* as that of a *man*. Or, more accurately, we might say that Marx's image of class *was* in fact the image of man, since "class" for him was very much a natural entity, very much a bodily unit. If capitalism was that monstrous machine whose "parts are human beings," class was that organic body within which those human "parts" could once again be united into a political whole.

"Class" in Marx was the effect of a generalization, then, not so much a primary category of thought as a projective or reflexive category, emanating from and imaged after the bodily subject, what (following Marx and Engels) we might call the figure of the "abstract individual." Of course, the "abstract individual" was the very thing Marx and Engels set out to critique, in their attack on Bruno Bauer and, most famously, in the eleven *Theses on Feuerbach*.[50] And yet it is possible to argue that the figure of the "abstract individual" was never so decisively foreign or antecedent to Marxism, that it was in fact quite at home in the Marxist concept of class, as in this description of the proletariat:

> Since the abstraction of all humanity, even of the semblance of humanity, is practically complete in the full-grown proletariat; since the conditions of life of the proletariat sum up all the conditions of

life of society itself in all their inhuman acuity . . . it follows that the proletariat can and must free itself. . . . The question is not what this or that proletarian, or even the whole of the proletariat at the moment considers as its aim. The quetion is *what the proletariat is*, and what, consequent on that *being*, it will be compelled to do.[51]

The proletariat here was an "abstract individual" in more senses than one. What especially interests me is the way it was imagined to be endowed with, to be a container of, a "being" that was politically and historically consequential. What empowered the proletariat, it would seem, was its very identity, what it objectively was and would be, its agency being not only contingent upon but actually imma-nent within that identity. It was this derivation of a historical neces-sity from an objective identity (and the attribution of that objective identity to a group of people) that made the proletariat an "abstract individual," a collective body generalized as a historical subject. And, since that subject was a metonymic container for "all the con-ditions of life," the unfolding of which was "practically complete in the full-grown proletariat," there was also a sense in which the progress of history would bring with it a human "whole," a univer-sal lack of differentiation. For this reason Marx wrote that, even though "proletariat and wealth are opposites . . . it is not sufficient to declare them two sides of a single whole." Rather, he argued, "when the proletariat is victorious . . . it is victorious only by abol-ishing itself and its opposite. Then the proletariat disappears as well as the opposite which determines it, private property."[52]

In this complex account of the end of history, the proletariat not only eliminated its antagonist but, in the same gesture, eliminated itself *as an antagonist*, and so ushered in a new breed of man, a new kind of entity, marked by its undifferentiated pristineness no less than by its dialectical completion.[53] From this perspective, the epis-temology of class would seem to rest on what Louis Althusser would call a postulate of "philosophical fullness" as well as a postulate of "simple original unity."[54] Of course, for Althusser, such postulates are sheer anathema, which he lays at the door of Hegel and, to some extent, of the early Marx himself.[55] What they amount to, he argues, is not only a fiction of origins but a fiction that equates the originary with the unitary:

For the unity of a simple essence manifesting itself in its alienation produces this result: that every concrete difference featured in the Hegelian totality, including the "spheres" visible in this totality (civil society, the State, religion, philosophy, etc.), all these differences are negated as soon as they are affirmed: for they are no more than "moments" of the simple internal principle of totality, which fulfils itself by negating the alienated difference that it posed; further, as alienations—phenomena—of the simple internal principle, these differences are all equally *indifferent*.[56]

Against this "indifferent" epistemology—one that turned all irreconcilable differences into epiphenomena, into "secondary" evidence—Althusser offers an elaborate defense, by painstakingly (and some would say casuistically) distinguishing the Marxist dialectic from its Hegelian precursor. Of course, the Hegelian legacy might be said to have influenced not only Marx but virtually every modern thinker, and most certainly Althusser himself.[57] Still, the point remains that, for Marx, the "indifferent" was nothing less than an epistemology, an epistemology I find especially troubling in his logic of metonymy, which, in its "indifferent" equation of the material and the immaterial, was thus tempted to generalize inductively, from a physical body to a political body, from an individual to a class. What ensued was a particular kind of imprecision: the reduction of the "collective" to a shadow effect, at best a generalized proposition, at worst a blurry image. Against this indifferent epistemology, I want to bring into focus one particular critique of Marxism (initiated by Engels, elaborated by Max Weber, Emile Durkheim, and, most recently, Anthony Giddens): a critique directed at the blurriness visited upon one specific category of the collective, what these critics loosely call the "social."

THE CATEGORY OF THE SOCIAL

This category, at once immaterial and nonindividual, has the most to suffer, I think, from the sort of generalizations imposed by a materialist and individualist philosophy. It suffers, that is, from analytic oversight, from a presumption of inferability, and it is helpful, in fact, to dwell on one moment of contrast, between the blurriness of the social in Marx and the sharp clarity of it in, say, Max Weber, or (perhaps most pertinent here) Emile Durkheim. I have in mind, in particular, the contrasting evidentiary domains that Marx and Durkheim constructed for what might appear an identical phenomenon, the division of labor.

For Marx, this was a phenomenon both well-defined and site-specific; it was an industrial arrangement, peculiar to the factory and the assembly line. He was at pains, indeed, to show that the "division of labor in the interior of a society, and that in the interior of a workshop, differ not only in degree, but also in kind." The former, the social division of labor, being pervasive and seemingly universal, was for that reason also unanalyzable, since it "springs up naturally," a "spontaneous growth," "caused by the differences of sex and age, a division that is consequently based on a purely physiological foundation."[58] True to his logic of bodily generalizations, society was figured here as a natural body, and social division of labor, being also natural, was thus a matter of analytic indifference to him.[59] All his critical energies were directed elsewhere, against the division of labor in the workshop, clearly no work of nature but a manmade horror, involving as it did the carving up of natural individuals into industrial parts. In short, for Marx, the domain of the "social" (to the extent that it was distinguishable from the economic), turned out to be only a secondary order of evidence, subsumable under the category of the "natural." Only the economic, only the primary evidentiary domain, merited the scope as well as the care of his analysis.

There was a hierarchy of evidence in Marx, we might say, a hierarchy seen all the more clearly when it is seen in reverse—when we turn, for example, to Durkheim. What was immaterial to Marx was consequential for that very reason to Durkheim. And so, tersely noting that "the division of labor [is] a fact of a very general nature, which the economists, who first proposed it, never suspected,"[60] Durkheim went on to discuss the phenomenon, not as a feature unique to the workshop but as a feature common to all organized society. As the principal investigatory site, the social also sustained the finest analytic distinctions in Durkheim. Far from being a cognitive shadow, or a collapsible epiphenomenon, it was here a field of primary relations, with an evidentiary domain in its own right, and out of whose complex differentiations Durkheim would elaborate an equally complex theory of social integration.

Durkheim's insistence on the social as primary evidence—his sense of its irreducibility to some other explanatory ground—serves as a challenge, not only to the evidentiary logic of Marx's economism,[61] but also to the logic of his bodily generalizations, his inductive reasoning from material entities to immaterial entities, from part to whole. The social might be seen, then, as a challenge to the very concept of a "whole." This was not, of course, Durkheim's own sense of its possible usage; for him, society was very much a "whole," and the "social" very much synonymous with the organically integral. Still, in rejecting a hierarchy of evidentiary planes, Durkheim himself would seem to be pointing the way toward a *non-*integral conception of society, predicated not on the generalizability from cause to phenomenon, from the material to the immaterial, but on some notion of intransitivity (or extreme permutability) in structural relays. Especially in the context of class, the social would seem to unsettle the very notion of "determination." Class, that is to say, can no longer be thought of as some genetic foundation, some "deep" causal ground, objectively inscribing (and unifying) a matching set of identities, identities coincidentally economic, social, and political. In short, by plying loose the metonymic entailment between the material and the immaterial, the social would seem to transform class into a vexed concept both on the axis of determination and on the axis of identity. It points toward a vision of class as a nonintegral formation: not an empirical unit, nor a body natural, but a strictly relational phenomenon, with no spatial location, no objective shape, no indwelling essence.[62]

Against Durkheim, then, and certainly against Marx, I invoke the social not only to challenge the logic of bodily generalizations but also to cast doubt on the actuality or even the potentiality of an integrated "whole" in any rigorous sense of the word. My thinking here is informed by Ernesto Laclau and Chantal Mouffe's powerful argument against our customary view of "society" as a "founding totality of its partial processes."[63] Taking seriously their suggestion that every social formation is "unsutured," I want to give particular emphasis to a number of concepts—concepts such as nonalignment and unevenness, permutability and intransitivity—that make bodily generalizations a little harder to naturalize and a little harder to defend. For my purposes, then, the social is less important as an autonomous domain than as a kind of conceptual pressure: an irritation and an affront to our entrenched habit of thinking about entities as "bodies," and thinking about bodies as bodies with "contents." Such a habit constructs for us a syntax of life structured by the preposition "in," a too familiar preposition, as Charles Taylor reminds us, carrying with it an epistemology of location and attribution that "comes to seem as fixed and ineradicable from reality as the preposition is from our lexicon."[64] And since the preposition is crucial not only to Marx but to a broad spectrum of modern epistemologies (beginning, perhaps, with Descartes's location of ideas "in" the mind, as mental "contents"),[65] I want to take this occasion to digress somewhat, and to examine some other contexts where the syntax of "in" might be usefully disturbed by the category of the social. I am thinking especially of our assumptions about what is *in* a literary text.

The social, in our current historicist turn, is, of course, adduced most often to give the preposition "in" a new literary meaning. The social is invoked, that is, to add substance and scope, to provide documentation and contextualization, to construct the text as a material artifact, a kind of linguistic container for a thing called History.[66] In our hasty retreat from deconstruction, we seem to have forgotten one of its crucial insights: that the "text" is neither a body nor a presence, that it has no spatial location or substantive identity, nothing that can be called its "inside." One conceivable implication of deconstruction might actually have been a radical challenge to the entire discipline of literary studies, a radical rejection of the practice of "reading," on the ground that there is nothing "in" a text to be read. Of course, this was not what in fact happened. New Historicism, to the extent that it reinstates "reading" as a legitimate practice—and to the extent that it posits an indwelling history as the subject of such readings—would seem to mark a return to an earlier epistemology, an epistemology of location and attribution, one that, in effect, reads History as the "identity" of Literature. The text is thus imagined once again to be a body with contents, contents historically disseminated, to be sure, but contents nonetheless, inferable if not ultimately provable. And the task of critic is, once again, to "read" those contents, by locating the historicity "in" the text and locating the text "in" history.

In what follows, I want to take issue with this epistemology of location and attribution. I want to propose, that is, a mode of literary studies not based on "reading" as a paradigmatic exercise, and not claiming its integrity on the ground of contents but owning up, forthrightly and unapologetically, to its lack of disciplinary boundaries, its necessary delineation through (as well as possible contribution to) other disciplines. Literary studies is justified, in other words, only as a field *without* an objective identity, a field of virtual relations, whose very virtualness must make the field interdisciplinary by necesssity and not by choice. Rather than invoking the social as an aid to interpretation—a way to localize a historical identity in a text—I invoke it in order to challenge the very concept of "identity,"[67] and to argue for a critical practice whose objective would not be to read a text at all, but to carry on various historical or philosophical conversations, amongst which and against which the text would appear only as a fitful and uncertain participant. And, rather than invoking the social to "enrich" the literary, I want to make a case for the latter's constitutive "poverty," a condition that (as Wallace Stevens suggests) not only frustrates the preposition "in," but also compels us to try out some other prepositions—"between," "in spite of," "adjacent to," "before," and "after"—prepositions that gesture not to a generalizable relation between part and whole but to a state of impossible wholeness.

MEN AT LEISURE

Toward that end, I want to examine Melville's "The Paradise of Bachelors and the Tartarus of Maids," a story that, almost providentially, brings together questions of part and whole, material and immaterial, and all within the context of a conspicuous (and problematic) relation between the literary and the social. As the title suggests, this is a diptych, a verbal whole made out of two clearly delineated parts. This is not the only Melville story so organized. Two other stories—"The Two Temples" and "The Poor Man's Pudding and the Rich Man's Crumbs"—also exhibit the same compositional principle. "The Paradise of Bachelors and the Tartarus of Maids" is unusual, however, in making that whole adequate to two forms of partitioning—along the line of gender as well as the line of class—making these two translatable one into the other. On one side, there is convivial ambience, culinary delight, and carefree association, a world inhabited not only by men but by a particular class of men. On the other side, there is desolate landscape, regimented labor, and physical misery, a world inhabited not only by women but by a particular class of women.

Taken by itself, neither the class partition nor the gender partition is especially remarkable. What is remarkable here, however, is the assumed relation between these two: they are presented not only as correlated but, it would seem, actually as coincidental and coextensive. One is perfectly translatable into the other, so that the category of gender neatly doubles as a category of class. It is this perfect "translatability" between the two categories that gives the story its spatial clarity, its status as a topographical whole made up of two categoric locations, "paradise" and "tartarus." This is very much a deliberate effect, of course, an effect achieved largely through the logic of metonymy. The strategy here, in other words, is to focus on the representative part of an adumbrated whole, a whole that is then generalized from that part. And so, a representative group of men—a privileged group of men—is made to stand in for the entire male population, making class privilege metonymically equivalent to a generalized maleness.

In this context, it is especially significant that the men here happen to be bachelors. For bachelorhood, here and elsewhere in Melville, is a species of manhood far more privileged than the more compromised kind, exemplified by the "Benedick tradesmen," who, being married, must spend their life worrying about the "rise of bread and fall of babies." The bachelors, by contrast, are free from all obligations, marital and paternal, a gender privilege that, in turn, is equated here with class privilege, with freedom from work. Of course, we know that the bachelors actually do work. They are practicing lawyers, hailing from such places as Grey's Inn and Lincoln's Inn. However, as they are here presented they are eminently at leisure, burdened neither by the exertions of the legal profession nor by the drudgery of domestic housework. The bachelors are portrayed, that is, as if they were gentlemen of means, characterized and unified by their pleasure in idleness. Flaunting as they do a specific gender privilege, they make up a class by themselves.

The mapping of an aristocratic identity upon a bachelor identity—the mapping of class upon gender—is, of course, something of a convention itself. As Eve Sedgwick points out, the "aristocratic," as perceived (no doubt wishfully) by the bourgeoisie in the nineteenth century, was marked by a cluster of associations, including effeminacy, unspecified homosexuality, connoisseurship, and dissipation, all of which were conveniently locatable in (or attributable to) the figure of the bachelor.[68] Sedgwick is speaking of nineteenth-century England, but her insight applies equally to nineteenth-century America, where an even keener suspicion of the "aristocratic" inspired the same depiction of class through gender, making the effete bachelor a metonym for the entire upper order, real or imagined. This is certainly the case with Ik Marvell's *Reveries of a Bachelor* (1850), which makes that most unmanly of luxuries, daydreaming, the essence of well-heeled bachelorhood. And it is the case as well with "The Paradise of Bachelors and the Tartarus of Maids," which, in making effete aristocrats out of effete bachelors, would seem to be operating within a well-defined tradition of class critique.

"The Paradise of Bachelors" is pervaded (and the ostentatious references to "paradise" notwithstanding) by an aura of the degenerate, an aura of declension from a heroic past to a feminized present: "The iron heel is changed to a boot of patent-leather; the long two-handed sword to a one-handed quill"; "the helmet is a wig." Instead of "carving out immortal fame in glorious battling for the Holy Land," as the Crusaders once did, the modern-day bachelor is now reduced "to the carving of roast-mutton at a dinner-board" (317–18). There is a time-honored quality to these charges brought against the pleasure-loving and leisure-flaunting bachelor, time-honored especially in America, where idleness had always been looked upon as untoward and effeminate. The Puritan ministers had long ago warned their congregation that "God sent you not into this world as into a Play-house, but a Work-house."[69] Later, in Revolutionary America, the chief bugbear in the Republican lexicon was of course "luxury," a perennial source of corruption. A burning concern for the Founding Fathers (here expressed by John Adams) was thus "to prevent riches from producing luxury," and "to prevent luxury from producing effeminacy intoxication extravagance Vice and folly."[70] It is not surprising, then, that European visitors from Tocqueville on were regularly struck by the inveteracy of the American work habit.[71] As late as 1849, Sir Charles Lyell, the eminent British geologist, noticed that this was a "country where all, whether rich or poor, were laboring from morning till night, without ever indulging in a holiday."[72] Another European visitor, Francis Grund, summed this up succinctly. Americans, he reported, "know but the *horrors* of idleness."[73]

Such "horrors of idleness" were denounced from a thousand pulpits, and in publications both eccleciastical and commercial. In 1843, when Henry Ward Beecher gave a series of Sunday evening lectures to his congregation (subsequently collected in his *Lectures to Young Men*), he devoted the first lecture to the subject of idleness, compiling a catalog of the "various classes of idlers, and leave the reader to judge, if he be an indolent man, to which class he belongs." To those who would dodge behind the excuse that "it is genteel leisure, not laziness; it is relaxation, not sloth; amusement, not indolence," Beecher had this to say: "Be not deceived: if you are idle, you are on the road to ruin, and there are few stopping places upon it. It is rather a precipice, than a road."[74] Shifting his metaphor, he also compared idleness to a somewhat different kind of topography:

> When Satan would put ordinary men to a crop of mischief, like a wise husbandman, he clears the ground and prepares it for seed; but he finds the idle man already prepared, and he has scarcely the trouble of sowing, for vices, like weeds, ask little strewing, except what the wind gives their ripe and winged seeds, shaking and scattering them all abroad. Indeed, lazy men may fitly be likened to a tropical prairie, over which the wind of temptation perpetually blows, drifting every vagrant seed from hedge and hill, and which—without a moment's rest through all the year— waves its rank harvest of luxuriant weeds.[75]

Such severe judgment (not to mention such figurative extravagance) might seem surprising. It is especially surprising coming from Beecher, who happened, after all, also to be the author of a popular novel, *Norwood* (1868), whose idealized hero, Reuben Wentworth, was not only idle once but downright unapologetic about it. Wentworth was blessed with a rich uncle, his uncle Eb, "an old bachelor of fifty years," whose "purse had carried him through college," given him "a year in Vienna, and one in Paris," and who, upon death, had left his nephew "an income that removed one motive for exertion." From the same bachelor uncle also came a long disquisition about what it took to be a gentleman. Asked by his nephew whether one could "be a gentleman in any respectable calling," he had answered, "Oh, dear, no. *My* gentleman must take all his time to it, spend his time at it, be jealous of everything else." Wentworth, of course, ended up not being a gentleman—he became a doctor—but what Uncle Eb said about the gentleman could equally be said of him: "He [is] so fine that he accomplishes more while doing nothing than others do with all their bustle."[76]

Elsewhere in Beecher, there are further examples of people who accomplish more while doing nothing than others do with all their bustle. In an essay entitled "Dream-Culture" (1854), for example, he resorted to the same metaphor of husbandry he had used earlier, in his lecture against idleness, though this time to a startlingly different end. Here, in a virtual parody of his earlier admonitions, Beecher suggested that "the chief use of a farm, if it be well selected, and of a proper soil, is, to lie down upon." He called this unusual kind of husbandry "industrious lying down," and contrasted it with the other, more usual, variety, practiced by farmers, which involved "standing up and lazing about after the plow or behind his scythe." *That* kind of farming was ordinary enough. "Industrious lying down," on the other hand, produced crops that are far more extraordinary: "harvests of associations, fancies, and dreamy broodings." And, to those who objected that such "farming" is "a mere waste of precious time," Beecher replied that it is completely justified "if it gives great delight . . . if it brings one a little out of conceit with hard economies, . . . and the sweat and dust of life among selfish, sordid men."[77]

Beecher certainly seemed to be speaking out of both sides of his mouth.[78] He was not alone, however, in being of two minds on the subject. There was very little agreement, in fact, in the mid-nineteenth century, about the relative merit and demerit of leisure and recreation.[79] The controversy attracted a good many commentators, especially clergymen, itself a significant fact. In a book called *The*

Christian Law of Amusement (1859), for example, James Leonard Corning, pastor of the Westminster Presbyterian Church in Buffalo, described the battle as being waged between those who denounced amusement "with most dogmatic intolerance as if nothing could be said in its favor," and those who praised it to the skies, "as if the progress of civilization depended on it."[80] However, this did not prevent Corning himself from joining the fray, determined as he was to prove that the necessity for amusement was a "Christian law."

In the case of Henry Ward Beecher, of course, the battle seemed to be going on inside his head and among his various pieces of writing. But there was a pattern as well behind these seemingly contrary pronouncements. The historian Daniel Rodgers, puzzling over them, has come up with what seems to be a crucial organizing principle. "The sermons explicitly directed at the young, the poor, or the working class tended also to be those in which the gospel of work was most prominent; in thinking of the prosperous, overtaxed businessmen in his congregation he often chose the counsel of leisure."[81] Such an assessment is borne out if we consider that, in *Norwood*, it was the gentlemanly Dr. Wentworth, who, alone of all the townspeople, could afford to be seen standing under a cherry tree, "watching with a kind of sober smile the workmen" laboring away at their tasks.[82] Clearly it made a difference to Beecher how the leisure was being used, and who was there to use it. Cheap amusements—such as the popular theater and the circus—were sinks of iniquity: a "universal pestilence," an "infernal chemistry of ruin," indeed "hell's first welcome."[83] More genteel pastimes, however—such as visiting the Louvre and the National Art Gallery, or summering in the country—actually turned out to be morally uplifting, and indeed were recounted by Beecher as fond episodes in his own life. *Star Papers*, his collection of occasional essays, offered a record of his tour of Europe as well as his "vacations of three summers."[84]

Beecher is something of a pivotal figure, from this perspective, testifying not only to a shift in cultural values in the nineteenth century but, more important still, to the transferability of class attributes, as the identities of class evolved over time. Leisure, once flung in accusation at the feet of the upper class, was fast becoming, by the second half of the nineteenth century, not only a birthright but something of a requisite for the middle class, at once identity-imparting and identity-certifying.[85] Leisure is class-inflected, then, not in the sense that it is tied to one particular class but in the sense it is variously marked, variously nuanced and accented, when it is invoked as the salient characteristic for different groups, when its semantic history bears the palpable imprint of social change. Given the shifting class location of any single trait, the social identity of class would seem to reside less in substantive definitions than in differential relations. Its profile at any given moment has everything to do with the contrasting assignment of attributes, rather than with the attributes as such. Once again, the social would seem to function here as an inflecting medium, a zone of mediate determinacy, whose articulations are more various, more complexly differentiated, and more possibly conflicting than might appear generalizable from any simple economic given. It is within this conception of the social that we can begin to gauge the dissonance in Beecher's own writings, or the dissonance between him and Melville. And it is within this conception of the social, as well, that we can begin to see the constitutive poverty of the text as a unit of analysis, its constitutive dependence on "extraneous" relations to make any sense at all, let alone *historical* sense. For the great interest of the Melville story is surely not what is "in" it: not the fact that leisure is here linked with degeneracy but the fact that it is so linked in accordance with an earlier, more populist, faintly anachronistic conception of class. Unlike the blandly decorous leisure in *Norwood* or *Star Papers*, leisure in "The Paradise of Bachelors" remains over-rich, sexy, wickedly alluring.[86] And, unlike Henry Ward Beecher, who apparently has come to accept leisure by accepting a selective version of it—the version newly sanitized by its association with the middle class—Melville has kept alive an older dynamics of attraction and revulsion, or attraction *as* revulsion, so that the spectacle of gentlemen at leisure becomes not so much a presumption in favor of leisure as a presumption against the gentlemen themselves, who, as leisured men, also turn out to be lesser men.

In this sense it is difficult to speak of a social critique "in" the story, for the critique is hardly located in the story, but exogenous to it, intelligible only in relation to Beecher, and only in relation to an earlier conception of class that, beginning in the mid-nineteenth century, was just about to be superseded. Furthermore, even within this relational matrix, the critique would not constitute a textual identity substantive enough or integral enough to warrant a singular reading. For the Melville story, in its very attempt to critique the leisured gentleman through the effete bachelor, also carries with it a range of polemical alternatives, some unintended, unexpected, and quite possibly unwelcome. One of them (and a somewhat unexpected one in the case of Melville)[87] is that, even though the story is obviously not "meant" to be homophobic, homophobia is nonetheless more than a dim shape on the horizons. Even as this complicates the story's profile, there is another sense in which the category of "textual identity" might be said to be in jeopardy as well. For in making gender the metonymic register for class, and in making the former fully a part of (and thus fully contained within) the latter, the story in effect resolves itself into a topographical whole, a "founding totality of its partial processes." Such a "whole" suggests yet another order of hazard for the text, one that, to my mind, is just as troubling. In the rest of this essay, I want to dwell on this problematic aspect of the story, especially as it bears on the fate of the counterpart to the effete bachelor, the woman worker in the second half of the story.

WOMEN AT WORK

The woman worker was, of course, one of the most significant creations of the nineteenth century, a figure cited as the most important part of the labor force by the earliest advocates of manufactures, Alexander Hamilton and Tench Coxe,[88] and, with the rapid expansion of the factory system, quickly becoming, by the second quarter of the nineteenth century, a permanent fixture on the social as well as the economic scene. In the Melville story, it is the woman worker who is made to stand metonymically for the entire working class—apparently a deliberate decision on Melville's part, for, as Judith A. McGaw points out, even though there were actually *both* male and female workers in the Dalton paper mill that Melville visited, the former was eliminated from the story.[89] This metonymic focus on the woman worker is in turn doubled upon itself, for the focus happens not to be on the woman generally but on her sexualized body specifically, the oppressions and deprivations of that body serving as a stand-in for the full range of her oppressions and deprivations. It is this double metonymy that makes female sexuality the representative sign for the generalized injuries of class. Beginning with the journey to the paper mill (a protracted affair, vividly rendered as a grotesque encounter with the female anatomy), the scene of labor is consistently imaged as a highly sexualized landscape, mechanical production here being dramatized as a kind of mechanical violation of the female body.

This sexualized landscape has traditionally been read in biographical terms, in terms of Melville's marital problems, domestic needs, the too-numerous births in his family. Here, I want to call attention to a somewhat different set of issues, having to do with the practice of metonymy, the practice of generalizing from part to whole. What especially concerns me is the status of gender when it is harnessed to this practice, when "woman" is invoked as a representative sign, and constructed as a signifying body to serve that purpose. Such a practice is both clarifying and obfuscating, I argue, clarifying, because the force of the indictment here is obviously considerable, but also obfuscating, because the mapping of class upon gender not only flattens out any possible nonalignment between the two, but also flattens out the figure of "woman" into a categoric unity, a signifying whole that, in its very singularity of feature, might end up being emptied of its claim to attention. The uniform abjection of the women also makes them, in a sense, uniformly uninteresting. It is with this provisional sense of hazard, then—this sense of the probable obfuscations of metonymy—that I return to the Melville story, to ask whether its emblematic clarity might not nonetheless generate a shadow of its own.

Along those lines, it is worth noting that the focus in the story is not only on female sexuality but most emphatically on deviant female sexuality. These are all girls, all unmarried, all unnaturally coupling with machines. Instead of fulfilling their wifely destinies, they are seen standing, "like so many mares haltered to the rack," tending machines that "vertically thrust up a long, glittering scythe . . . look[ing] exactly like a sword" (329). And instead of laboring naturally, as in childbirth, the women workers labor unnaturally, giving birth, not to babies but to industrial products. The narrator reports a "scissory sound . . . as of some cord being snapped, and down dropped an unfolded sheet of perfect foolscap . . . still moist and warm" (332). In short, the sights and sounds of industrial production cruelly mimic the sights and sounds of biological reproduction, underscoring, at every turn, the drama of perverted womanhood.

Of course, Melville was not the only one to have seized on the image of the denaturalized woman as a metonym for the sufferings of the working class. Joan Wallach Scott, studying the representation of women workers in France during the same period, has come upon images strikingly similar, images of female sexual disorder also used to represent the problems of the entire industrial order. As Scott points out, this mode of cultural figuration—this mapping of a class critique upon the symbolic body of gender—is not altogether disinterested. Indeed, as she documents it, political economists such as Jules Simon (who wrote a book called *L'Ouvrière*) not only routinely lamented the sexual plight of the women workers but also proposed, as a remedy, "the return of the mother to the family," for, as he said, "It is necessary that women be able to marry and that married women be able to remain at home all day, there to be the providence and the personification of the family." Given this view of things, it is not surprising that, according to Michelet, "ouvrière" was an "impious, sordid word that no language has ever known." Jules Simon, meanwhile, went so far as to say that "the woman who becomes a worker is no longer a woman."[90]

There is, of course, nothing quite so outspoken in "The Paradise of Bachelors and the Tartarus of Maids," nor anything to hint of the Cult of True Womanhood, the American counterpart to those pronouncements offered by Michelet and Simon.[91] Still, given Melville's anxieties about his literary career in an environment dominated by "scribbling women," it is certainly possible to see, in this story about "blank-looking girls" working on "blank paper," a half-resentful, half-wishful, and not especially well-disguised fantasy about women who wrote too mechanically and too much.[92] Biographical speculations of this sort fall outside the purview of this essay, although it is worth noting that, from a variety of perspectives (not the least being his self-regarding individualism), Melville would seem to have reason for assigning to "women" a metonymic character, turning them into representative bodies, bodies that not only encapsulate their identity but encapsulate as well the identity of a larger whole, a whole fully generalizable from its emblematic part.

THE LIMITS OF GENERALIZATIONS

A metonymic practice such as this bears more than a resemblance, of course, to our own practice as critics, our practice to speak of the "body" of the text, a body of encapsulated contents. I have referred to this as an epistemology of location and attribution. It is this epistemology that persuades us to see each text as a miniature container of the historical whole, a historical whole that (at least for some critics) is assumed to be *generalizable* from the text, as an attribute resident "in" its body. Given my dissatisfaction with this preposition—and given my sense of the radical disparity between the text as a composed object and as an epistemological moment—I want to suggest a different critical practice, premised not on the full presence of history in literature but on the impossibility of such an event: an impossibility whose consequences I take to be pragmatic, rather than self-deprecatingly rhetorical.

In other words, since the horizons of intelligibility for a text are never fully encapsulated by its moment of production, and never fully contained by the textual body itself, any attempt to locate within that body a set of historical "contents" is necessarily presumptuous, if not ultimately foolish. Rather than trying to derive historical generalizations from literary texts—rather than trying to read literature as the ground of intelligibility for history—we might want to invert the entire process, and attend instead to those moments when the text seems most intractable, most stubbornly incapable of some larger meaning, using these moments to question the very notion of "generalizability" itself. Only with some working skepticism toward that concept—some sense of the possible nonalignment between history and literature, and some sense of the possible silence of the latter—can we resist the temptation of seeing history simply as the identity of a literary text, disclosable through reading. And only then can we free literary criticism itself from its perennial need to construct a subject of predication out of what a text supposedly "is."

Having no wish, then, to construct a subject of predication for "The Paradise of Bachelors and the Tartarus of Maids," I want instead to use the figure of the woman worker to trouble the very notion of a unitary historical subject, by examining her through other texts, other accounts of factory life. And indeed, she was nothing if not an emblematic figure in the 1830s and 1840s. Gleefully adduced—by company officials and by ecstatic foreign visitors—she was the pride of America and was routinely contrasted with the debased operatives in Manchester, England.[93] Charles Dickens, who admitted to having "visited many mills in Manchester and elsewhere," reported with much-dramatized surprise that the American women workers "were all well dressed. . . . They were healthy in appearance, many of them remarkably so, and had the manners and deportment of young women: not of degraded brutes of burden." Indeed, "from all the crowd I saw in the different factories that day, I cannot recall or separate one young face that gave me a painful impression; not one young girl whom, assuming it to be a matter of necessity that she should gain her daily bread by the labour of her hands, I would have removed from those works if I had had the power."[94]

For Dickens, the American woman worker cut a different figure for obvious reasons: in being so happily unrecognizable to the English reader, she cast shame on her English counterpart and on everything that was wrong with industrial England. She was as much a metonym here as she was in the Melville text: in both cases, she was a part generalizable into a whole, although the "whole" she bodied forth here could not have been more contrary to Melville's purposes. This was, in any case, the standard identity assigned her by English visitors. The Reverend William Scoresby, who visited the "factory girls" expressly to report to his congregation in Bradford, England, devoted chapters of his book, *American Factories and Their Female Operatives* (1845), to "Their Literary Pursuits," "Their Leisure Employments," "Their Moral Condition," and "Causes of Their Superiority." Scoresby found that these women were "clothed in silks, and otherwise gaily adorned," that it was "a common thing for one of these girls to have five hundred dollars (a hundred guineas, nearly) in deposit" at the Lowell Institution for Savings, that their literary publication, the *Lowell Offering*, was "fair and comely," quite "a phenomenon in literature," and that, in short, though "having no possible motive for flattering our transatlantic sisters," he must nonetheless conclude that in "general moral character, or superior intelligence, or great respectability—these factory girls do greatly surprise and interest us," and that they must commend themselves to "those who feel an interest in the improvement of the condition of our working population."[95]

These glowing nineteenth-century accounts are echoed by some twentieth-century historians, who, reacting against mainstream labor history, have called attention instead to the *benefits* of factory work for women.[96] Thomas Dublin, in particular, emphasizes the importance of industrialization not only to women's individual well-being, but also to their potential for collective action. Dublin finds that—contrary to our usual view—the New England factory girls had not been driven to work by dire necessity. Indeed, according to him, the property holdings of the fathers put them in the broad middle ranges of wealth in their home towns; fully 86 percent of the fathers had property valued at $100 or more. These women came because they wanted to, he argues, because they wanted the freedom of urban living, away from their rural families, and what they gained, as well, was a sense of solidarity born out of the social relations of production. Work-sharing at the mills and communal living at the company boardinghouses socialized the women in a way that the household economy would not, and that experience led directly to the collective action exemplified by strikes of the 1830s and the Ten Hour Movement of the 1840s, which saw the growth of a permanent labor organization among women, the Lowell Female Labor Reform Association, founded in December 1844. Dublin concludes that the factory experience "placed the Lowell women squarely within the evolving labor movement and indicated that crafts traditions were not the only legitimating forces in labor protests of the period."[97]

Such conclusions, striking in their own right, do not pose as severe a challenge to the Melville story as they do to our current practice of reading. Any attempt to localize within the text a historical "identity"—any attempt to read it metonymically, as the index to a historical whole—seems to me seriously misguided, for what is most striking about the story is surely its inorganic relation to the lives of nineteenth-century women workers, its nonencapsulation of anything that might be called "social reality," and hence its resistance

to any direct historical generalizations. There is no explanatory fullness inductively derivable from the text, no compression of a historical whole. Rather than seeing history as the identity of literature,
then, we might want to set aside this identitarian premise, in favor
of concepts such as discrepancy, noncoincidence, off-centeredness.
To acknowledge this is not, of course, to abandon the project of his-
toricization altogether. It is, however, a proposal to rethink its terms
and its method: to make it less metonymic, less confident about the
genetic alignment or interpretive concentricity[98] between text and
history, and less assured of a generalizable relation between part and
whole.

BODY AND MIND

For the nineteenth-century women workers themselves, such a concession to (or rather, such an insistence on) the limits of generalizations was not only cognitively salutary, but also psychologically necessary.[99] Their stories and poems, letters and memoirs were thus ani-
mated by a stubborn refusal to bear witness to a principle of
integration, a refusal that might help us rethink the not absolutely
transitive relation between body and consciousness, class and gender, the universal and the specific. Almost without exception, these
women, even those writing for house organs such as the *Lowell
Offering*, commented on the physical ordeal of work, the fatigue and
often the disfigurations endured by the body. In a series entitled
"Letters from Susan," one author, Harriet Farley, complains that

> the hours seemed very long . . . and when I went out at night the
> sound of the mill was in my ears, as of crickets, frogs, and jewsharps,
> all mingled together in strange discord. . . . It makes my feet ache and
> swell to stand so much, . . . they almost all say that when they have
> worked here a year or two they have to procure shoes a size or two
> larger than before they came. The right hand, which is the one used
> in stopping and starting the loom, becomes larger than the left.[100]

What is remarkable, however, is that, such bodily afflictions notwithstanding, Farley also went on to report, in the same letter, that, while
the factory girls "scorn to say they were contented, if asked the question, for it would compromise their Yankee spirit. . . . Yet, withal,

they are cheerful. I never saw a happier set of beings. They appear
blithe in the mill, and out of it."[101] From aching ears and swollen
feet, it might seem a long way to cheerfulness, happiness, and
blitheness, and if Farley left the exact passage—the exact sequence of
relays—unspecified, a partial account was offered by Harriet Hanson
Robinson, who started working in the Lowell mills in 1834, at the
age of ten, and gave an account of that experience in her memoir,
Loom and Spindle, published in 1898 when she was seventy-three
years old. From the distance of some sixty years, she could still
remember the excitement of gainful employment, of having money
in the pocket for the first time, and of the magical transformation the
women underwent:

> [A]fter the first pay-day came, and they felt the jingle of silver in
> their pockets, and had begun to feel its mercurial influence, their
> bowed heads were lifted, their necks seemed braced with steel, they
> looked you in the face, sang blithely among their looms or frames,
> and walked with elastic step to and from their work. And when Sun-
> day came, homespun was no longer their only wear; and how sedate-
> ly gay in their new attire they walked to church, and how proudly
> they dropped their silver four-pences into the contribution-box! It
> seemed as if a great hope impelled them,—the harbinger of the new
> era that was about to dawn for them and for all women-kind.[102]

For women not accustomed to having earnings of their own, not
accustomed to the luxury of city clothes, or the luxury of church
patronage, leaving home and working in a factory brought with it a
psychological well-being that shone forth in full view of the physical
ordeal of repetitive labor and long working hours. One was not
reducible to the other, or generalizable from the other, and that was
precisely the point. For what was most remarkable about these
accounts of factory life was surely the incessant mismatch—the lack
of absolute determinacy or logical entailment—between standards
of discomfort and states of mind, between the generalized conditions of work and the specific affect reported by the women workers. The women workers were workers, to be sure; they were bodies
bound to machines, bodies that became aching ears and swollen feet.
But they were women as well, and, as women, they had a prehistory
significantly different from that of the male workers, and a capacity

for transformation (not to mention a capacity for benefit) also significantly different. The experience of industrialization, it would seem, was not at all an integral experience, not at all evenly registered or universally shared, but locally composed for each particular group, its composition being directly related to the antecedents out of which that group emerged.[103] In the case of the women workers, coming as they did from under the shadow of the patriarchal household, the emotional satisfaction as newly independent wage-earners might turn out to be as nontrivial a benefit as the physical drudgery of labor was nontrivial an oppression. It is here, in the perpetual lack of adequation between these two registers, that we can speak of the "nontrivial" as a crucial evidentiary category, a crucial challenge to any explanatory model of compulsory transparency. And it is here, as well, that we can speak of gender as an exemplary instance of the nontrivial, both in the relays it multiplies between body and mind, in the limits it poses to the logic of generalizations.

What emerged, then, from these writings by women workers, were a set of determinations that, while acknowledged, were also carefully kept from being too controlling. Between the body and the individual, and between the individual and the class, there was always the possibility for nonalignment: always the possibility for inconclusive mappings and intransitive relays. The bodies of the women told one story, their inspirations and aspirations told another, and their organized strikes, it would seem, told yet a third. Lucy Larcom was speaking not as an abstract worker generally but as a woman worker specifically when she wrote,

> One great advantage which came to these many stranger girls through being brought together, away from their own homes, was that it taught them to go out of themselves, and enter into the lives of others. Home-life, when one always stays at home, is necessarily narrowing. That is one reason why so many women are petty and unthoughtful of any except their own family's interests. . . . For me, it was an incalculable help to find myself among so many working-girls, all of us thrown upon our own resources, but thrown much more upon each other's sympathies.[104]

She was speaking not as an abstract worker generally but as a woman worker specifically when she mentioned that she was "dazzled" by the thought of "Mount Holyoke Seminary . . . as a vision of hope," and that "Mary Lyon's name was honored nowhere more than among the Lowell mill-girls."[105] And it was certainly not as an abstract worker generally but as a woman worker specifically that Sally Rice wrote the following letter, explaining why she did not want to leave the factory and go home to the "wilderness":

> I can never be happy in among so many mountains. . . . I feel as though I have worn out shoes and strength enough walking over the mountains. . . . And as for marrying and settling in that wilderness, I won't. If a person ever expects to take comfort it is while they are young. . . . I am most 19 years old. I must of course have something of my own before many more years have passed over my head. And where is that something coming from if I go home and earn nothing. . . . You may think me unkind but how can you blame me for wanting to stay here. I have but one life to live and I want to enjoy myself as well as I can while I live.[106]

We would be hard put to find a generalizable identity in these letters and memoirs by women workers.[107] What confronted us instead was a series of momentary postures, at once unevenly developed and imperfectly aligned. The women were not speaking out of a singular body called the "working class." They were not even speaking out of a singular body called the "person." For the "person," in every respect, turned out to be less than a singularity, but also more than a body. It resembled, if anything at all, a composite image, multiply exposed, an image of uncertain focus and spectral outlines, no part of which—neither the swollen feet, nor the letter-writing self—could give an adequate idea of the whole, the very idea of which was shown to be something of a fiction.

In this sense, the writings of the women workers suggest one way to think about Rebecca Harding Davis's *Life in the Iron Mills* (1861), to my mind one of the most interesting variations on the practice of metonymy in the nineteenth century, a variation sustained not in spite of but because of Davis's obsessive interest in the generalizability from material conditions to material bodies, and from material bodies to immaterial persons.[108] What is unusual and compelling about her novel is the explanatory limit she herself insisted on: the carefully specified nodal points where the story's transparency of

determination was allowed to become opaque, to mutate into a relation of impermeability, indirection, or nonalignment. One such
moment revolves around the central female character, Deborah,
whose "thwarted woman's form," "colorless life," and "waking stupor
that smothered pain and hunger" would seem to make her "fit to be
a type of her class."[109] Her typicality is by no means guaranteed, however, for, generalizable as she might seem, one can nonetheless never
be sure she is just that, and no more than that. Certitude extends, in
other words, only to what is verifiably there, not to what is unverifi-
ably not. There is no final proof, for instance, that there is

> no story . . . hidden beneath the pale, bleared eyes, and dull, washed-
> out-looking face, [where] no one had ever taken the trouble to read
> its faint signs: not the half-clothed furnace-tender, Wolfe, certainly.
> Yet he was kind to her: it was his nature to be kind, even to the very
> rats that swarmed in the cellar: kind to her in just the same way. She
> knew that. And it might be that very knowledge had given to her face
> its apathy and vacancy more than her low, torpid life. (22)

If the opaqueness of Deborah begins with a postulate of the unveri-
fiable, something that might or might not be in her, it ends with
something like a tribute to the inexhaustible, a condition that makes
any generalized cause inadequate to the felt effects. Of course, what
is inexhaustible here turns out to be Deborah's capacity for suffering,
a capacity well in excess even of what her "low, torpid life" so amply
supplies her. This fact, lamentable from one point of view, nonetheless gives Deborah, from another point of view, something almost
akin to the cheerfulness, happiness, and blitheness reported by Harriet Farley, Harriet Robinson, and Lucy Larcom—akin in the sense
that it also saves her from being a transcript of her material conditions, and affirms in her a density and an obscurity of relays. Her
greatest suffering comes not from her bodily deprivations but from
the particular sort of *kindness* with which she is treated. In this unexpected fastidiousness (where one would have imagined simple grat-
itude), Deborah emerges less as an identity than as the impossibility
of identity. She cannot be read metonymically for just that reason,
for her identity is both overflowing and undersaturated, both unex-
hausted by her materiality, and only partially accounted for by its
determinations.

In the enigma of affect that Davis puts at the heart of a story that is otherwise relentlessly transparent, relentlessly generalizable, *Life in the Iron Mills* stands as a concession: to the limits of explanation, and perhaps to the limits of cognition itself. And yet, it is in just this concession—in the breakdown of its epistemological assurance, the breakdown of its ability to integrate part to whole either in the collective life of the working class or in the circumscribed life of a woman named Deborah—that a concession is made as well to the nonabsurdity of hope. On the strength of that hope, and against the legible markings of *its* own body (identifying it as "literature," as a "story"), *Life in the Iron Mills* invites us not to a reading, not to an exercise in location and attribution, but to a political theory as fruitfully seen against Marx as against Melville: a theory that imagines persons as something other than bodies and societies as something other than wholes, a theory that, thus far, would seem to be not only more humanly bearable but also more humanly precise.

NOTES

1. Emerson, "The American Scholar," in *Selections from Ralph Waldo Emerson*, ed. Stephen E. Whicher (Boston: Houghton Mifflin, 1960), 64.

2. Henry David Thoreau, *Walden and Other Writings*, ed. Brooks Atkinson (New York: Modern Library, 1950), 41.

3. Chapters 1–3 of *An Inquiry into the Nature and Causes of the Wealth of Nations* (1776) bear the respective titles, "Of the Division of Labour," "Of the Principle which gives occasion to the Division of Labour," and "That the Division of Labour is limited by the Extent of the Market." Smith was not the first one to hit upon the concept. Sir William Petty, in *Political Arithmetic* (1690), and Bernard Mandeville, in *The Fable of the Bees* (1714), also wrote approvingly of the division of labor.

4. Smith, *Wealth of Nations*, 15.

5. Ralph Waldo Emerson, "Doctrine of the Hands," lecture on December 13, 1837, at the Masonic Temple, Boston, in *Early Lectures of Ralph Waldo Emerson*, eds. Stephen E. Whicher, Robert E. Spiller, Wallace E. Williams, 3 vols. (Cambridge, Mass.: Harvard University Press, 1959–1972), II:230.

6. John Ruskin, *The Stones of Venice*, in *The Complete Works of John Ruskin*, ed. E. T. Cook and Alexander Wedderburn, vol. 10 (London: George Allen, 1904), 196.

7. Karl Marx, *Capital*, trans. Samuel Moore and Edward Aveling, 2 vols. (New York: International Publishers, 1967), 1:339, 345.

8. Ibid., 360.

9. Jakobson sees metonymy as a principle of contiguity, and contrasts it with metaphor as a principle of equivalence. He associates the former with Realist narrative and the latter with Romantic poetry. See his "Linguistics and Poetics," in Richard T. de George and Fernande M. de George, eds., *The Structuralists From Marx to Lévi-Strauss*, (Garden City, N.Y.: Doubleday, 1972), 85–122. See also Jakobson, "Two Aspects of Language and Two Types of Aphasic Disturbances," in Roman Jakobson and Morris Halle, eds., *Fundamentals of Language* (The Hague: Mouton, 1956).

10. Kenneth Burke, *A Grammar of Motives* (Berkeley: University of California Press, 1969), 503–11. I should point out that Burke distinguishes between metonymy and synecdoche, associating the former with reduction and the latter with relations between part and whole. However, as he readily allows, the tropes "do shade into one another," and "metonymy may be treated as a special application of synecdoche." In short, even though Burke's "metonymy" is narrower than Lakoff's, the former can nonetheless be assimilated to the latter.

11. For instance, as Lakoff points out, the subcategory "working mother" is actually defined against a silent normative category, "housewife-mother," who presumably does not "work." For Lakoff's interesting "culturization" of metonymy, see his *Women, Fire, and Dangerous Things: What Categories Reveal about the Mind* (Chicago: University of Chicago Press, 1987), 77–90.

12. Hayden White, *Metahistory: The Historical Imagination in Nineteenth-Century Europe* (Baltimore: Johns Hopkins University Press, 1973), 281–330.

13. Charles Taylor, *Sources of the Self: The Making of the Modern Identity* (Cambridge, Mass.: Harvard University Press, 1989), 176, 177.

14. Marx, *A Contribution to the Critique of Political Economy*, ed. Maurice Dodd (New York: International Publishers, 1970), 20.

15. Sandel, for example, has critiqued Rawls for assuming that "the bounds of the subject unproblematically correspond to the bodily bounds between human beings." See Michael Sandel, *Liberalism and the Limits of Justice* (New York: Cambridge University Press, 1982), 80.

16. Aristotle, *The Nicomachean Ethics*, trans. Martin Ostwald (Indianapolis: Bobbs-Merrill, 1962), 125–27.

17. Taylor, *Sources of the Self*, 186–92. Actually, in his respect for the concrete particular, Aristotle is much less committed to ontic logos than Plato is, a point noted by Taylor, and by Martha Nussbaum, among others. So, in citing Aristotle, we are already encountering the lowest common denominator of the tradition of ontic logos.

18. Adelmannus of Brescia, *Epistle to Berengar; Sentences of Florian*, 66; Alger of Liege, *On the Sacraments*, I.17; William of Saint-Thierry, *On the Sacrament of the Altar*, 12. All quoted in Jaroslav Pelikan, *The Christian Tradition. Vol. 3. The Growth of Medieval Theology (600–1300)* (Chicago: University of Chicago Press, 1978), 191.

19. 1 Corinthians 10:16–17.

20. Augustine, *Exposition of the Gospel of John*, 26.15, quoted in Pelikan, *The Christian Tradition*, 3:191.

21. Hugh of Breteuil, *On the Body and Blood of Christ*, quoted in Pelikan, *The Christian Tradition*, 3:199.

22. Berengar of Tours, *On the Holy Supper*, quoted in Pelikan, *The Christian Tradition*, 3:192, 194.

23. Guitmond of Aversa, *De corporis et sanguinis Christi veritate in eucharistia*, quoted in Pelikan, *The Christian Tradition*, 3:197.

24. Berengar of Tours, *Fragments*, quoted in Pelikan, *The Christian Tradition*, 3:198.

25. Ibid., 3:203.

26. In the Thomistic formula, the effects of the Fall chiefly involved the disordering of the faculties and the rebellion of the senses against reason. See Barbara Lewalski, *Protestant Poetics and the Seventeenth-Century Religious Lyric* (Princeton: Princeton University Press, 1979), 15.

27. Galileo, *Dialogue Concerning the Two Chief World Systems* (1632), quoted in Ian Hacking, *The Emergence of Probability* (Cambridge: Cambridge University Press, 1975), 26.

28. Pelikan, *The Christian Tradition*, 3:185, 201.

29. Ernest H. Kantarowicz, *The King's Two Bodies: A Study in Medieval Political Theology* (Princeton: Princeton University Press, 1957).

30. Edmund Plowden, *Commentaries or Reports*, quoted in Kantorowicz, *The King's Two Bodies*, 9.

31. Bacon, *Post-nati*, 651, quoted in Kantorowicz, *The King's Two Bodies*, 448.

32. Frederic W. Maitland, "The Crown as Corporation," first published in *Law Quarterly Review* (1901), reprinted in *Collected Papers*, 3 vols., ed. H. A. C. Fisher (Cambridge: Cambridge University Press, 1911), 3:249.

33. See Christopher Lawrence, "The Nervous System and Society in the Scottish Enlightenment," and Steven Shapin, "Homo Phrenologicus," both in Barry Barnes and Steven Shapin, eds., *Natural Order: Historical Studies of Scientific Culture* (Beverly Hills: Sage, 1979), 19–40, 41–71; Simon Schaffer, "States of Mind: Enlightenment and Natural Philosophy," in G. S. Rousseau, ed., *Languages of Psyche: Mind and Body in Enlightenment Thought* (Berkeley: University of California Press, 1990), 233–90; John W. Yolton, *Thinking Matter: Materialism in Eighteenth-Century Britain* (Oxford: Basil Blackwell, 1984).

34. See especially Michael McKeon's chapter on "The Evidence of the Senses: Secularization and Epistemological Crisis," in *The Origins of the English Novel, 1600–1740* (Baltimore: Johns Hopkins University Press, 1987), 65–89.

35. On this point, see Alasdair MacIntyre, *After Virtue* (Notre Dame, Ind.: University of Notre Dame Press, 1981), esp. 79–108.

36. Indeed, from a certain perspective, materialism and dualism might turn out to be the same thing. For this stunning point, see Richard Rorty, *Philosophy and the Mirror of Nature* (Princeton: Princeton University Press, 1979).

37. This "Enlightenment" Marx is currently embraced by some Marxists. See, for example, the interview with Lucio Colletti in *New Left Review* 86 (1974), and, especially, Sebastiano Timpanaro, *On Materialism*, trans. Lawrence Garner (London: Verso, 1980). For a response to Timpanaro, see Raymond Williams, "Problems of Materialism," *New Left Review* 109 (1978):3–17.

38. Michel Foucault, *The Order of Things: An Archaelogy of the Human Sciences* (New York: Vintage, 1973), 251.

39. Marx and Engels, *The Holy Family* (Moscow: Foreign Languages Publishing House, 1956), 172. This particular chapter was written by Marx.

40. Ibid., 173.

41. Marx, *The Economic & Philosophic Manuscripts of 1844*, ed. Dirk J. Struik (New York: International Publishers, 1964), 180, italics in original. This "corporeal" aspect of materialism has been largely overlooked. For a notable exception, see Elaine Scarry's brilliant reading of materialism as corporealism in *The Body in Pain: The Making and Unmaking of the World* (New York: Oxford University Press, 1985), 242–77.

42. Marx and Engels, *The Holy Family*, 173.

43. MacIntyre, *After Virtue*, x.

44. Karl Marx, *Grundrisse. Introduction to the Critique of Political Economy*, trans. Martin Nicolaus (New York: Vintage, 1973), 83.

45. Ibid., 472–73.

46. Ibid., 474, 483.

47. Karl Marx, *The Economic and Philosophic Manuscripts of 1844*, trans. Martin Milligan, ed. Dirk J. Struik (New York: International Publishers, 1964), 112. To my mind, Marx's discussion of the relation between individual life and species life is by far the most interesting aspect of his account of alienated labor. Marx writes,

> In estranging from man (1) nature, and (2) himself, his own active activity, estranged labor estranges the *species* from man. It changes for him the *life of the species* into a means of individual life. . . . It is just in his work upon the objective world, therefore, that man first really proves himself to be a *species being*. . . . In tearing away from man the object of his production, therefore, estranged labor tears from him his *species life*, his real objectivity as a member of the species and transforms his advantage over animals into the disadvantage that his inorganic body, nature, is taken from him.

The notion of "species-being" appears again in late Marx, though in a somewhat modified form, as when he suggests that man "appears originally as a species-being, clan being, herd animal" (*Grundrisse*, 496).

48. Marx, *Economic and Philosophic Manuscripts*, 101–2.

49. In the last chapter of *Capital*, Marx seemed to be moving away from his longstanding conception of class identity as objective interests. He wrote, "What constitutes a class?—and the reply to this follows naturally from the reply to another question, namely: What makes wage-labourers, capitalists, and landlords, constitute the three great social classes?" And he went on to say, "*At first glance*—the identity of revenues and sources of revenue," which would seem to suggest that he was about to change his mind (or at least to offer an amendment). However, since the manuscript broke off at just this point, the amendment was never developed. See *Capital* 3:886; italics mine.

50. The critique of Bruno Bauer is developed in *The Holy Family* (1844), the critique of Ludwig Feuerbach in *The German Ideology* (1845) and in *Theses on Feuerbach*, where Marx observes that Feuerbach reduces all historical process to the "abstract individual," an "inward dumb generality which naturally unites the many individuals." Against this view, Marx argues that "the essence of man is no abstraction inherent in each separate individual. In its reality it is the *ensemble* (aggregate) of social relations." See *Theses on Feuerbach*, "Appendix" to *The German Ideology*, ed. R. Pascal (New York: International Publishers, 1947), 198–99.

51. Marx and Engels, *The Holy Family*, 52–53.

52. Ibid., 52, 53.

53. Marx further clarifies this point in his preface to *A Contribution to the Critique of Political Economy* (1859), where he suggests that "the bourgeois mode of production is the *last* antagonistic form of the social process of production, . . . but the productive forces developing within bourgeois society create also the material conditions for a *solution* of this antagonism." See *A Contribution to the Critique of Political Economy*, ed. Maurice Dobb (New York: International Publishers, 1970), 21; italics mine.

54. Louis Althusser, *For Marx*, trans. Ben Brewster (New York: Vintage, 1970), 127, 197.

55. See, for example, "Contradiction and Overdetermination" and "On the Materialist Dialetic" in ibid., 87–128, 161–218; and "Marxism is not a Historicism," in Louis Althusser and Etienne Balibar, *Reading Capital*, trans. Ben Brewster (London: New Left Books, 1975), 119–44.

56. Althusser, *For Marx*, 203.

57. In all his writings, and especially in "On the Materialist Dialectic," Althusser refers routinely to a "pre-given complex structured whole."

58. Marx, *Capital*, 1:354, 351, 356, 351.

59. In this sense, Marx's position in *Capital* actually represents a retreat from (and a simplifying of) his earlier position, articulated for example in *The German Ideology*, where he concedes the involuntary character of the social division of labor, and at least entertains the possibility of a parallel between it and the industrial division of labor. See *The German Ideology*, 22.

60. Emile Durkheim, *The Division of Labor in Society*, trans. George Simpson (New York: Free Press, 1964), 41.

61. Marx's economism is qualified, of course, by his observation, in his unfinished 1857 "Introduction" to the *Critique* (subsequently published as "Introduction" to the *Grundrisse*), about the "uneven development of material production relative to e.g. artistic development" and (he further adds) "legal relations." See *Grundrisse*, 109. The phrase "uneven development" has been a major inspiration for political theorists and literary critics, though it remains asserted rather than elaborated in Marx. And, in any case, since the 1857 "Introduction" was not published until 1903 in *Die Neue Zeit*, and the *Grundrisse* not published until 1939 in Moscow, Durkheim certainly would not have known about it when he published *The Division of Labor in Society* in 1893.

62. In this sense, we have yet to learn from the definition of class put forward by E. P. Thompson, who argues that class is to be understood not "as a 'structure,' nor even as a 'category,' but as something which in fact happened (and can be shown to have happened) in human relationships." See the "Preface" to *The Making of the Working Class* (New York: Vintage, 1966).

63. Ernesto Laclau and Chantal Mouffe, *Hegemony and Socialist Strategy: Towards a Radical Democratic Politics* (London: Verso, 1985), 95.

64. Taylor, *Sources of the Self*, 186.

65. The scholarship on this point is voluminous. For a standard account, see Anthony Kenny, *Descartes* (New York: Random House, 1968), 96–125.

66. My previous book, *Empire for Liberty: Melville and the Poetics of Individualism* (Princeton: Princeton University Press, 1989) was certainly one example of this practice. But then, that book was among distinguished company.

67. My polemic, here and throughout this essay, against "identity" is informed by Judith Butler, *Gender Trouble: Feminism and the Subversion of Identity* (New York: Routledge, 1990).

68. Eve Kosofsky Sedgwick, *Between Men: English Literature and Male Homosocial Desire* (New York: Columbia University Press, 1985), esp. 83–96.

69. Perry Miller, *The New England Mind: The Seventeenth Century* (Cambridge, Mass.: Harvard University Press, 1954), 44.

70. Adams to Jefferson, December 21, 1819, in *The Adams-Jefferson Letters*, ed. Lester J. Cappon (Chapel Hill: University of North Carolina Press, 1959), II:551.

71. Tocqueville wrote, "In the United States a wealthy man thinks that he owes it to public opinion to devote his leisure to some kind of industrial or commercial pursuit or to public business. He would think himself in bad repute if he employed his life solely in living." See *Democracy in America*, ed. Phillips Bradley (New York: Vintage, 1945), 161.

72. Charles Lyell, *A Second Visit to United States* (New York, 1849), quoted in Allan Nevins, *American Social History as Recorded by British Travellers* (New York, 1932), 333.

73. Francis J. Grund, *The Americans in Their Moral, Social, and Political Relations*, 2 vols. (London: Longman, Rees, Orme, Brown, Green, and Longman, 1837), 2:1–2.

74. Henry Ward Beecher, *Lectures to Young Men* (1844; rpt. New York: J. C. Derby, 1856), 16, 40, 41.

75. Ibid., 35–36.

76. Henry Ward Beecher, *Norwood: or, Village Life in New England* (New York: Charles Scribner, 1868), 22, 28, 23, 24.

77. Henry Ward Beecher, "Dream-Culture," in *Star Papers: Experiences of Art and Nature* (New York: J. C. Derby, 1855), 263, 268, 263, 269.

78. Nor was this the only occasion he was known to do so. William C. McLoughlin, for example, has compared Beecher's "massive inconsistency" to Whitman's. See *The Meaning of Henry Ward Beecher: An Essay on the Shifting Values of Mid-Victorian America, 1840–1870* (New York: Knopf, 1970), 30.

79. This was true, of course, not just of America, but also of industrial England. See, for example, E. P. Thompson's groundbreaking essay, "Time, Work-Discipline, and Industrial Capitalism," *Past and Present* 38 (December 1967):56–97.

80. James Leonard Corning, *The Christian Law of Amusement* (Buffalo: Phinney and Co., 1859), 7.

81. Daniel T. Rodgers, *The Work Ethic in Industrial America, 1850–1920* (Chicago: University of Chicago Press, 1978), 98.

82. Beecher, *Norwood*, 16. The idea that leisure is properly enjoyed only by those entitled to it is not unique to Beecher, of course. Addison, for example, in *The Spectator* 411 (June 21, 1712), had long ago suggested that "there are, indeed, but very few who know how to be idle and innocent, or have a relish of any pleasures that are not criminal." I am indebted to John Buck for bringing this to my attention.

83. Henry Ward Beecher, "Popular Amusements," in *Lectures to Young Men*, 249, 250, 251. As Lawrence Levine has persuasively demonstrated, the theater was polular entertainment in the nineteenth century, quite different from the exclusive pastime it has become today. See "William Shakespeare in America," in his *Highbrow/Lowbrow:*

The Emergence of Cultural Hierarchy in America (Cambridge, Mass.: Harvard University Press, 1988), 11–82.

84. Beecher, Preface to *Star Papers*.

85. See Richard H. Brodhead, *Culture of Letters* (Chicago: University of Chicago Press, 1993).

86. The allure of such a world as found in "The Paradise of Bachelors" was personally experienced by Melville himself, during his visit to London in December 1849, when he was wined and dined by the literary and legal community.

87. See, for example, Robert K. Martin, *Hero, Captain, and Stranger: Male Friendship, Social Critique, and Literary Form in the Sea Novels of Herman Melville* (Chapel Hill: University of North Carolina Press, 1986). For a more troubling view of Melville, see Eve Kosofsky Sedgwick, *Epistemology of the Closet* (Berkeley: University of California Press, 1990), 91–130.

88. Tench Coxe argued, for example, that, with the development of manufactures, "the portions of time of housewives and young women, which were not occupied in family affairs, could be profitably filled up." See Coxe, *A View of the United States of America* (1794; rpt. New York: Augustus Kelley, 1965), 55. Alexander Hamilton argued, meanwhile, that "it is worthy of particular remark that in general, women and children are rendered more useful, and the latter more early useful, by manufacturing establishments, than they would otherwise be," and that "the husbandman himself experiences a new source of profit and support, from the increased industry of his wife and daughters, invited and stimulated by the demands of the neighboring manufactories." See Hamilton, "On the Subject of Manufactures," in *Industrial and Commercial Correspondence of Alexander Hamilton*, ed. Arthur Harrison Cole (New York: Augustus M. Kelley, 1968), 259.

89. Judith A. McGaw, *Most Wonderful Machine: Mechanization and Social Change in Berkshire Paper Making, 1801–1885* (Princeton: Princeton University Press, 1987), 335.

90. Joan Wallach Scott, " 'L'ouvrière! Mot impie, sordide . . .': Women Workers in the Discourse of French Political Economy," in *Gender and the Politics of History* (New York: Columbia University Press, 1988), 158, 155.

91. The pioneering and still useful account of the doctrine is Barbara Welter, "The Cult of True Womanhood, 1820–1860," *American Quarterly* 18 (1966):151–74. Since then, a vast body of scholarship has sprung up on the subject. For a good summary of the now diverse positions, see Linda Kerber, "Separate Spheres, Female Worlds, Woman's Place: The Rhetoric of Women's History," *Journal of American History* 75 (1988):9–39.

92. For a reading along these lines, see Michael Newbury, "Figurations of Authorship in Antebellum America," Ph.D. dissertation, Yale University, 1992. See also Michael T. Gilmore, *American Romanticism and the Marketplace* (Chicago: University of Chicago Press, 1985).

93. For extensive discussions of this point, see Thomas Bender, *Toward an Urban Vision: Ideas and Institutions in Nineteenth-Century America* (Baltimore: Johns Hopkins University Press, 1975), 21–93; John F. Kasson, *Civilizing the Machine: Technology and Republican Values in America, 1776–1900* (New York: Penguin, 1977), 53–106.

94. Charles Dickens, *American Notes* (1842; rpt. New York: St. Martin's, 1985), 60–61.

95. William Scoresby, *American Factories and Their Female Operatives* (1845; rpt. New York: Burt Franklin, 1968), 54, 55, 69, 82, 88, 51.

96. Christine Stansell, for example, has emphasized the benefits of factory work, as opposed to the take-home "outwork," which not only paid less but also "bolstered up older forms of patriarchal supervision and curtailed the ways in which single women could turn manufacturing work to the uses of independence." See her *City of Women: Sex and Class in New York, 1789–1860* (Urbana: University of Illinois Press, 1987). The upbeat conclusions of Stansell (and Thomas Dublin, discussed below) need to be supplemented, however, by the work of other historians, who call attention to the persistent low pay, job segregation, and the failure of women workers to break free from traditional families. See, for example, Mary Blewett, *Men, Women, and Work: A Study of Class, Gender, and Protest in the Nineteenth-Century Shoe Industry* (Urbana: University of Illinois Press, 1988); McGaw, *Most Wonderful Machine.* For critiques of mainstream labor history as insufficiently attentive to questions of gender, see Sally Alexander, Anna Davin, and Eve Hostettler, "Labouring Women: A Reply to Eric Hobsbawn," *History Workshop* 8 (Autumn 1979):174–82; Joan Wallach Scott, "Women in *The Making of the English Working Class,*" in her *Gender and the Politics of History,* 68–92; Susan Levine, "Class and Gender: Herbert Gutman and the Women of 'Shoe City,' " *Labor History* 29 (Summer 1988):344–55; Alice Kessler-Harris, "Gender Ideology in Historical Reconstruction," *Gender and History* 1 (Spring 1989):31–37. For a useful survey of the vast scholarship on this subject, see Ava Baron, "Gender and Labor History," in Ava Baron, ed., *Work Engendered* (Ithaca: Cornell University Press, 1991), 1–46. For a more general discussion of the methodological entanglements between Marxism and feminism, see Heidi Hartmann, "The Unhappy Marriage of Marxism and Feminism: Towards a More Progressive Union," in Lydia Sargent, ed., *Women and Revolution: A Discussion of the Unhappy Marriage of Marxism and Feminism* (Boston: South End Press, 1981), 1–42.

97. Thomas Dublin, *Women at Work: The Transformation of Work and Community in Lowell, Massachusetts, 1826–1860* (New York: Columbia University Press, 1979), 89.

98. Sacvan Bercovitch has described this as "the imperial claims implicit in the concentricity of self, text, and interpretation." See *The Rites of Assent* (New York: Routledge, 1993), 270.

99. This is, in fact, something of a convention in their writings. Harriet Robinson insists, for example, "When I look back into the factory life of fifty or sixty years ago, I do not see what is called 'a class' of young men and women going to and from their daily work, like so many ants that cannot be distinguished one from another" (Harriet Hanson Robinson, *Loom and Spindle, or Life Among the Early Mill Girls* [1898; rpt. Press Pacifica, 1976], 37). In the same vein, Lucy Larcom suggests that every woman should "ask herself whether she would like to hear herself or her sister spoken of as a shop-girl, or a factory-girl, or a servant-girl," and "if she would shrink from it a little, then she is a little inhuman when she puts her unknown human sisters who are so occupied into a class" (*A New England Girlhood* [1889; rpt., Gloucester, Mass.: Peter Smith, 1973], 200).

100. Benita Eisler, ed., *The Lowell Offering: Writings by New England Mill Women, 1840–1845* (Philadelphia: J. B. Lippincott, 1977), 52.

101. Ibid., 53.

102. Robinson, *Loom and Spindle*, 43.

103. Here I am giving voice to a position well articulated by women historians. See, for example, Sally Alexander, "Women, Class, and Sexual Difference," *History Workshop* 17 (Autumn 1984):125–49; Ava Baron, "Women and the Making of the American Working Class: A Study of the Proletarianization of Printers," *Review of Radical Political Economics* 14 (Fall 1982):23–42; Emily Hicks, "Cultural Marxism: Nonsynchrony and Feminist Practice," in Sargent, ed., *Women and Revolution*, 219–38; Sonya Rose, "Gender at Work: Sex, Class, and Industrial Capitalism," *History Workshop* 21 (Spring 1986):113–21; Joan Wallach Scott, "Work Identites for Men and Women," in her *Gender and the Politics of History*, 93–112.

104. Larcom, *A New England Girlhood*, 178–79.

105. Ibid., 223.

106. Nell Kull, " 'I Can Never Be So Happy There Among All Those Mountains': The Letters of Sally Rice," *Vermont History* 38 (1970):49–57; quoted in Dublin, *Women at Work*, 37.

107. For an important collection of letters by the factory women, see Thomas Dublin, ed., *Farm to Factory: Women's Letters, 1830–1860* (New York: Columbia University Press, 1981). Also valuable is the Harriet Hanson Robinson Collection at the Schlesinger Library, Radcliffe College, which includes letters from the Currier sisters.

108. For a complex discussion of *Life in the Iron Mills* along these lines (and linking questions of reduction or irreduction to market culture), see Mark Seltzer, *Bodies and Machines* (New York: Routledge, 1992), 121–45.

109. Rebecca Harding Davis, *Life in the Iron Mills* (Old Westbury, N.Y.: Feminist Press, 1972), 22.

II THE CULTURE

OF CLASS

3 LITERARY CRITICS AS INTELLECTUALS

CLASS ANALYSIS AND THE CRISIS OF THE HUMANITIES

John Guillory

> *The struggle of classifications is a fundamental division of class struggle. The power of imposing a vision of divisions, that is, the power of making visible and explicit social divisions that are implicit, is the political power par excellence: it is the power to make groups, to manipulate the objective structure of society.*
> —PIERRE BOURDIEU, *"Social Space and Symbolic Power"*

THE POLITICAL CLASS

In his introduction to a recent volume of essays entitled *Intellectuals: Aesthetics, Politics, Academics,* Bruce Robbins notes that the subject of intellectuals is "back on the agenda" after a long period when, for a number of reasons, the very category had disappeared from critical discussion.[1] The recession of interest in the analysis (or self-analysis) of intellectuals was universally seen to coincide with their disappearance as public, adversarial figures "grounded in a social constituency, project, or movement" (xi). If rumors of their demise (or alternatively, their devolution into a disengaged professoriate) were premature, the renewal of interest in the category may be taken to signify a willingness on the part of the professoriate to dust off a coat of arms to which it indeed has a claim. To say that the subject of intellectuals is "back on the agenda" is to say that there exists a particular social group inclined at this moment to say, "we are the intellectuals."

Now this genealogical claim, as in an old romance, might well have gone unasserted had it not been for the fact that the intellectuals have of late been *called out*, drawn from their institutional retreats into the sphere of publicity. In brief, they have been attacked. Their supposed transformation from the activists of the sixties into "tenured radicals" has become a matter of public notice, the main event in a public controversy now all too familiar.[2] The argument to follow is not a rehearsal of that controversy but a consideration of what is implied by the specific accusation against them, which might be summed up as: "They have politicized the humanities!" This accusation has had the effect of "interpellating" the intellectuals— chiefly in the strict lexical sense of that word: to ask a person formally for an explanation of his or her action or policy—but also in the sense given currency by Althusser, and which is not to be evaded here.[3] For the intellectual is interpellated now as a peculiar kind of *political subject*, the name, as we shall see, of "the political class."

Just as interesting as the effect of interpellation is the circumstance that what began as an attack upon university teachers for "politicizing" their disciplinees, an attack that seemed to repeat a charge by Benda long ago against the "treason of the intellectuals,"[4] has become the occasion for response by these same teachers to a *left* critique of academics as politically disengaged, as having abdicated their responsibility as critics of the social order for the perquisites and security of a mere profession. In the face of that equally disturbing critique (elaborated most recently by Russell Jacoby in his *The Last Intellectuals* but certainly expressing a prevalent unease among left academics themselves), the event of being so violently attacked by right-wing journalists has been in some ways gratifying.[5] Mobilizing the profound anti-intellectualism of American culture, the reactionary polemic has at least enabled academics to reclaim the title of public intellectual, a noble title that might be traced all the way back to its origin in the Dreyfus affair. The dialectical relation between reaction and reentitlement (we are speaking here of what may be called a "petty dialectic" as opposed to a grand, Hegelian one) is witnessed by the very publication of such volumes as the one quoted above and from which I will offer another definitive statement: "*Thanks to the Reaganite backlash*, much of the public has thus learned that, for better or worse, the left is a forceful presence in American cultural life" (x; italics mine). It would seem that such a backlash was necessary in order to bring the intellectuals back into the public sphere; but once there, they have been compelled (or enabled) to reclaim the very public, political status that defined their nature as intellectuals. They have been compelled (or enabled) to recognize that what Robbins very aptly calls their "grounding" in the university did not represent an abdication of their responsibility to take up a political position but the emergence of a "new, perhaps already incipient, politics of intellectuals" (xxv).

If recent commentary on the subject of intellectuals has thus had to respond to critique from both the right and the left, the existence of this double front has required a defense of both the constitutively political nature of intellectuals and of the university as an appropriate site for the development of that politics. With regard to the right-wing agenda, there is no question that one must always endorse the defense of intellectuals against a culture that has historically regarded them with an implacable hostility. In fact, one must remark that the very phenomenon of anti-intellectualism in American culture is still very insufficiently analyzed. Just as important, one must reject the mythological history of intellectuals as, in Mannheim's well-known formulation, institutionally "free-floating,"[6] since the autonomous "public sphere" intellectuals were supposed formerly to occupy was nothing other than the sphere of journalism, itself subject to institutional pressures emanating from both political and economic sources. Nevertheless, I would like to express a reservation about the tenor of recent commentary on the subject of intellectuals, specifically its seizing upon the occasion of the reactionary backlash to affirm a constitutively political identity of academic intellectuals.[7] This reservation is not at all intended to locate intellectuals in some domain of political neutrality, as we can be sure that such a domain will always be politically conservative by default. Rather, my reservation responds to the very paradox implicit in the reemergence of the category of "intellectuals" in the wake of the reactionary backlash. If the political identity of the intellectuals is dependent in some way upon the very "publicity" that is the effect of reaction, that identity is peculiarly vulnerable to the vicissitudes of publicity itself. If the commentators on the right had been a little shrewder, they might have deduced that intellectuals are more effectively neutralized politically by a strategy of indifference than by their projection into the domain of publicity under the sign of notoriety, the negative version (but not the negation) of the principle of *celebrity*. But that does not mean, on the other hand, that the reactionary backlash was simply a tactical error; on the whole, a good deal of harm was done, in conjunction with a concerted effort by successive Republican administrations to defund the universities, and to further dismantle the public educational system. I would suggest that the dialectic of reaction and reentitlement was considerably more complicated than either a narrative of repression, or a paradoxical self-assertion of the intellectuals, can possibly convey. (It is perhaps too soon to tell whether, after the passing of the Republican Party from executive power, the same conduits to publicity will remain open to academic intellectuals.) Without undertaking to analyze here the phenomenon of publicity itself in its current form, we might wonder whether all politics has to be routed through the publicity system, with its regnant principle of celebrity, and perhaps also whether the notoriety produced by the reactionary backlash makes the best case for claiming an "incipient politics of intellectuals."[8]

The dialectic of reaction and reentitlement was premised on the assumption that the constitutive element of intellectual identity is political position-taking. But such position-taking is of course neither an exclusive property of intellectuals, nor is it entirely consistently of the left or the right among them. If the intellectuals appeared historically as an identified *group* (writers, artists, scholars) at the moment of their political organization into an adversarial movement (the Dreyfus affair), that moment of identification introduced an ambiguity into the discourse of intellectuals that has perplexed it ever since. Thus, while it has always seemed necesssary to define intellectuals by their inclination to dissident political stances, it has also been possible to ground the analysis of intellectuals in the socioeconomic domain by positing a constitutive distinction between intellectual and manual labor, a distinction that for good historical reasons implicates intellectual labor in the system of economic exploitation. It is quite difficult on that basis to demonstrate how the fact of intellectual labor becomes the condition for the innate tendency to progressive or even leftist politics that is assumed to characterize intellectuals. Yet we cannot deny that what is at stake in the discourse of the intellectuals *about themselves* is their critical responsibility in relation to the exercise of political power. It is no wonder then that the figure of the intellectual circulates in the political imaginary as innately progressive, always potentially subversive. Such a construction of the intellectual still guides most recent commentary on this subject, even arguments that begin with the distinction between intellectual and manual labor. Stanley Aronowitz, for example, argues that the present "epoch is marked by the domination of intellectual over manual labor" and that "in these societies in which the knowledge mode of production prevails and culture is an ineluctable feature of social rule, intellectuals may become the only genuine political class."[9] One perceives in such arguments, even those that have been purged of the kind of naive optimism that was supposed to compromise Alvin Gouldner's famous argument for the revolutionary destiny of the "New Class" intellectuals, a desire nonetheless that intellectuals might constitute a political *movement*, and thus that they can be perceived always to be moving in a direction that it would be difficult to conceive as anything but progressive.[10] In this way intellectuals are defined as a political and not a socieconomic identity.

What troubles such an account is certainly not its "optimism of the will," to use Gramsci's phrase, but rather an unfounded optimism of the intellect, an analysis of intellectuals in which their identity is defined by generalizations about their innately progressive political nature or tendencies. Such an analysis is complicated by the fact that the initial attack upon university intellectuals in the 1980s was mounted by other disaffected professors (Allan Bloom and William Bennett) whose denunciations of their colleagues were then taken up into the realm of publicity, of the journalistic meda. It is surely a peculiar circumstance that these right-wing academics could indulge in the most hyperbolic generalizations about the leftist tendencies of academic intellectuals, as though they themselves did not belong to the same professional category as those they condemned. One might conclude on this basis that no *necessary* position in the political spectrum is implied by the profession of "academic," and that one can at most speak of a certain political *tendency* predominating among certain sectors of intellectuals in the academy. It is a mistake, then, to imagine intellectuals in general—if intellectuals are supposed to be equivalent in public discourse now to academics— moving in one direction through the medium of history, like a flock of birds whose mysteriously coordinated flight signifies at once a transcendent perspective upon the social order and an uncanny sense of the direction of historical change. The fact that even in the university intellectuals may dispose themselves along the whole of the political spectrum suggests that it should at least be difficult to make political generalizations about them. But one suspects that such generalizations, if they were at the time of the Dreyfus affair the product of a particular conjunctural situation of writers, artists, and scholars, are now the product of an equally conjunctural situation in which the status of a particular *sector* of academic intellectuals has been generalized as that of intellectuals per se, and in such a way that writers and artists (as opposed to academics) now occupy a some- what more nebulous domain of peripheral intellectuality (indicated by the somewhat vexed relations between academics and freelance writers and artists). In this later conjuncture what Aronowitz calls the "knowledge mode of production" limits the qualifications for belonging to the group of "intellectuals" on behalf of sustaining the equation between intellectuals and "the political class." What emerges from the foregoing discussion is a question about this equa- tion, a question I shall attempt to answer in this essay by proposing an integration of Pierre Bourdieu's sociology of intellectuals with a particular aspect of Antonio Gramsci's class analysis of this group.[11]

THE POLITICS OF POLITICIZATION

Gramsci famously wrote in his discussion of intellectuals that "all men are intellectuals . . . but not all men have in society the function of intellectuals."[12] One might also say that all academics are intel- lectuals, but that not all academics have in society the *name* of intel- lectuals. The reservation I propose at this point asks us to give seri- ous consideration to the fact that the calling out of the intellectuals in the past decade hardly concerned most disciplines of the univer- sity professoriate, but was addressed to specific disciplines of the humanities, and preeminently among them, literary criticism. Bruce Robbins notes that all but three of the contributors to his anthology are literary critics, a fact that he cites as evidence of what Stuart Hall calls "the deeply *cultural* character of the revolution of our times."[13] If literary critics speak now for culture in general, what developments within society have authorized this representational claim? What does it mean that it is at this *site* within the university that the question of intellectuals is so conspicuously "back on the agenda"?[14] Not to consider this fact is to disregard what is surely a crucial issue in the reemergence of interest in the problem of intellectuals, its determination by objective social conditions. What is at issue here is not the distortion that may result from a disciplinary lens—one might possibly correct for such a distortion—but the more interesting question of why the self-recognition of the intellectuals might be vested at this moment in literary criticism, or in select adjacent disciplines.[15] If it should happen that the reactionary backlash has occasioned not the general self-recognition of university professors as intellectuals but a self-recognition specific to certain disciplines within the university, one should nevertheless insist that the qualities defining intellectual membership not be restricted to the qualities of this select group, and thus that its particular situation not be falsely generalized. For it may be the case that what is most interesting about this conjuncture is the very *uniqueness* of the situation specific to these particular disciplines, the peculiar way in which these disciplines have become associated with political position-taking or, in current right-wing discourse, "politicized."

In retrospect, it would seem that "the intellectuals" have reappeared in the public realm as a consequence of the attack upon certain disciplinary practices (structuralist and poststructuralist theory, deconstruction, feminism, Marxism, New Historicism, multiculturalism) in the mainstream media; and that the identity of intellectuals has been projected from the caricature of these practices in the media. The specific direction of interpellation can be appreciated by recognizing that the journalists themselves played the role of Zola: "J'accuse le president de la . . . *MLA*." But if one were to extrapolate intellectual identity from another direction, beginning with the recognition that a very large sector of the populace is engaged in intellectual labor, then it would be immediately apparent that the intellectuals who provoked so virulently anti-intellectual a reaction, and thus were interpellated as intellectuals, exhibited an *anomalous* relation to the domain of publicity among dissident intellectuals specifically (of the type, say, of Noam Chomsky), and intellectual laborers in general. For we are not speaking here of intellectuals who pause in the pursuit of their labors to take up a political stance with respect to some issue of the day (signing petitions, organizing, lobbying, etc.), but rather of academics who undertake to *thematize* the political in the "everyday" practice of their disciplines.[16] Now this thematizing of the political, of *subject matter* itself, is obviously much less possible within the scientific and technical disciplines; it is only really possible in the humanities and the social sciences—and it is only really *unexpected* in the humanities. The discipline of "political science," for example, can scarcely be perceived as "politicized" by virtue of its taking the political as its object; but the same cannot be said for literary criticism or philosophy or even history. It is as though the space of the normative practice of these disciplines had been vacated and reoccupied by another practice. Let us pose a question, then, which is eminently historical: what conditions—disciplinary, institutional, social—underlie the present thematizing of the political in the disciplines of the humanities?

We might reject at the outset certain pseudo-empirical speculations that have considerable currency on both the right and on the left: the politicization of the disciplines was surely not the result of a migration of sixties leftists into the humanities, where they are supposed now to be "tenured radicals"; surely these former activists were dispersed among very many disciplines, professions, jobs. It is much more likely that the space of "politicization" was already beginning to open up in the 1960s as a result of the historical transformation of the disciplines themselves, particularly that of literary criticism. I will argue specifically that the transformation recognized in the discourse of the right as "the crisis of the humanities" represents not the deliberate self-immolation of these disciplines through a process of politicization but rather the effect of their marginalization over the long term in relation to other disciplines that have become more integral to the needs of what has come to be called the "professional-managerial class."[17] More and more, as Barbara and John Ehrenreich argued in the groundbreaking essay on the formation of this class, these technical disciplines serve the purpose of reproducing the socioeconomic system by resupplying its intellectual labor and by disseminating an ideology of technobureaucratic "productivity" and upward mobility. I hope to demonstrate in this argument that the politicization of the humanities is an effect of the latter's marginalization and not the other way around. If this is indeed the case, then one should be able to acknowledge the full significance of an equally important fact: the relative decline of political engagement (and of left/liberal politics) among *intellectuals in general* (that is, the very large sector of intellectual labor) since the 1960s and 1970s. The calling out of the intellectuals among the disciplines of the humanities is not unrelated to this other fact.

The phenomenon of politicization is also overdetermined in its relation to the journalistic media that flushed the intellectuals from their university covert in the 1980s. Here we can propose a hypothesis that recovers the historical relation between the domains of journalism and literary criticism, an intimate relation that Habermas discovered at the very origin of the "public sphere," defined as a domain of private citizens engaged in public discourse—a "print culture" that had emancipated itself from domination by the church and the state but was not yet wholly subject to domination by the market. The emergence of that sphere in the eighteenth century was coterminous with the emergence of the "bourgeois reading public. . . . This public remained rooted in the world of letters even as it assumed political functions; education was the one criterion for admission—property ownership the other."[18] During the period within which this public sphere assumed such large political significance, its successful functioning depended entirely upon *literary* education to provide private citizens with the means (literacy, a standardized language, a common set of cultural texts) of both identifying itself as a class with common interests and of negotiating these interests in a "public" domain separate from (that is, not dominated by) that of the state. Hence it was neither possible nor desirable to make a sharp distinction in the eighteenth century between the domains of journalism and literary production, and both realms remained quite permeable to each other until well into the next century. With the gradual incorporation of journalistic media as capitalist enterprises, these domains ceased to be coincident, and there occurred what Habermas calls the "structural transformation of the public sphere," marked by an intensifying division of labor between journalistic and literary producers.

The domain of journalism was increasingly subjugated to specific economic and political interests within the socioeconomic order even while the domain of literary production was relegated to that of private consumption. This history is usually repressed in our representations of the contemporary public sphere that, insofar as it is now a domain of "mass culture," operates according to structural principles that are very different from those of its "bourgeois" precursor. Hence the practices of journalism and of literary criticism can continue to confront each other as *mirrors* in which they see not their respective relations to the mass cultural form of publicity but an idealized image of their former Enlightenment identity (their identity *with each other*), an image of their former function as autonomous critics of politics and culture.

Habermas's historical argument allows us to see that the "politicization" of the disciplines and the reaction of the journalists are profoundly complementary phenomena. Together they express a nostalgia by social agents in both domains for the public sphere of the eighteenth century and, perhaps more powerfully, the survival of an imaginary or simulacral version of that sphere. The circumstance of being "publicly" attacked can thus be experienced after the fact as both the confirmation of a dissident intellectual identity and a further entitlement to "political" speech. If this mutual provocation can now take the form of staged public debates between, for example, Stanley Fish and Dinesh d'Souza, the actual political convictions of the parties to this debate will finally matter less than their representative functions in a public performance, their respective public identities as university intellectual and right-wing journalist. We can also be sure that the conflict between these siblings will repress the ambiguous, nonidentical relation between the simulacral public sphere and the mass cultural form of publicity. This repression operates on both the left and the right; it is as characteristic of Russell Jacoby as it is of Allan Bloom. In this context, one must agree with Barbara Ehrenreich's pointed response to Jacoby: "I am a little afraid that Jacoby's 'public intellectual' is really a *famous* intellectual."[19]

If the expression of political engagement by the intellectuals is really so dependent upon the form of publicity—of fame—then it will only ever be possible for a few figures to enter that arena. This is not to say that opportunities should not be seized when available, but that it is a mistake not to recognize that the domain of contemporary publicity is not the *same* as the public sphere in which the literarily educated once exercised a crucial political function. One has at least to reckon the consequences that follow from the fact that opinion must be commodified in order to enter the realm of publicity at all (usually this will entail its being consumable as *entertaining*, a condition thoroughly understood, for example, by Camille Paglia). But more than that, one has to observe a certain double misrecognition determining the relations of academics to publicity: if the sphere of mass publicity is often mistaken for the old bourgeois public sphere, academics have also failed to recognize that the quite real (if also limited) public sphere in which they do operate—one of a number of such counter- or micro-public spheres in contemporary society—is increasingly being transformed into a simulacrum of the mass publicity sphere. This transformation is visible in the rapid turnover of intellectual fashions, the reconstruction of academic careers on the model of celebrity, and the pervasion of scholarly writing by a certain nervous tendency to allude to mass cultural phenomena.

Habermas's argument is further helpful in suggesting that the decline of the old bourgeois public sphere was in fact the condition for the emergence of intellectuals *so-called*: "Only then did there arise a stratum of 'intellectuals' that explains to itself its progressive isolation from, at first, the public of the educated boureoisie as an—illusory—emancipation from social locations altogether and interprets itself as 'free-floating intellectuals.'"[20] This narrative would account for the subsequent oscillation among the intellectuals between a cathexis of disengagement and a nostalgia for engagement, the latter expressed usually as a nostalgia for the very public sphere that functioned historically in the *absence* of a socially identified group of "intellectuals." This oscillation appears alternatively as a double bind in which intellectuals have felt compelled historically to assume the specific political responsibility of leading mass movements—thereby betraying (the "treason of the intellectuals") the very conditions of autonomous inquiry that defines them as intellectuals—or to defend the conditions of free and disengaged inquiry, thereby abdicating their political responsibility.[21] The historical category of the intellectuals names this contradiction in the division of labor, a point that we may now develop with reference to the work of Pierre Bourdieu.

The very complexity of the historical formation of the intellectuals means that a phenomenon such as the "politicization" of the disciplines will not yield its significance to a hypothesis so simple as the internal exile of unrepentant activists into the humanities. Nor is it necessarily the case that something in the very nature of these disciplines lends itself to "politicization" and hence that they are especially privileged with respect to the formation of intellectuals. Rather we should look to conjunctural conditions underlying the public calling out of the intellectuals for an explanation of these phenomena, in much the way that Pierre Bourdieu has recently attempted to account for the events of May '68 in *Homo Academicus*:

> The crisis as conjuncture, that is to say as conjunction of independent causal series, supposes the existence of *worlds* which are separate but which participate in the same *universe* both through their motive forces and through their contingent functioning: the independence of causal series which "develop in parallel," as Cournot says, supposes the relative autonomy of the fields; the meeting of these series supposes their relative dependence as regards the fundamental structures—especially the economic ones—which determine the logics of the different fields. It is this independence in dependency which renders the *historical event* possible.[22]

The "independent causal series" that come together in Bourdieu's account refer to 1) an increase in the size of the student population, which occasions at once a "downclassing" of the traditional disciplines and a crisis of falling expectations; and 2) a "conflict of the faculties" (Kant) in which the social capital embodied in the legal and medical professions is increasingly in tension with the intellectual capital embodied in the sciences and social sciences.[23] In this conjuncture the social sciences (*les sciences humaines*) play a particularly significant role, indexed by the pressure they exerted from the advent of structuralism to the present upon the high canonical discipline of philosophy in the French educational system. Bourdieu makes this genealogy explicit by describing his sociology as "fieldwork in philosophy."[24] The conditions determining the French mas-

ter theorists' sublimation of "the human sciences" into a philosophical problematic are lost to view when these theorists (Derrida, Foucault, Lacan et al.) cross the Atlantic as paradigmatic texts for a new
literary criticism, as "theory"; but this deracination of French
thought really reflects the fact that the position of philosophy in the
French university is actually homologous with that of literary criticism in America. If the erstwhile centrality of the humanities in
Western educational systems is belied by their actually peripheral
status in the production of new and valued knowledges, then the
"center" of this periphery was clearly philosophy in France, literary
study in America.

In any case, the conjuncture of the 1980s in the United States
interpellated the intellectuals in a manner rather different from the
events of May '68 in France, or for that matter, the sixties in America, when it was mainly the social sciences and public policy disciplines that were the sites of politicization in the university. The
present notoriety of American literary critics vis-à-vis the practice
of politicization is an effect of "parallel" developments in the
spheres of mass culture, where journalism is increasingly subject to
pressures that accentuate its distinction from the academic field,
and in the university, where the humanities have occupied a progressively smaller area of the curriculum in relation to the disciplines reproducing the technical and managerial professions. In
the face of what Bourdieu calls a kind of "structural declassing,"
only partially compensated by the mimetic "professionalization" of
disciplines within the humanities, these disciplines, especially literary criticism, have become the likely sites for "politicization," the
very thematizing of dissidence that in turn provokes the fraternal
hatred of the journalists.

The above analysis is only a preliminary sketch, however, an
opening of the subject in the direction of a sociological analysis; but
this analysis suggests already that generalizations about intellectuals
will remain dubious if they do not account for the conjunctural circumstances in which intellectuals appear *as such*. That is, such generalizations continue to regard the identity of intellectuals as something that can be claimed only in the act of political position-taking,
a theoretical stance that is always in danger of lapsing into mere vol-
untarism. In this context, Foucault's distinction between universal

and specific intellectuals appears to be more problematic than its reception would suggest, as it forgoes precisely the kind of analysis that would explain *which* specific intellectuals are likely to engage in *what* political position-taking. Dismissing the claims of "universal" intellectuals as nothing more than a repetition of the Enlightenment bourgeoisie's claim to be the bearer of universal values, such an analysis remains incapable of accounting for the fact that it is only *some* specific intellectuals who are likely to be politicized in any given configuration of what Foucault calls the discourses of truth. Foucault proposes the scientist as the typical specific intellectual (the relation between science and the politicization of literary theory will concern us presently), but there is no necessary relation between specificity itself and politicization. The example of Oppenheimer, cited by Foucault as marking the transition from the universal intellectual (the "great writer") to the specific, testifies especially against the point he wants to make, since it is precisely the scientist who is now least likely among the specific intellectuals to be politicized in any adversarial way. Within the university, moreover, scientists are more inclined than social scientists to second the demand of the journalists that teachers of the humanities return to their historical mission of transmitting universal truths and values. But perhaps one has to be located in a certain place—where, for example, one might *read Foucault*—in order to recognize oneself as one of the specific intellectuals. This place turns out to have the same characteristics of perspectival universal that the very concept of specificity calls into question.[25]

In practice, it is difficult to identify "specific" intellectuals *as intellectuals* except by reference to their political positions, which always address something other and larger than questions that arise only in the practice of their disciplines. Consider, for example, the following identification by Stanley Aronowitz of the specific intellectuals of our era: "Today the left intellectual is a feminist, an ecologist, a critic of science and technology, a person of color. Right-wing intellectuals still occupy those universal spaces once the province of the left and liberals."[26] But what spaces are these? Is a feminist or an ecologist a specific intellectual by virtue of being a feminist or an ecologist, and not by virtue of being located in the system of production as a specific kind of intellectual laborer—a literary critic, a scientist, a doctor, a lawyer? It must be said too that one's identity as a minority, which might indeed ground a certain practice of resistance, has no necessary relation to one's labor, intellectual or otherwise. And why should it? What is the relation, then, between the political positions in question and one's place in the world of work? What sense does it make to derive the identity of intellectual from the act of taking a specific political position? Aronowitz defines the left intellectual by a political *position*, the right by a *space*. Surely all intellectuals must be defined by both, or more accurately, by a determinate relation between a social space and a political position. Let us at least acknowledge the fact that it is paradoxically at the site where one would most expect to find old-style *universal* intellectuals—the humanities—that one is most certain to find all the varieties of "left intellectual" named by Aronowitz, in other words, the supposedly "specific" intellectuals. Does this paradox not suggest that it was precisely the long-term crisis of this institutional space, the very crisis that divided intellectual labor into so many specificities, that gave rise at a particular conjuncture to the "politicization" of the traditional humanities, to the transformation of these declassed and evacuated "universal" spaces into the basis for a mode of political self-assertion that was at once of the left, and that claimed not to be universal but "specific" to a variety of constituencies and causes? Such a development would conform to a principle Bourdieu has articulated as follows: "The space of positions tends to command the space of position-takings."[27] In this case, the very obsolescence and disarray of those disciplinary paradigms that once grounded the claims of humanities teachers to be "universal" intellectuals now ground claims that are no less universal (only now *crypto*-universal) for being described as "specific" to women, minorities, etc.

Hence the paradox of intellectual identity: defined by nothing more than political positions that might conceivably be held by any politically aware person, and yet inexplicably clustered within certain disciplines or sites in the larger domain of intellectual labor. I propose to follow Bourdieu in disputing this implicitly voluntarist construction of the intellectuals, defining them instead as laborers who are possessed of certain kinds of what Bourdieu calls "cultural capital." In this way I also hope to avoid the covert elitism of the discourse of the intellectuals that produces the intellectual as an *honorific* title just by virtue of the claim to be the constitutively "political class." This elitism is sustained even when the "universal intellectual" is ritually dethroned in theory, because the ritual of dethronement represses the fact that there *is* a determinate relation between social location in the sphere of production and one's public identity as an "intellectual." Let us recall that the only other constitutively "political class" history reveals to us is the aristocracy, who were defined by their mode of political domination. The intellectuals have, conversely, but according to the same logic, been defined by their mode of political *resistance*. We must learn instead to recognize that when the intellectuals appear as such, as simultaneously called out and self-nominated, we are really seeing only a particular *sector* of intellectual labor come into public view, most likely that sector that is thrown into crisis.

THE SPACE OF POSITIONS

An alternative analysis of intellectual identity would attempt to preserve a sense of the determinate relation between the intellectuals so-called and the total domain of intellectual labor. If the category of "universal intellectuals" is vulnerable to question (and of course it is), it remains an insufficiently analyzed fact that "specific intellectuals" seem to occupy virtually the same social locations as their universal predecessors. The figure of the universal intellectual has thus been overthrown by rejecting the concept of "universality" on behalf of new political commitments, but without interrogating the positioning of the intellectual in social space. I will argue for the reverse procedure: a sociological analysis of intellectuals that rigorously reduces the tendency of their political position-taking to an effect of their position in the socioeconomic order. This no doubt offensive determinism is only instrumental, however; in fact, it is not a determinism at all, but a necessary analytic exercise the purpose of which is to demonstrate that the conditions for producing desirable political positions *must themselves be produced*. These conditions are defined by a certain measure and kind of *autonomy*, a measure of work autonomy, a kind of intellectual autonomy. From this point of view, the concept of the "universal" will not induce the phobic response so characteristic of our current discourse of the intellectuals, because the quality of "universality" will not be attributed exclusively to the social group of self-nominated intellectuals but to *intellectuality in general.* I propose, then, that an analysis of the intellectuals that is truly analytic, that evinces the determinate relation between intellectuals so-called and the larger domain of intellectual labor, must be directed not toward the overthrow of the universal intellectual but toward the universalization of intellectuality. But having ventured this quixotic theme, let me hasten to add that it is not original: in what follows I have undertaken to "translate" an argument that runs through the oeuvre of Pierre Bourdieu, and which is indicated by his advocacy of a "corporatism of the universal"—a thinking of the universal through the medium of the particular interests of intellectual labor.[28] This translation, however, should be set off in double quotation marks, first of all because it is an attempt to "translate" into homologous American contexts certain of Bourdieu's arguments that make constant reference to French culture and to the French educational system; and second, because this "translation" is necessarily a mistranslation, a deliberate deflection of Bourdieu's argument into the context of an American debate in which the status of "class" as an analytic concept is very uncertain.

It is to the latter issue that I would turn first, by acknowledging the fact that the theoretical problem posed by the intellectuals has seemed to damage beyond repair the apparatus of class analysis, particularly in its Marxist form. Perhaps the debate might be most efficiently evoked by first raising the question of *classification,* of the specific theoretico-political work being done by such as concepts as the "New Class," or the "Professional-Managerial Class." For both Gouldner in his *The Future of Intellectuals and the Rise of the New Class* and for the Ehrenreichs in their article on "The Professional-Managerial Class," the social groups thus nominated include the intellectuals *so-called* without being identical to their self-perception. At least since Gramsci, the very project of attempting to account for the class position of intellectuals has required extending that designation far beyond the group of self-nominated intellectuals, at the same time that it has raised questions about the basic two-class model of bourgeoisie and proletariat. Notwithstanding such compromise formulations as that of Poulantzas, who attempted to assimilate what U.S. theorists call the "New Class" to the traditional Marxist category of the petty bourgeoisie,[29] it has been difficult to deny that the increasing size and diverse functions of the group in question require a significant revision of class theory. These revisions have tended to accent a fundamental and long-standing methodological tension between theoretical constructions that define class according to economic position and constructions that define class according to the cultural practices that produce the experience or perception of class identity.[30] It would seem that the most obvious way to resolve such a theoretical tension would be to redefine class in such a way that it assumes both economic and cultural constituents. This strategy is employed, for example, by the Ehrenreichs in their essay. There a class is defined by both a "common relation to the economic foundations of society" and by a "coherent social and cultural existence."[31] While this recourse to a combinatory analysis is methodologically strategic, if not unavoidable, we should not forget that the Professional-Managerial Class is more than simply the object of such a combined analysis. As the *occasion* of this methodological compromise, the challenge posed to class analysis by the group in question is precisely that of a class in which the cultural constituent appears to be definitive, and in which its mode of cultural or "knowledge" production is *uniquely* related to the system of production.

Without venturing too far into the complexities of what has become a highly scholastic debate, we might attempt to characterize as concisely as possible a certain aspect of this unique relation. The Ehrenreichs contend, for example, that the Professional-Managerial Class emerged in the process of "appropriating" the "skills once vested in the working class" and thus must be seen historically as agents of the essentially exploitative program of the capitalist economy. The incompatibility of economic interests between the New Class and the working class is complemented by strategies of cultural distinction deployed elsewhere than in the workplace. At the same time, however, the Professional-Managerial Class is not simply identical to the "ruling class," if by that is meant the owners of capital, as its interests are not wholly coincident with the interests of that group. Let us recall that in *The Communist Manifesto* Marx did not hesitate to regard emergent New Class figures as wage-labor: "The bourgeoisie has stripped of its halo every occupation hitherto honoured and looked up to with reverent awe. It has converted the physician, the lawyer, the priest, the poet, the man of science, into its paid wage-labourers." Interpreting the same relation of antagonism a century later, Gouldner projects the victory of these wage-laborers over the bourgeoisie, which he sees as the victory of cultural over material capital. If these accounts of the position of the New Class are not simply contradictory, in the sense in which one or the other must be true, the differences between them suggest the great difficulty posed for class analysis by the hypertrophic development of cultural capital, a difficulty we might represent as a kind of theoretical torsion. In this conception capital and labor need not define two classes fixed in immutable identities by their opposition to one another, but classes *in process*, defined by the alternatives of capitalization and proletarianization.[32] These potentialities project a social continuum, the two poles of which might be twisted in opposite directions. Straddling the center of this continuum, at the point of maximum torque, is the "New Class." For this reason the torque embodied in intellectual labor can be released in the direction either of capitalization or proletarianization. This to say both that knowledge, like money, is only capital when it is capitalized, when it produces the effect of *embourgeoisement*; and conversely, that knowledge can be devalued in such a way that its possessors become indistinguishable from wage-labor—a process of proletarianization marking the history of, for example, primary-school teachers and secretaries.[33]

A similar theoretical torsion is implied by Bourdieu's description of "intellectuals" as "a dominated fraction of the dominant class."[34] If Bourdieu's "intellectuals" are representative figures of the New Class, they cannot be described as simply powerless on account of their being so dominated. Nor is their power exercised solely in their relations with the working class. We will have to say that a certain kind of power vis-à-vis the "dominant fraction" is derived from the very dependency of the latter upon the New Class, the fact that the New Class's organizational knowledge is essential to the domination of labor, or that its knowledge products are essential to the development of the forces of production, or that its cultural artifacts and symbolic constructs are essential to the ideological reproduction of the system as a whole. These several indispensible functions are different in rather consequential ways, as we shall see, but the exercise of each of them entails a measure of "autonomy." The Ehrenreichs put this point as follows: "The roles that the Professional-Managerial Class was entering and carving out for itself—as technical innovators, social mediators, culture producers, etc.—required a high degree of autonomy, if only for the sake of legitimization."[35] The principle of legitimization through autonomy is perhaps best understood in the historical context of "professionalization," the form of association or incorporation by which this autonomy is established and safeguarded. By renegotiating through the medium of such corporate structures the *exchange-value* of its commodified knowledge, the New Class "wage-laborers" secured not only increasing compensation (sufficient often to convert wage income into capital) but an increasing measure of autonomy. This autonomy represents not simply a "contradiction" between capital and labor embodied in the Professional-Managerial Class, but a political effect produced by the torsion of these forces, the emergence of "self-government" among the professions. This political form is distinct from the form of *domination*, the government of *others*, the very power that is exercised by sectors of the Professional-Managerial Class in its management of the productive process.

How then is one to understand the condition of autonomy as a distinct form of "political" power? One can be sure that the dominant fraction of the dominant class will wish to yield only as much autonomy to its dominated fraction as is required for the latter's legitimation or efficient functioning. The hypothetical upper limit of such autonomy would then be defined by that point at which its exercise would be perceived to constitute a threat to the power of capital or of the state.[36] Just because it is a terrain of struggle, autonomy is always relative—in the sense of limited—and it would be a mistake (perhaps Gouldner's mistake) to posit this autonomy as even potentially absolute. Autonomy is always also relative in another sense: it is the autonomy of what Bourdieu calls a *field*—the cultural field, the economic field, the political field—in relation to another field.[37] Thus, autonomy from the state does not necessarily imply autonomy from other fields, such as the market. Relative autonomy always defines a certain ratio between autonomy and *heteronomy*, the domination that emanates from another field in a social space consisting always of more than two fields.[38] Working with this multi-field model of the social universe, Bourdieu has attempted to reconstruct a historical sociology of the intellectuals in which the crucial moment of their formation is not their self-nomination in the Dreyfus affair but the achievement by cultural producers in general of relative autonomy from church and state in the eighteenth century *at the same time* that these producers became increasingly subject to "structural domination" by the market.[39] One must even say that it is paradoxically their subordination to the market that secures their autonomy from church and state. Autonomy, then, is always the object of struggle between fields, and as such can be won or lost, accumulated or spent, in relation to one field or another. This analysis grounds Bourdieu's understanding of that second origin of the intellectuals in the Dreyfus affair: "Only at the end of the [nineteenth] century, when literary, artistic and scientific fields attained a high degree of autonomy, did the most autonomous agents of these autonomous fields realize that their autonomy was not identical with a rejection of politics, and that they could intervene in politics as artists, writers and scholars."[40] What one always needs to remember, however, is that autonomy from political domination does not imply an equal measure of autonomy from "structural domination by the market, and hence the struggle for relative autonomy from that realm could be waged in other arenas than that of political position-taking—for example, in the struggle of the historical avant-garde against the normalizing effects of the bourgeois market upon cultural production. Autonomy, in brief, is always a relational fact, and not a quantum possessed in any absolute measure by any social group.[41]

At this point we must introduce another fold in the complication of this analysis: just as the New Class performs a variety of indispensible functions in modern societies, the *modes* of autonomy specific to those functions are correspondingly different. Here it will be necessary to make a distinction between work autonomy and intellectual autonomy, but with the important qualification that all work autonomy is potentially intellectual autonomy. That is, any reflection on the conditions of work designed to maximize the autonomy of those conditions can potentially become a reflection on the general conditions of work within a field, on relations between fields, and on the social system as a totality of relations between fields. However, if a measure of work autonomy is necessary in all the sectors of intellectual labor in order for that work to be accomplished at all, it does not follow that all sectors of intellectual labor are granted the same measure of work autonomy, or the same *potential* intellectual autonomy. In fact, one might observe here a certain inverse relation between the organic significance of sectors of intellectual labor to the process of production and the measure of work autonomy (and thus potential intellectual autonomy) granted to those sectors.[42] Intellectual laborers in the administrative and managerial spheres certainly possess less work autonomy than artists, scholars, or scientists; but that low degree of autonomy is inversely related to the degree of domination they exercise over workers in the production process. This domination can also be exercised over *other sectors of intellectual labor*, as in the management of scientific research by corporate or state agencies. Relations of domination within the intellectual field are further complicated by the tendency of institutions composed largely of intellectuals (universities or professional associations) to develop a stratum of managers, often recruited from their own ranks, who exercise domination over other intellectuals. The struggle for autonomy takes place at many levels, between and within fields; it may even take the form of a struggle by individuals against the normative practices imposed on individuals by the professions themselves.

The New Class is internally divided, then, along multiple lines of fracture and in response to multiple sources of conflict; the contested ratio of autonomy to heteronomy between fields is reproduced within the field of intellectual labor as the conflict between different sectors of that field. This is the context in which one has to recognize that the appearance of the *category* of the intellectuals so-called has a conjunctural determination. It is the index of a particular conjunctural situation that is only intelligible if one can read it first in relation to the total interrelations between the sectors of intellectual labor, and then to the relation between the intellectual and other fields. Within that sector of the intellectual field that defines academics and their labor, for example, we can tentatively identify different ratios between intellectual and work autonomy as the source of a politically significant division between the humanities and the sciences. The same systemic features that make it unlikely that scientists would be called out as "political" intellectuals—except under extraordinary circumstances—also make it very likely that university teachers in the humanities and in some of the social sciences would be so called. It is a question, then, of the location of teachers in a complexly divided social space, and specifically of the ratio of autonomy possessed by these agents. If the experience of work autonomy in the sciences remains only *potentially* a form of intellectual autonomy, this is obviously a function of the much greater integration of the knowledge-products of science into the system of production, a kind of subtle intellectual heteronomy that tends to produce in scientists (not exclusively but tendentially) a tacit endorsement of those systemic relations that guarantee their work autonomy. Thus, scientific progress can always be cited as a confirmation of the wisdom of the present political order, because that order is supposed (entirely uncritically, of course) to be conducive to scientific progress. It follows that the assertion of intellectual autonomy among the scientists (of a potential intellectual *identity*) is most likely to occur as a consequence of restraints imposed upon their work autonomy.[43]

I would propose here that the distinction between intellectual autonomy and work autonomy can be mapped roughly but not inaccurately in relation to Gramsci's famous distinction between traditional and organic intellectuals. If the autonomy possessed by humanist or "traditional" intellectuals apparently entails a much weaker endorsement of contemporary systemic relations, that is because this autonomy has another source altogether, their investment in the *historical* rather than the contemporary conditions of their identity:

> Since these various categories of traditional intellectuals experience through an "*esprit de corps*" their uninterrupted historical continuity and their special qualification, they thus put themselves forward as autonomous and independent of the dominant social group. This self-assessment is not without consequences in the ideological and political field, consequences of wide-ranging import. The whole of idealist philosophy can easily be connected with this position assumed by the social complex of intellectuals and can be defined as the expression of that social utopia by which the intellectuals think

of themselves as "independent," autonomous, endowed with a character of their own, etc.[44]

As Gramsci's analysis makes clear, the great perplexity in the discourse of intellectuals derives from the fact that the traditional intellectual's self-identification seems to be equated in the professional imaginary with autonomy itself. Gramsci goes on to demonstrate that the relation between traditional intellectuals and the order in which they find themselves may be more oblique, more mediated, than that of "organic" intellectuals, but that they are not on that account absolutely independent, absolutely autonomous. In fact, the emergence of a dominant class, which entails the development of intellectuals who are "organic" to that class, always also entails the "assimilation" and even "conquest" of the traditional intellectuals. This conquest is specifically named as "ideological" and its successful prosecution implies that the traditional intellectuals are continually refunctioned in the service of what Gramsci usually calls "hegemony"—though this refunctioning or "conquest" occurs in different ways and in different measure at different times.

Gramsci's distinction between traditional and organic intellectuals emphasizes constitutive *divisions* within the total group of the intellectual functionaries, and thus potential *conflicts* between sectors of intellectual labor. An analysis that incorporates this recognition would necessarily refrain from drawing conclusions about the political character of intellectuals in general on the basis of the particular sector of intellectual labor that is interpellated as such. Such an analysis would recognize instead that the category of the intellectuals so-called always indexes the specificity of a conjuncture: that is, the conjunction of specific conflicts between the sectors of intellectual labor, as well as the specific alliances possible among sectors of intellectual labor in response to heteronomous pressures emanating from the political and economic fields. Such an alliance is the basis for the conjunctural recategorization of these temporarily allied sectors as "the intellectuals." The contingency of such alliances can be confirmed by the fact that in the former Soviet Union the category of "dissident intellectual" included traditional intellectuals such as Solzhenitsyn, but also, and equally prominently, scientists such as Sakharov.[45] The prominence of scientists among the Soviet intellectuals attested to the extraordinary degree of heteronomy exercised by the bureaucratic ruling class, the *nomenklatura,* who did not have to compete with the capitalist corporation for the service of scientists, and who therefore did not have to negotiate autonomy as a form of compensation for work.

In the meanwhile, it should be possible to integrate Gramsci's distinction between traditional and organic intellectuals into a schema that can be extrapolated from Bourdieu's analysis of autonomy and heteronomy. The formula by which Gramsci seems to assign autonomy per se to the traditional intellectuals can be modified in the recognition that the specific sites designated by Gramsci's distinction between traditional and organic intellectuals actually represent certain ratios of autonomy (intellectual or work autonomy) to heteronomy (domination by others and domination of others). Gramsci speaks of measuring "the degree of organicism of the various intellectual strata," Bourdieu of the degree of autonomy and heteronomy. An integration of these ratios would look as follows:

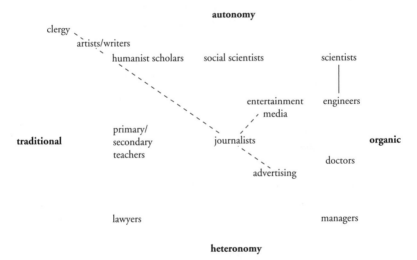

The schema can be glossed as follows:

- The two axes register comparative relations and not quanta; we can at most say that a particular site represents more or less autonomy, more or less organicity in relation to some other site. The horizontal axis also defines a temporal progression not possessed by the vertical, which measures the degree of autonomy or heteronomy at any point along the temporal axis. The line connecting the bottom and the right side of the diagram defines the contiguity of the Profession-al-Managerial Class with the domains of State and Capital.

- Obviously only the upper stratum of the diagram names the "intellectuals" in conventional usage. A Gramscian perspective requires, however, that we regard all of the positions on the diagram as the names of "intellectual functionaries." The purpose of the diagram is precisely to compel us to see that the discrepancy between inclusive and exclusive definitions of intellectuals in Gramsci's account, or in theories of the Professional-Managerial Class, describes a social reality—the occlusion of intellectual functionaries by the discourse of "intellectuals"—and is therefore not a mere defect in theory.
- The functionaries at the bottom of the diagram represent the source of heteronomy, a power they exercise in relation to the functionaries of the upper tier in greater or lesser measure, but most extensively (in the case of the numerically very large group of managers) in the realm of production. It is also the case that they themselves possess little work autonomy since the bureaucratic mode of domination assures that every such agent is responsible to higher agents.
- Lawyers and doctors appear somewhat distantly from each other in the schema, despite their social congruity, primarily because lawyers retain a measure of their identity as traditional intellectuals (they were the "organic" intellectuals of the early modern absolutist states). They are at once the most "conquered" of the traditional intellectuals and, as the group from which the state recruits its highest functionaries, the most politically ambivalent. That ambivalence virtually defines the spectrum of political position-taking for the citizenry. Doctors, on the other hand, while they too have traditional origins (their premodern social status was in fact very low), have effected a break from those origins by virtue of the extreme professionalization and scientization of their practice. At the same time they remain much closer to the domain of heteronomy than scientists as a consequence of

the great social capital that is embodied in the identity of doctor, the most aristocratic of the technocrats.

- Journalists, as organic intellectuals of the old bourgeoisie, are located equidistantly from every pole in order to indicate the fact that they define at least "structurally" a public sphere (however actually limited and simulacral) in which any and every interest is theoretically capable of being expressed. The dotted line indicates their historically cognate relation to the traditional intellectuals, as well as their ongoing assimilation into the adjacent domains of mass culture (advertising and mass media). The greater "organicity" of the journalists permits them to adopt a heteronomous (that is to say, censorious) relation to academics; conversely, the love-hate relation between the traditional intellectuals and the domain of "publicity" can become the conduit for the latter's entry into the system of publicity and thus for their "structural domination" by the forms of mass culture, that is, by the economic field.

The disposition of professions along the two axes allows us to describe the conjunctural conditions for a calling out of the intellectuals in the 1980s as determined *externally* by relations between humanist academics and the journalists, and *internally* (within the university) by relations among humanist scholars, social scientists, and scientists. This conjuncture excludes the clergy (despite the fact that they function now, as they have since the early modern period, as the model in the professional imaginary for the distinction between intellectuals and the laity), because their autonomy is now an effect of their legislated exclusion from the political field. The conjuncture also somewhat distances the traditionally defined artists and writers who were still integral to the field of intellectuals at the time of the Dreyfus affair. Without pausing here to take up the altogether interesting question of why the very great intellectual autonomy of artists and writers (they are, as it were, the most free to starve of all intellectual laborers) no longer readily interpellates them as intellectuals, we can at least pose the question correctly. For the purpose of the schema is not to show that intellectuals have all *become* academics but to raise the question of why among intellectual functionaries it is only academics—and only certain *kinds* of academics—who tend now to be interpellated as intellectuals.

The schema confirms first of all an inverse relation between the degree of intellectual autonomy and the degree of organicity of a discipline. Hence, while we can easily enough identify a high degree of intellectual autonomy as a *condition* for dissident political position-taking, this condition is nonetheless not in itself sufficient to account for such position-taking. Dissident politics, for example, does not necessarily characterize the clergy, despite their high degree of autonomy from political and economic heteronomy, although such politics is always possible. And when it does occur, the very fact of this great autonomy means that religious expressions of dissidence can be quite extreme, either more reactionary or more radical than the spectrum defined by the legal profession.

If intellectual autonomy alone, however, were sufficient to account for such position-taking, we would be forced to return to a conception of the intellectuals as "the political class," as somehow *innately* dissident. In the case of the traditional intellectuals in the humanities we shall have to take into account the correlative condition of their increasingly "inorganic" relation to the system of production—we will have to recognize that in their case, an additional condition of their interpellation as intellectuals is a long-term crisis of the humanities, namely the declining value of the cultural capital embodied in their knowledge-products in relation to the cultural capital produced and reproduced in the legal, technical, and managerial disciplines.[46] This declining organicity is very different from the condition of inorganicity that may be said to characterize the clergy, whose crisis vis-à-vis the cultural capital of its knowledge-products came long ago. Here it is important to recall that the way in which the humanist intellectuals of the early modern period (some of whom of course were still clergy) were conquered by the dominant bourgeois class in the later eighteenth century was precisely by giving to them the important function of producing—primarily through the educational system—a cultural distinction between the bourgeoisie and the lower classes. The schools made possible a kind of mimetic identification of bourgeois culture with aristocratic culture. The cultural distinction between classes has operated since the early modern period as a mode of ideological domination of the working class, a strategic doubling of the class hierarchy as a status hierarchy. However, the cultural capital constituting such distinction has slowly but progressively diminished in significance with the emergence of the New Class, inasmuch as the management of the lower classes is effected now more through an ideology of "productivity" and "upward mobility" and less through the old bourgeois status hierarchy. While the culture of the Professional-Managerial Class has not of course replaced that of the bourgeoisie in any simple historical dialectic, it has in fact undermined the basis for the *cultural homogeneity* of the owners of capital. The older cultural markers of the status hierarchy remain in place, then, but in a seriously etiolated form. As the management of the productive process has been more and more entrusted to the Professional-Managerial Class, and thus to those teachers in the sciences and social sciences, the legal and managerial fields, who reproduce this class, the social function of the traditional intellectuals has been increasingly marginalized.

The paradoxical effect of this marginalization has been to enlarge the domain of intellectual autonomy for traditional intellectuals (as a result of what we may think of as the inattention of political power) at the same time that the value of their cultural capital has been falling. This paradox marks the long-term crisis of the humanities and is the condition for dissident political position-taking among the humanist academics. However, in order to understand the *latest* crisis of the humanities, which is really its passage into a new phase, we shall have to observe further that in the last several decades traditional intellectuals have responded to the decline in the value of their cultural capital in new ways, and that these new strategies have in turn become the conditions for the most recent "crisis of the humanities" marked by the "politicization" of the disciplines.

We know that over the course of the century, the disciplines of the humanities have been increasingly "professionalized," and that this strategy has actually succeeded to a certain degree in ameliorating the worser effects of the crisis. Professionalization has entailed renouncing older individualist notions of vocation for the newer modes of professional association. Nevertheless, this strategy has enhanced the value of the cultural capital of traditional intellectuals by a paradoxical renunciation of work autonomy, a renunciation that takes the form of a mimetic bureaucratization of the working life, the submission of scholarly labor to the norms of "productivity" and institutional competition. The effects of this mimetic bureau-cratization are very familiar anecdotally as everything associated with such phrases as "publish or perish," but what is not yet fully acknowledged by academics is the fact that it was only by yielding to "structural domination" by the market, that the knowledge-products of traditional intellectuals could continue to circulate as cultural capital. Despite the acceleration of this process in recent decades, however, it did not represent a permanent and completely successful solution to the declining organicity of the humanities. The process of professionalization has also been supplemented by a strategy of "scientization," by which the disciplines of the humanities came under increasing pressure to restructure basic methodological para-digms along the lines of more scientific principles, primarily by a mimesis of the social sciences.[47] It was this mimesis that formed the immediate conditions and pretext for the emergence of "theory," whose deep problematic was precisely the sublimation of *les sciences humaines* into the traditional disciplines of the humanities.[48] In this context I believe it is essential now that we begin to take seriously Bourdieu's argument in *Homo Academicus* and elsewhere for recon-sidering the relation between the social sciences and the intellectual projects of such master theorists as Foucault and Derrida. In the case of the former, Bourdieu has suggested that "screen concepts" such as "genealogy" actually "help to provide a cover for an ambitious enter-prise in social history or genetic sociology." In the case of the latter, he argues similarly that Derrida "knows how to suspend 'decon-struction' just in time to prevent it tipping over into a sociological analysis bound to be perceived as a vulgar 'sociologistic reduction,' and thus avoids deconstructing himself *qua* philosopher."[49] The enterprise of theory is long since due for such a "sociologistic reduc-tion," which would of course be something quite other than a *rejec-tion* of theory. On the contrary, the master theorists have nothing to lose by such a reduction except the mystifying aura lent by the *name* of theory. Their "reduction" would mean that we are learning to read them in historical context, which is in any case how we have come to read their precursors, Nietzsche, Freud, Saussure et al.[50]

While the sublimation of the human sciences into "theory" was mediated in the U.S. by being routed through continental thinkers, it always proceeded in the context of a disciplinary practice institutionally *adjacent* to the practices of the social sciences. Making reference once again to the schema above, we can acknowledge the full force of this adjacency in historical terms. For the social sciences represent the most charged domain of ideological production in the university—it is no accident that the earliest form of social science was political economy, whose specific mission in the eighteenth century was to lay the groundwork for a social as well as for a political rationalization of the capitalist system. But the social sciences occupy a curiously ambiguous position in the topography of the disciplines, if one recalls that political economy is a disciplinary practice that constituted itself by effecting a break from its origins in "humanistic" discourses—moral and political philosophy—and then pursued a career in which its agenda of ideological justification was better served by "scientizing" its practice. This process of scientization produced "economics" as the dubiously mathematized discipline occupying a place aggressively contiguous to that of the natural sciences. But insofar as the social sciences in general are situated *between* the humanities and the natural sciences in the social space of the disciplines, they are ambiguously the site of both ideology and of ideology-critique.

Let us try to assess this ambiguity for its effect upon the humanities, and in particular for its effect upon literary criticism as the most egregiously "politicized" of the disciplines. I should like to claim now that the mimetic scientization of the humanities in response to the long-term crisis of its specific cultural capital was the immediate condition of a "politicization" of the disciplines—especially literary criticism in the 1980s. The disciplinary "contamination" of the humanities by the social sciences opens the space for politicization, but the transformed disciplinary paradigm that results from this contamination is not mimetic in any simple sense, nor is it yet successful enough to be regarded as legitimate by the social sciences. It is presently a very inchoate and troubled paradigm, at once insufficiently scientized to circulate as a legitimate new social science, but also still committed to certain aspects of its older ideological agenda. Hence "politicization" sometimes falls to the level merely of *thematizing the political,* a rereading of literature that foregrounds political and social themes in a manner reproducing the "ethical" mode of criticism that defined the disciplinary paradigm of literary criticism in its bourgeois heyday.

At the same time, the lesser degree of organicity characterizing the humanistic disciplines continues to support a large measure of intellectual autonomy, a circumstance that has several interesting effects. First, this autonomy is uniquely privileged vis-à-vis the social sciences themselves, in that it is the basis for a critique of what is "ideological" in those sciences, of what is merely mimetic of the natural sciences in them, and hence of how they disseminate a techno-scientific ideology of productivity. In that sense the humanistic disciplines have become the site of a reflection on social science not often enough undertaken by social scientists themselves. This fragile transitional state, of a not yet legitimated social scientificity, which by virtue of that fact is potentially a critical reflection on social science, means that what Bourdieu calls "reflexive sociology" is more likely to be found in the U.S. in the humanities than in the social sciences themselves, which remain highly scientized on the model of natural science. At the same time, this reflexive sociology is not necessarily of a very high order, since it is practiced in the context of very haphazard and unintegrated political agendas that are constantly in danger of lapsing into mere political position-taking and, even worse, moral posturing.

The second effect follows directly from the fact of "politicization." This development very quickly came to the attention of the journalists (thanks to native informants), and thence to the attention of the state, which, like the Cyclops aroused from its stupor, took a predictable swat at the former "nobodies," the humanities professors. Insofar as the "attention" of the journalists and of the state paradoxically opened a conduit to the domain of "publicity" for these professors, the very phenomenon of the reactionary backlash seemed to revalue upward the knowledge produced by the humanities, according to the economic logic of celebrity (the most "politicized" professors became—and not unjustly—the most sought after), at the same time that it provoked an attempt to limit the intellectual autonomy of these teachers (either by harrassment or by more direct interventionary measures). The reaction was dialectically completed by the "reentitlement" or interpellation of these academics as "intellectuals." But it is important to recognize that this latest self-assertion of the intellectuals, insofar as it projected literary critics into the glare of publicity, constituted a much narrower interpellation than that which characterized, for example, the ferment in France before and after May '68, or the contemporaneous events in the United States. The sequence of professionalization-scientization-politicization charting successive responses to the long-term crisis of the humanities in the U.S. did not produce "the intellectuals" as an *alliance* of humanists and social scientists (much less scientists) and this represents its most serious limitation. Whether or not it will be possible to produce such an alliance on the basis of a critique of the organicity of the latter two fields, of a reflection on the *real* limitations imposed upon intellectual autonomy by that organicity, it is clear that the further development of a new disciplinary paradigm in literary criticism and in the humanities generally must proceed in two directions that are very much in tension with each other: 1) an increasing incorporation of the most critical and the most sophisticated methodological resources of the social sciences; and 2) a continued self-critique of any merely mimetic appropriation of scientificity.

THE CORPORATISM OF THE UNIVERSAL

What I am proposing here is the necessity of what may look at first like a return to an earlier moment in the history of the disciplines, when the new social science of "sociology" was detaching itself from the highly scientized (and also ideologized) discipline of political economy. It is worth remarking that this disciplinary origin was effected by its original practitioners (Durkheim, Simmel, Weber et al.) in part through a process of liberal borrowing from the fields of literary criticism, history, and philosophy.[51] Drawing a lesson from this remarkable and still unappreciated fact, I think it would be a mistake to undertake the reconstruction of the humanities simply by deferring to the disciplinary paradigms of the social sciences; for that would be to lose precisely the possibilities opened up by the erosion of disciplinary boundaries, an earlier instance of which gave birth to the discipline of sociology. It may well be the case that the social sciences themselves now exhibit an exhaustion that is the effect of the uncritical scientificity of their practices, and that the very disarray of literary criticism and of the humanities generally may provide both occasions and models for a reformation of social science. At any rate, one may remark here that the recent tendency of the humanities and some of the social sciences to project new disciplinary paradigms under such names as "New Historicism," "Cultural Studies," or the "new social history," suggests that the disciplines of the humanities have reached a certain limit in the degree of their specialization and that what is happening now is the *convergence* of the disciplines (via their breakdown) into several forms of historical sociology. But this is a hopeful reading of the situation, and the further development of this positive scenario depends a good deal on the resistance new forms of historical sociology put up to a practice that merely thematizes the political, or that forgets the real knowledge accumulated in the disciplines of the humanities without learning what historical sociology once knew, and may know again.

On the basis of the disciplinary deformation and reformation represented by these developments, an alliance may be possible that may reconstitute "the intellectuals" a little more broadly than at present. This alliance must, however, be formed more with the immediate agenda of a reflection on the conditions of disciplinary practice than on the basis of political position-taking. To repeat: in order to make strategic use of the determinations that lie behind political position-taking, one must work to produce the conditions that determine desirable political position-taking. One must, so to speak, *extend* the crisis by exposing to a sociological critique the pervasion of heteronomy in the sectors of the intellectual field that are less inclined to self-reflection.

It is for this reason that Bourdieu makes an argument that may otherwise seem surprising in the context of American academics' fervid reduction of intellectuality to taking political stands: "The first objective for a movement of intellectuals is to work collectively towards the defense of their own interests and towards the means necessary for the protection of their autonomy."[52] If Gramsci's analysis of the intellectuals reminds us that there are constitutive divisions and thus conflicts within the intellectual field, Bourdieu's analysis reminds us that conflicts are always ipso facto matters of alliance. Every such alliance reintroduces the possibility of what was too soon and too easily dismissed as the "universal." The possibility of a "corporatism of the universal," or what Bourdieu also calls a "republic of intellectuals" (dismissing once and for all the pseudo-aristocratic self-identification of the intellectuals)[53] would thus depend especially upon promoting the recognition that intellectual autonomy—and therefore intellectuality—is always potentially at stake in work autonomy, which is at stake in every sector of intellectual labor, and of labor in general. The politics of such an alliance would have to acknowledge as its necessary condition that some sectors of intellectual labor must struggle with other sectors, on behalf of universalizing the conditions of intellectuality and the conditions of work autonomy that are its immediate support. The self-assertion of the intellectuals is a strategic mode of "corporatism" that should never imply the *identity* of the universal with the intellectuals so-called. The historical appearance of "the intellectuals" on the contrary names a certain general crisis in the division of labor, the other and local name of which is "the crisis of the humanities."

NOTES

1. Bruce Robbins, ed., *Intellectuals: Aesthetics, Politics, Academics* (Minneapolis: University of Minnesota Press, 1990).

2. The "tenured radical" thesis is Roger Kimball's, in his *Tenured Radicals: How Politics Has Corrupted Our Higher Education* (New York: Harper and Row, 1990). In rejecting this thesis, I do not mean to imply that many leftist academics were not actually activists in the sixties, or do not consider themselves to be radical still. Nevertheless, what this thesis does not explain is why the center of dissident political expression in the academy shifted from the social sciences to the humanities in the past two decades, that is, why the humanities seem to offer a home for political dissidence, despite the fact that in the sixties they were not especially remarkable for encouraging political activism. See also Allan Bloom, *The Closing of the American Mind* (New York: Simon and Schuster, 1987); Dinesh D'Souza, *Illiberal Education: The Politics of Race and Sex on Campus* (New York: Free Press, 1991); and Alvin Kernan, *The Death of Literature* (New Haven: Yale University Press, 1990). Articles in the journalistic media are too numerous to cite here, but for a typical intervention see the *Wall Street Journal* of February 2, 1988, "From Western Lit to Westerns as Lit."

3. For Althusser's concept of interpellation, see his "Ideology and Ideological State Apparatuses," in *Lenin and Philosophy* (London: New Left Books, 1971).

4. Julien Benda, *The Treason of the Intellectuals*, trans. Richard Aldington (New York: W. W. Norton, 1969).

5. Russell Jacoby, *The Last Intellectuals: American Culture in the Age of Academe* (New York: Basic Books, 1987).

6. See Karl Mannheim, *Ideology and Utopia*, trans. Louis Wirth and Edward Shils (New York: Harcourt Brace Jovanovich, 1936).

7. For a classic statement of the equation between intellectual identity and political position, see Edward Shils, *The Intellectuals and the Powers, and Other Essays* (Chicago: University of Chicago Press, 1972).

8. The reservation expressed here is to be distinguished from an argument such as Regis Debray's, in his *Teachers, Writers, Celebrities: The Intellectuals of Modern France* (London: Verso, 1981). Debray's rejection of the intellectual as celebrity, while it is supported by some very shrewd analysis, puts the case against the "mediatic" intellectual too simply by contrasting this figure with an idealized predecessor. The point of the present analysis is neither to idealize the supposedly autonomous intellectuals of a former historical order, nor to dismiss the possibilities of critique that may very well inhere in the spaces of the mass media. It is rather to analyze the uncritical equation between the mass media and the "public sphere" among intellectuals themselves. In the absence of an analysis of the relation between the institutional space of academia and the space of the media, political discourse by "mediatized" intellectuals is *to some degree* vitiated by transformation into what Debray calls "spectacle value." In this context it is significant that Debray dates the mediatization of French intellectuals to the fateful year of 1968, the same political moment that seems to have inaugurated in the U.S. the supposed withdrawal of the intellectuals into the universities. For an argument analogous to Debray's, see Zygmunt Bauman, "Love in Adversity: On the State and the Intellectuals, and the State of the Intellectuals," *Thesis Eleven* 31 (1992):81–104.

9. Stanley Aronowitz, "On Intellectuals," in Robbins, ed., *Intellectuals*, 52.

10. Alvin Gouldner, *The Future of Intellectuals and the Rise of the New Class* (New York: Oxford University Press, 1979). Gouldner's argument is in my view somewhat more complex than the above remarks suggest, particularly as regards the relation between socioeconomic position and political identity.

11. Among Bourdieu's many works dealing directly or indirectly with the question of intellectuals, I shall be making reference primarily to *An Invitation to Reflexive Sociology* (Chicago: University of Chicago Press, 1992); *Homo Academicus*, trans. Peter Collier (Stanford: Stanford University Press, 1988); "The Corporatism of the Universal: The Role of Intellectuals in the Modern World," *Telos* 81 (1989):99–110; "The Market of Symbolic Goods," *Poetics* 14 (1985):13–44; "The Field of Cultural Production, or: The Economic World Reversed," *Poetics* 12 (1983):311–56; and "The Intellectual Field: A World Apart," in *In Other Words: Essays Towards a Reflexive Sociology*, trans. Matthew Anderson (Stanford: Stanford University Press, 1990).

12. *An Antonio Gramsci Reader*, edited by David Forgacs (New York: Schocken, 1988), 304.

13. *Intellectuals*, xxi. But this representative relation of literary critics to culture is by no means necessary. Contrast the Robbins volume, for example, with the Scandinavian anthology, Ron Eyerman et al., eds., *Intellectuals, Universities, and the State in Western Modern Societies* (Berkeley: University of California Press, 1987), whose contributors

are exclusively social scientists. What seems to be the predominantly "cultural character" of our times is in fact, as Aronowitz certainly knows, an effect of the international division of labor, a division in which the old factory modes of production have not disappeared but have relocated to Third World sites of cheap labor. The predominance of information production and thus of the Professional-Managerial Class in the First World no doubt accounts for the fact that the First World (the U.S. in particular) has become more a producer of cultural products than of traditional factory-made commodities. In the absence of any established discipline of mass cultural studies in the U.S., the task of such analysis has fallen by default to literary critics, who thus stand in a certain representative relation to culture in general as the typical "intellectuals." The ambivalence provoked by this representative relation is confirmed by countless depictions in the mass media of "English teachers" as absurd, exotic, or irrelevantly devoted to policing the anachronistic norms of Standard English along the border between high culture and low.

14. The calling out of literary critics as the intellectuals is confirmed repeatedly in the media, which typically conflate all forms of literary criticism as versions of left politics. Thus we read in an article in the *New York Times* announcing the appointment of a new president for Duke University that "in recent years Duke has gained national attention as a basketball powerhouse and intellectual hothouse, roiling over issues like political correctness and deconstructionism, the literary theory" (*New York Times*, December 12, 1992, A24). Such statements lend credence to Debray's complaint about the reduction of intellectual matters to "spectacle value"—the equivalence of basketball and deconstruction—which is not to say, however, that real passions and interests are not engaged in and through this spectacle.

15. As exemplified, for example, in such studies as Jim Merod's *The Political Responsibility of the Critic* (Ithaca: Cornell University Press, 1987).

16. There is a very real difference, then, between the sense in which it can be said that literary criticism was always "political," and the sense in which it is currently "politicized." The former refers to the fact, easily confirmed by historical research, that literary pedagogy has always served political agendas, and has thus always had political consequences. These agendas were typically advanced by ethico-normative techniques of literary pedagogy, as well as by more straightforward objectives of social control, such as the teaching of Standard English. The techniques employed historically on behalf of these agendas did not, however, demand the thematization of the political as a *content* of literary texts, and in fact were more usually advanced by positing the ethico-normative content of literature as transcending any merely political concern. The technique of politicization obviously rejects such transcendentalizing gestures, although, as we shall see, it does not necessarily reject an ethico-normative objective of literary pedagogy.

17. Barbara Ehrenreich and John Ehrenreich, "The Professional-Managerial Class," in Pat Walker, ed., *Between Labour and Capital* (Montreal: Black Rose Press, 1979).

18. Jürgen Habermas, *The Structural Transformation of the Public Sphere: An Inquiry into a Category of Bouregois Society*, trans. Thomas Berger (Cambridge, Mass.: MIT Press, 1989), 85.

19. *Intellectuals*, 177.

20. *Structural Transformation*, 174.

21. On this question, see Bourdieu, "The Corporatism of the Universal."

22. Bourdieu, *Homo Academicus*, 174.

23. Ibid., 163.

24. See "Fieldwork in Philosophy," in *In Other Words*.

25. Foucault's comments on the subject of intellectuals are contained primarily in two interviews: "Truth and Power," in *Power/Knowledge: Selected Interviews and Other Writings, 1972–1977* (New York: Pantheon, 1980), 125ff.; and "Intellectuals and Power," in *Language, Countermemory, Practice: Selected Essays and Interviews* (Ithaca: Cornell University Press, 1977), 205–17. There are tensions in Foucault's comments on intellectuals that only begin to be suggested by the remarks in the text above. It should be pointed out, however briefly, that Foucault's distinction between universal and specific intellectuals is driven by two polemical objectives, both of which are now somewhat outdated: first, a refusal of the Marxist construction of the universal intellectual as necessarily proletarian, or as developing the "universal" perspective of the proletariat; and second, a refusal of the valorization of the "great writer" over the technical expert or university professor. Both of these refusals are aimed preeminently at the figure of Sartre, although Foucault himself may very well have replaced Sartre precisely as the public auteur-intellectual whose obsolescence he proclaimed. Foucault's comments on intellectuals remain valuable for drawing our attention to the always potential and sometimes actual politicization of "truth" within the disciplines and sciences, but they remain inadequate for failing to make distinctions within the aggregate of specific intellectuals. These distinctions will be proposed at a later point in this essay.

26. *Intellectuals*, 41.

27. *Invitation to Reflexive Sociology*, 105. I have somewhat broadened the sense of "position-taking" in Bourdieu's formulation, where it refers more narrowly to moves within the field of a given cultural or institutional practice. Entirely in the spirit of Bourdieu's argument, I have regarded "politicization" as a kind of "position-taking" *within* a field, even when its content makes reference to everything exterior to the field, or to the field of the political self.

28. See "The Intellectual Field," 146: "The fact remains that the specific interests of cultural producers, in so far as they are linked to fields that, by the very logic of their functioning, encourage, favour or impose the transcending of personal interest in the ordinary sense, can lead them to political or intellectual actions that can be called universal." Bourdieu does not of course mean that these "specific interests" are always ipso facto "universal" by virtue of one's identity as a cultural producer or "intellectual"— but this is a qualification that is seldom considered in the context of most discussions of intellectuals.

29. See Nicos Poulantzas, *Classes in Contemporary Capitalism*, trans. David Fernback (London: Verso, 1974); also André Gorz, *Farewell to the Working Class: An Essay on Post-Industrial Socialism*, trans. Michael Sonenscher (Boston: South End Press, 1982); this subject is also considered extensively in Eyerman et al., eds., *Intellectuals, Universities, and the State*.

30. For Bourdieu's views on this issue, which I have kept in mind throughout the following discussion, see "The Social Space and the Genesis of Groups," *Theory and Society* 14 (1985):723–44; and "Social Space and Symbolic Power," in *In Other Words*, 123–39.

31. "The Professional-Managerial Class," 11.

32. In this formulation I have followed Etienne Balibar and Immanuel Wallerstein, *Race, Nation, Class: Ambiguous Identities* (London: Verso, 1991). Balibar comments: "Let us accept once and for all that classes are not super-individualities, neither as objects nor as subjects; in other words, they are not castes. Both structurally and historically, classes overlap and become meshed together, at least in part. In the same way that there are necessarily bourgeoisified proletarians, there are proletarianized bourgeois" (179). Similarly, Wallerstein remarks that "at a certain level of expansion of income and 'rights,' the 'proletarian' becomes in reality a 'bourgeois,' *living off the surplus-value of others*, and the most immediate effect of this is on class consciousness. The twentieth-century bureaucrat/professional is a clear instance of this qualitative shift" (122).

33. It is also of course no accident that the proletarianization of a given profession follows all too often upon the entrance of women into such professions. It is well known that secretaries, for example, were predominantly men in the nineteenth century, as were most teachers at all levels of the school system. The articulation of the sexual division of labor with the class system is both a support of, and supported by, that system.

34. See "The Intellectual Field," 145; and "The Field of Cultural Production," 319ff.

35. "The Professional-Managerial Class," 22.

36. Bourdieu, "The Intellectual Field," 145ff.

37. For extensive comments *passim* on the subject of "fields," see *Invitation to Reflexive Sociology*.

38. Bourdieu, "The Field of Cultural Production," 319; see also André Gorz, *Critique of Economic Reason*, trans. Gillian Handyside and Chris Turner (London: Verso, 1989), 32: "I term *sphere of heteronomy* the totality of specialized activities which individuals have to accomplish as functions co-ordinated from outside by pre-established organization."

39. Bourdieu, "The Intellectual Field," 145: "This domination is not exercised any longer, as it used to be, through personal relations (like that between a painter and the person who has commissioned a painting or between writer and patron), but takes the form of a structural domination exercised through very general mechanisms, such as those of the market."

40. "The Corporatism of the Universal," 100–1.

41. See *Homo Academicus*, 53: "The most heteronomous positions are never entirely free of the specific demands of a field officially orientated towards the production and reproduction of knowledge, and the most autonomous positions are never entirely free of the external necessities of social reproduction."

42. See "The Intellectual Field," 145, on the different autonomies of the "expert or technician" and the "intellectual."

43. This point seems to me significant enough to be worth supporting with a brief case study: the emergence of a scientific "intellectual"—Richard Feynman—into the public sphere as a result of investigations into the explosion of the space shuttle *Challenger* in January 1986. Now this incident is particularly rich in conjunctural significance because it entered the national imaginary as an unassimilable rebuke to a conviction of national technological superiority that was being steadily undermined by devel-

opments in many domains of international competition. In the subsequent investigation of the accident it became apparent that the judgment of the engineers that the space shuttle was unsafe to be launched on that day was overruled by corporate managers who were apparently acting in response both to internally generated bureaucratic imperatives and to tacit political pressures. The public hearings into the accident were dominated in the media by the participation of Nobel Prize-winning physicist Richard Feynman, who succeeded in exposing the actual physical cause of the accident. In his later account of the investigation, *What Do You Care What Other People Think?* (New York: Bantam, 1989), Feynman expressed much amazement at the fact that engineers, who are after all scientists too, could be overruled by administrative personnel. But this amazement really indexes the quite different ratio of autonomy to heteronomy governing the site of Feynman's intellectual practice, a research university. The engineers, who were employees of corporations, were powerless either to prevent the accident or to confirm that its proximate cause was not a scientific "fact" but their very domination by the managers. If the status of the engineers thus seemed to be "proletarianized," the peculiar circumstance of a public investigation permitted Feynman himself to appear *as an intellectual.* He took on this identity not simply because he was a physicist but because he found himself in the position of defending the autonomy of scientific practice against the managerial sector of intellectual labor, and against the forms of political and economic heteronomy constraining scientific practice. More interestingly still, his momentary interpellation as an intellectual enabled him to recognize intellectuality in places where no one would have been inclined to recognize it before, for example, in the mere "workers" who assembled a part of the rocket: "The assembly workers had other observations and suggestions. . . . The suggestions weren't very good, but the point is, the workers were *thinking!* . . . They were very interested in what they were doing, but they weren't being given much encouragement."

If the moral of this fable is only too apparent, its gesture toward the theme of the universal is interestingly counterpointed by the circumstance that oddly overdetermined the *Challenger* disaster, the fact that this particular flight was intended to serve a propaganda function by the inclusion of a high school science teacher in its crew. Whether or not then-President Reagan's intention to exploit this occasion in his State of the Union address may have constituted a tacit form of heteronomous pressure on the managers who overruled the engineers, the "teacher in space" is easy enough to read as a piece of ideology. The agents of the Reaganite plan to defund the educational system could employ no more clever strategy than to enlist teachers themselves in its cause, wittingly or not. In this way the shuttle was made to perform a "circus" function, celebrating as an accomplished fact the very social project—the reproduction of a scientific corps—which was in the process of being abandoned. That the cynical exploitation of a science teacher then became the occasion for the calling out of a scientific intellectual was both an "accident," a very spectacular one, and no accident at all. The pressures militating against the interpellation of scientists as intellectuals were very great, and required such an accident in order to be overcome at all.

44. *Gramsci Reader,* 303.

45. See Bill Martin and Ivan Szelenyi, "Beyond Cultural Capital: Toward a Theory of Symbolic Domination," in Eyerman et al., eds., *Intellectuals, Universities, and the State,* 46, for a comment on this fact.

46. It should be evident at this point that my use of the term "crisis" is not intended to endorse the right-wing rhetoric that has popularized the "crisis of the humanities." There *is* a long-term crisis of the humanities, but it is a crisis of the cultural capital of its knowledge-products.

47. The process of scientization, as will be apparent, is no less ambiguous than the process of professionalization. Scientization subordinates the ethico-normative function of traditional literary pedagogy to the norms of autonomous inquiry. This inquiry can be motivated (personally, politically, or otherwise), but its scientificity is instituted in the process of "objectification," through which the object of study is defined, and a methodology specific to this object is developed. On the other hand, while the strategy by which professions may scientize themselves obviously enhances the cultural capital of their knowledge-products, there is no guarantee that such a strategy will be anything more than mimetic, or that the discipline in question will go on to produce a critique of its own scientificity, what Bourdieu calls the "objectification of the process of objectification." The question of whether literary criticism in any of its recent forms can be said to constitute a science can only be broached here, on behalf of suggesting that this is not a question that can be answered simply in the negative. The construction of criticism as a "sublimated" social science is intended to argue for the inadequacy of identifying criticism with either an unreflective mimesis of natural science or with the alternative of that impressionism which can trace its genealogy all the way back to the rhapsode. Finally, let us also recall that mimetic techniques for enhancing the exchange value of knowledge-products are nothing new. The medieval guilds achieved a similar effect by a technique of mimetic "sacralization," that is, by excluding access to their knowledge in such a way as to constitute that knowledge as quasi-sacred—in the language of the time, as a "mystery." For the "lay person" of the present, natural scientific knowledge itself can still circulate as "mystery," which is to say that its position in the hierarchy of knowledges is homologous to that of theology during the feudal era.

48. It is perhaps time to reconsider the invention of theory by none other than Althusser, in "On the Materialist Dialectic" and other texts of the sixties. Whatever one might wish to say about the "theory of theoretical practice," it is a fact of some relevance that Althusser's notion of theory is developed out of a deliberate engagement between philosophy and science. This theory eventuates, moreover, in the positing of a "structure in dominance" that performs a "decentering" of structuralism's version of social science precedent to Derrida's more canonical decentering operation in "Structure, Sign, and Play." Another origin of theory, then, but displaced in the canonical history. For Althusser's consideration of the mimetic relation between the humanities and the human sciences, see his text of 1967, "Philosophy and the Spontaneous Philosophy of the Scientists," in *Philosophy and the Spontaneous Philosophy of the Scientists*, ed. Gregory Elliott (London: Verso, 1990), 95ff. On this and other questions, I have benefited from astute responses to my essay from Jonathan Kramnick.

49. *Homo Academicus*, xxiv; also the comments on Derrida in *Distinction: A Social Critique of the Judgment of Taste*, trans. Richard Nice (Cambridge, Mass.: Harvard University Press, 1984), 494ff. One necessary implication of such a "sociologistic reduction" is that we must deemphasize to a certain extent the break between "structuralist" and "poststructuralist" theory, in the recognition that these movements constitute moments in the ongoing scientization of the humanities. If poststructuralism seemed

to call into question precisely the scientific pretensions of structuralism (its projection of what Fredric Jameson has called a "universal mathesis" in his superb "Periodizing the Sixties," in *The Ideologies of Theory* [Minneapolis: University of Minnesota Press, 1988], vol. 2, 186), the positing of an antithetical "indeterminacy" emptying out the positive content of theoretical knowledge merely displaced scientificity from the site of knowledge-content to the site of *method*, where a scientistic practice was all the more fetishized under the name of "rigor." The negative knowledge embodied in method-ological rigor maintained the purity of its negativity—a more deeply sublimated scien-tificity—only briefly, however; with the emergence of "politicized" criticism in the 1980s, poststructuralist theory has been driven to rediscover in its very negative knowl-edge a positive political content, which now subtends such projects as Derrida's com-mentaries on apartheid or developments in Eastern Europe.

50. The resist of theory to a "sociologistic reduction" is interestingly exemplified in Derrida's well-known essay, "The Principle of Reason: The University in the Eyes of Its Pupils," *Diacritics* (Fall 1983):3–20, first delivered as a lecture on the occasion of Derrida's accepting a Cornell University "professorship at large." The lecture under-takes to interrogate the very "principle of reason" that is the university's "reason for being," or its ungrounded ground. Derrida's interrogation of this ground converges upon the same problematic of autonomy that exercises Bourdieu; and just as vehe-mently as Bourdieu, Derrida protests the "external" determination of university research by heteronomous government and market forces. Inasmuch as heteronomy is inscribed within the principle of reason itself, as the "end-oriented" nature of reason, the Derridean methodology, which we shall not be so tedious as to rehearse here, draws a certain predicatable conclusion: if the university, as an *institution*, objectifies the prin-ciple of reason, which is nothing other than the founding principle of *philosophical* dis-course, then any effective critique of the institution must pass through the philosophi-cal discourse. Only from this position internal to the thought of reason and to the prac-tice of philosophy will it be possible to "threaten . . . the fundamental axiomatics and deontology of the institution, its rhetoric, its rites and procedures." Such a thought must bypass, in other words, a *sociological* critique, which would in Derrida's view lead back once again to an uninterrogated principle of reason: "Whatever may be their sci-entific value—and it may be considerable—these sociologies of the institution remain in this sense internal to the university, intra-institutional, controlled by the deepseated standards, even the programs, of the space they claim to analyze" (16). The sociologies in question are lumped together as "Marxist or neo-Marxist, Weberian or neo-Weber-ian, Mannheimian, some combination of these or something else entirely"—but the very mention of these names should compel us to recall that these figures already pro-posed a scientific practice that was nothing if not suspicious of the instrumental or tech-nical rationality Derrida seems to be discovering for the first time. By declining to indulge in mere sociology, Derrida is in the end driven to celebrate the notoriety of his own "double gesture" of standing within and without the university ("unbearable to certain university professionals"); that is to say, he is forced to ground his critique in his *charismatic authority* as master theorist, and thus to recapitulate the very dynamic between charisma and institution that Weber had analyzed "sociologically." For this reason Derrida finally identifies himself not as an academic but with the figure of Kierkegaard, "one of those thinkers who are foreign, even hostile to the university, who

give us more to think about, with respect to the essence of the university, than academic reflections themselves." Thus, the "community of thought" that Derrida would propose to constitute as thinkers of his radical thought, and who "reflect on what is beyond the principle of reason," somehow completes the "double gesture" inaugurated by the master theorist who stands at once within and without the university. The thought of the "professor at large" is taken up by the "disciples at large," who likewise mystify themselves by imagining that they can stand "outside" the university without considering at all the very relationship between mastery and discipleship that enables such imaginary exteriority, and that is itself institutionally grounded. The fact that charismatic authority (of which "theory" is only the latest incarnation) has always constructed itself as occupying such an "at large" position with respect to institutions escapes the notice of the thought too radical for mere sociology, and too secure in its institutional place to analyze the sociological dynamic of its own authority.

51. See Wolf Lepenies, *Between Literature and Science: The Rise of Sociology*, trans. R. J. Hollingdale (Cambridge: Cambridge University Press, 1988). Lepenies argues for the intimate and mutually ambivalent relation between sociology and literary criticism, and more particularly for regarding literary criticism in England in the nineteenth and twentieth centuries as a form of "concealed sociology," what I have called analogously a sublimation of social science. From this perspective both the literary theory of the sixties and seventies and the historico-cultural criticism of the eighties and nineties continue to negotiate an ever more complex subterranean disciplinary relation with social science. In recovering the historical origins of this process of sublimation, something both more and other than an "institutional history" of criticism will be required. The objective proposed here is rather to grasp the formation of disciplines in the interrelations of historically precedent discourses.

52. "The Corporatism of the Universal," 103.

53. Bourdieu's recourse to a notion of "republic" (and even to an "international") of intellectuals, it should be acknowledged, is not without its own ambiguous implication, if we do not also emphasize that such a notion risks reintroducing the very elitism it is intended to supersede. This paradox points to certain real tensions in Bourdieu's thought, between a sociology that seeks to analyze the pervasion of the intellectual field by heteronomous forces, and a much less developed gesture toward "forms of organization which permit the creation of a voice for a *large collective of intellectuals*" ("The Corporatism of the Universal," 108). Thus, while demonstrating that "intellectuals have not escaped the universal temptation to universalize their particular interests," Bourdieu seeks to hold open the possibility of a "modest redimensioning of their mission" that would necessarily have to be expressed in collective practices that recognize 1) that intellectual autonomy is vested in *specific* sites within the field of labor, and even within the intellectual field itself; and 2) that it is this very specificity that any collectivity of intellectuals must seek to undo by universalizing intellectuality.

4 REGIONALISM AND THE UPPER CLASS

Richard H. Brodhead

In American literature in the second half of the nineteenth century regional fiction presents an especially instructive instance of the history of literary opportunity. Focused on the ground of literary forms, this familiar if rather tepidly admired genre presents an easily identified set of formal properties. It requires a setting outside the world of modern development, a zone of backwardness where locally variant folkways still prevail. Its characters are ethnologically colorful, personifications of the different humanity produced in such nonmodern cultural settings. Above all this fiction features an extensive written simulation of regional vernacular, a conspicuous effort to catch the nuances of local speech. Edward Eggleston tells his reader in the preface to *The Hoosier Schoolmaster* (1871) that his labor in writing has been "to preserve the true *usus loquendi*" of "the provincialisms of the Indiana backwoods." Thomas Nelson Page's *In Ole Virginia* (1887) begins by underscoring that "the dialect of the Negroes of eastern Virginia differs totally from that of the Southern Negroes, and in some material points from that of those located farther west," then offers a pronunciation guide for the dialect it records.[1]

But focused within the history of authorship, the genre defined by these place-centered literary features also possesses an unexpected further feature, namely that it served as the principal place of literary access in America in the postbellum decades. Regionalism was not the career vehicle for Henry James and William Dean Howells, the most heavily professionalized among post–Civil War writers. But virtually every other writer of this time who succeeded in establishing himself as a writer did so through the regional form. Eggleston became an author by becoming the literary recorder of rural Hoosier culture. Twain (admittedly a more complicated case) became the author of a midwestern life only somewhat further west. George Washington Cable established his literary self by taking what his first book called *Old Creole Days* (1879) as his subject. Sarah Orne Jewett and Mary Wilkins (later Freeman) made themselves writers by making remote New England villages their literary concern.

But more interestingly for my purposes, this genre did not just create a place for writers: in the later nineteenth century regionalism was so structured as to extend opportunity above all to groups traditionally distanced from literary lives. Regional fiction set as the competence required to produce it the need to know how to write, but it set this entry requirement unusually low: since this form was heavily conventionalized in formulas that barely changed from the 1860s to the century's end, it did not require the more highly elaborated writerly skills that other forms asked for their successful performance. (The fact that authors in this mode typically had their first efforts published suggests how little special training the form required, how adequate it was found in its most conventional versions.) The other knowledge this form required was familiarity with some cultural backwater, acquaintance with a way of life apart from the culturally dominant. In this respect regionalism made the experience of the socially marginalized into a literary asset, and so made marginality itself a positive authorial advantage. Through the inversion of customary privilege built into its formal logic this genre created a writer's role that women were equipped to perform, especially women from small towns and peripheral locations—like Mary E. Wilkins, of the nonmetropolitan Randolph, Massachusetts; or Rose Terry Cooke, from rural Connecticut; or Tennessee's Mary Noailles

Murfree, Iowa and Arkansas's Alice French ("Octave Thanet"), or Louisiana's Grace King. Ann Douglas has noted that local-color writing provided the door into literary careers for women in the postbellum decades that the domestic-sentimental novel had afforded in the antebellum years;[2] but women were by no means the only socially disparaged figures that this form paradoxically advantaged. The vernacular requirement of the local-color form made the folkways and speechways known to African Americans—heretofore a mark of their inferior "civilization"—into a valuable literary capital; and by trading on the value this form gave to the knowledge of black vernacular, members of America's principal subjugated minority— Charles Waddell Chesnutt and Paul Lawrence Dunbar, in particular—broke into the ranks of American authors. The form extended a comparable opportunity to those disparaged in other ways. Hamlin Garland, the first farmer to have entered American literature, felt humiliatingly handicapped for authorship by his provincial origins and immersion in manual labor. But in Garland's case a farm worker was enabled to become an author by the regional form, which converted his rural background into a career-funding resource. American literary writing in all its branches was a monopoly of the native-born throughout the nineteenth century. But when an ethnic immigrant first succeeded in establishing himself as a writer outside his ethnic group it was again with the assistance of the regional mode. I am thinking of Abraham Cahan, who won a general American audience in *Yekl* (1896) and *The Imported Bridegroom, and Other Stories of the New York Ghetto* (1898) by figuring out how to adapt the dialect-tale formula to the "region" of the Lower East Side.

Historically, then, nineteenth-century literary regionalism yielded more than a place of access. It effected a revision of the traditional terms of literary access, a major extension of the literary franchise. This fact gives the genre its importance for the history of access at large. But if we place it within that history we will right away face a question: why should this genre have made the difference I have discussed? What was it about this form that let it so re-form the field of possible authors? I have said that regional fiction could alter the demographics of authorship because it enfranchised a new set of social knowledges as a source of literary expertise. But this reasoning cannot say why the genre should have entered the literary field when it did, or how it won the power, there, to establish its practitioners in careers. Those matters are functions of its cultural life and standing; and to know how this form created enablement we need to inquire into the terms of its historical social life.

One reason regionalism could win public places for those who wrote it in the later nineteenth century, we might begin by observing, is that this genre was an object of special demand. A kind of writing that has been the target of much milder interest at other times and places was the focus in America, from the 1860s well into the 1890s, of intense and steady readerly desire. Sample circulation histories—the fact that Sarah Orne Jewett's first volume, *Deephaven* (1877), went through twenty-three editions in its first nineteen years, or that Mary Noailles Murfree's *In the Tennessee Mountains* (1884) went through seventeen editions in its first two years—attest to the market for such wares in these years. In recognition of this market, American publishers of the Gilded Age not only eagerly received but actively encouraged the production of this commodity. In 1867 one publisher contracted to pay Bret Harte, the pioneer creator of local-color fiction in its far western variant, $10,000 for exclusive rights to whatever he might write in the coming year. Regionalism, this publisher clearly believed, was the current form of limitless demand, the work for which a publisher could not pay too much. In the wake of Murfree's 1878 discovery of southern Appalachia for local color (regionalism's nineteenth-century history is that of a search for new locales by which to renew a standard formula), another publisher sent another would-be author—Sherwood Bonner, or behind her pseudonym, Katherine Sherwood Bonner MacDowell—on a flying visit to learn how to "do" Tennessee mountainfolk and cash in on Murfree's success. Bonner was raised one county seat away from Faulkner's Oxford, Mississippi but her life story more nearly resembles Scarlett O'Hara's. After the war this strong-willed belle left her weakling husband and child to parlay her charm into a more powerful career, as an author. The terms of her success show the opportunities for the ambitious that regionalism's demand created. Virtually recruited into authorship by the need for local color, she found a comparably ready market for her tales of black life south of Memphis and of downstate Illinois.[3]

Bonner's case demonstrates how the public demand for regionalism produced the opportunity it offered. During the time when readerly desire attached to such fiction, virtually anyone who could supply this commodity could get his or her work into print, and so win public recognition for an asserted literary self. But if its popularity was the condition for the opening it afforded, this fact only drives our inquiry back a step. What was the condition for its popularity, we would now need to ask: what gave this of all genres such appeal at this time?

A historiography long attached to regional fiction offers one explanation for the interest it held.[4] Regionalism became a dominant genre in America at the moment when local cultural economies felt strong pressure from new social forces, from a growingly powerful social model that overrode previously autonomous systems and incorporated them into translocal agglomerations. This genre's great public flowering began with the Northern victory in the Civil War, in other words with the forcible repression of sectional autonomy in favor of national union and the legal supplanting of the locally variant by national norms of citizenly rights. Regionalism's heyday was in the years of rapid corporate-capitalist industrial development in America, with its reinsertion of agrarian and artisanal orders into a new web of national market relations. (The national brand and national corporation—Coca-Cola and Standard Oil—are other inventions of regionalism's years.) The linkage of American railroads into a transcontinental network helped further incorporate once self-enclosed social communities into a national commercial grid. The great American cities that grew up at the new junctures of transportation and commerce in the Gilded Age—Chicago, Cleveland, Pittsburgh, and the rest—embody another supersession of an older localism. Such cities drew in population from small towns and the rural countryside, a now-"older" world they helped devitalize and deplete.

Such familiar Gilded Age histories have an obvious relevance to the regional genre, and in their light it has seemed easy to say what office it must have performed. The cultural work of nineteenth-century regionalism, the emotional and conceptual service this writing performed that made it meet a profound social *need*—for the historical demand for regionalism bespeaks not just taste but need—has been assumed to be that of cultural elegy: the work of memorializing a cultural order at that moment passing from life and of fabricating, in the literary realm, a mentally possessible version of a loved thing lost in reality. Nineteenth-century regionalism can be said to have manufactured, in its monthly renewed public imaging of old-fashioned social worlds, a cultural version of D. W. Winnicott's transitional object: a symbol of union with the premodern chosen at the moment of separation from it. Certainly the works of nineteenth-century regionalism read their function in these terms. Many of them specify the incursion of forces of modern development upon once-autonomous cultural islands as the occasion for their recording of local lifeways: in *Oldtown Folks* (1869) Harriet Beecher Stowe announces that she wants to register the New England village order of "ante-railroad days" because those days are "rapidly fading"; in *In the Tennessee Mountains* the imminent arrival of the railroad drives Murfree to want to capture endangered Cumberland Mountains ways.[5] Many of these works, similarly, offer themselves as a surrogate memory of a life now passing into the past. Their memorial function is announced in their titles: *Oldport Days; Oldtown Folks; Old Creole Days; Old Times on the Mississippi; In Ole Virginia;* "The Old Agency"; and so on.

There is no reason to doubt that the regionalist genre had the array of forces bound together under the word "development" as a prime historical referent; and it would not be wrong to assume that this form's ability to articulate the dislocations development engendered was a major cause of its nineteenth-century popularity. But it is worth at least wondering, I think, whether this familiar account tells the whole story of regionalism's cultural operation. This account's general historiography, after all, is not inevitable. The recent historical work affiliated with the label "new rural history" has shown that there was no unilinear or invariant suppression of local cultural economies in the period of intense capitalist-industrial development in the United States, indeed that such cultures persisted, adapted, and even established themselves during the years of their purported demise.[6] Such work reminds us that nineteenth-century regionalist fiction—the form of rural history operative in its time—did not simply record contemporary reality but helped compose a certain version of modern history. Its elegaism, further, has a clear and suspicious relation to what recent anthropologists have seen in traditional ethnographic writing (regional fiction is also a nineteenth-century ethnography): the habit while purporting to grasp an alien cultural system of covertly lifting it out of history, constituting it as a self-contained form belonging to the past rather than an interactive force still adapting in the present.[7] For the United States, regionalism's representation of vernacular cultures as enclaves of tradition insulated from larger cultural contact is palpably a fiction. This would suggest that its public function was not just to mourn lost cultures but to purvey a certain story of contemporary cultures and of the relations among them: to tell local cultures into a history of their supersession by a modern order now risen to national dominance.

Further, the received account of regionalism's cultural operation implies that it helped readers in general work through the emotional difficulties of shared contemporary history. But if we were to track it to the scene of its historical operation we would find that this genre was highly localized in its late-nineteenth-century life, active in some cultural places and not others. In nineteenth-century America regional writing was *not* produced for the cultures it was written about, which were often nonliterate and always orally based. It was projected toward those groups in American society that made a considerable investment in literary reading; but even here we can discriminate. In its early avatars, such writing most often appeared within the middle-class domestic reading world. Susan Warner wrote early regionalism in the "Aunt Fortune" sections of *The Wide, Wide World* and elsewhere; Stowe, the triumphant "literary domestic" of the antebellum decades, shifted into regional writing with *The Pearl of Orr's Island* (1862) and *Oldtown Folks*; Eggleston's *The Hoosier Schoolmaster*—a regionalist classic whose cultural provenance is marked by its concern with graded elementary schools and noncorporal discipline—was serialized in *Hearth and Home*, a family-entertainment-and-instruction magazine that Stowe helped edit. But beginning in the 1860s, then decisively after 1870, regionalism shifted its mode of cultural production and began to be featured in a different kind of place. The Bostonian *Atlantic Monthly* gave Bret Harte the celebrity contract for his fables of California. It also serialized Twain's *Old Times on the Mississippi*, the stories of Murfree's *In the Tennessee Mountains*, and the bulk of Jewett's tales of coastal

Maine, to name no more. The New York-based *Harper's Monthly* sent the Mississippi-born Sherwood Bonner to soak up the color of eastern Tennessee. It also printed Wilkins Freeman's tales of insular New England villages and Constance Fenimore Woolson's stories of rural Ohio, Michigan, and Florida. George Washington Cable's tales of New Orleans Creole society were sought out and printed not in New Orleans but in the North, in *Scribner's Monthly* and its successor *The Century Magazine*. This New York-based magazine also serialized the *Adventures of Huckleberry Finn* (1884) and Thomas Nelson Page's *In Ole Virginia*, among other regional works.

The names of such place of appearance are not a neutral fact of publishing history. These journal titles specify a highly particular provenance: they say that regional fiction was published within a certain historical formation of the literary, and beyond that, of culture at large. Lawrence Levine and others have documented the profound reformulation of "culture" as a social and artistic category that took place in America after 1850. These historians have reconstructed the process by which a previously more unitary culture, in which artistically mixed programs played to mixed social audiences, got broken apart, and a now-separated "high" culture asserted over against a now-distinct "low" opponent. The segmentation and stratification that produced a separate high culture is seen in the splitting off of a nonpopular "legitimate" theater from the older theater that had played Shakespeare with farcical interludes; in the midcentury remaking of a museum from a popular hall of miscellaneous wonders (like Barnum's 1841 American Museum) to a monumentalized shrine for classical masterpieces (like the 1870 Metropolitan Museum of Art); and in the supplanting of popular band programs by the newly institutionalized symphony orchestras that specialized performance to the classical repertory—the Chicago Symphony, the Boston Symphony, and the like.[8]

This stratification in the cultural realm happened not alone but in complicated interaction with a parallel stratification in the social realm, the articulation of a new-style "high" social class. Ronald Story, E. Digby Baltzell, Burton Bledstein, and others[9] have told the story of the formation of a translocally incorporated social elite in place of an older locally based gentry order in the mid-nineteenth century. (Story calls this process "the shaping . . . of a durable upper class within a capitalist order.") The new elite of the post–Civil War period was composed of various subgroups—inheritors of older wealth and of older local-gentry status, mercantile and managerial groups grown rich in the new corporations, the new-order professionals of this professionalizing period; and elements of the earlier self-articulated middle class eager to distinguish themselves from a now more clearly defined working class strongly identified with this new elite formation as well, especially after the 1860s. The point about the postbellum upper class is that it was not an already-integrated "group" but a group in the process of self-grouping, a coming together of elements with a common need to identify themselves as superior. And in this process of self-definition Culture played a crucial role. In the 1860s and later the newly formed elite identified itself very centrally through the artistic culture it enjoyed. In consequence, in the postbellum United States a now-segregated high culture became a chief sign of elite status and chief weapon of elite social sway. In this period it was the social segments just described that devoted themselves to high art and founded its social institutions. This group turned out the audience for such art and trained itself to appreciate such art—so that the young Jane Addams, like most upper-middle-class girls of her generation, was brought up in a self-devotion to Culture that would have been aimed toward domestic or religious goals a generation earlier. In the late nineteenth century this group also promoted the culture it valued as a means to subordinate the differently cultured *to* its values—as genteel librarians used their institutional control over reading habits to try to change the living habits of the lower sort, or as genteel art patrons strove to recivilize the public through the public display of classical works.[10]

In the years between 1860 and 1900, the *Atlantic Monthly*, the *Century Magazine*, and *Harper's Monthly Magazine* achieved an identification as the three American "quality journals." This means that these three journals produced the same high or distinguished zone in the literary realm that the classical museum or symphony orchestra produced in art or music, a strongly demarcated high-status arena for high artistic practice. And though actual audiences are notoriously hard to establish, there is reason to think that they produced literary writing toward a similarly constituted social public.

Sometimes these periodicals say whom they address quite overtly: the 1878 *Atlantic* article "Three Typical Workingmen" speaks of its readers as "cultivated" people and explains how the textual format of such journals' articles—particularly their length—sets them outside the world of working-class reading.[11] But these journals specify their assumed audience just as overtly on every page of every issue, in the work they elect to publish. The nineteenth-century *Atlantic, Harper's*, and *Century* can be searched in vain for articles that address the interests of factory workers, immigrants, farm laborers, miners, clerks, shopgirls, and secretaries. To a student of mid-nineteenth-century domestic periodicals they will seem equally notable for their non-address to classic middle-class interests: the discourse of evangelical piety, the childrearing essay, and the lesson in good housekeeping, the staple genres of that group's reading, are wholly absent from their pages. Instead, their selections speak to interests highly particular to the new upper class and its imaginative adherents.

The great staple of these journals, the virtually mandatory item in their program of offerings, is the short piece of touristic or vacationistic prose, the piece that undertakes to locate some little-known place far away and make it visitable in print. The mental habits these pieces rehearse are, in sociohistorical terms, quite strongly localized. It is pertinent here to remember that the late-nineteenth-century American elite self-defined through its care for high art was also identified by its other distinctive leisure practices—its new sports, for instance: golf, tennis, yachting; and particularly its arts of leisure travel. The postbellum period is when the American elite perfected the regimen of the upper-class vacation: the European tour, for the whole family or—if the father's business pressed—for the wife and daughters, of the length of four months or more; or the comparable summer in the country, at the seashore or at mountain resorts. The American abroad—rarity in the 1830s but commonplace in the 1870s—is one manifestation of this Gilded Age class phenomenon. The gentry summer resorts newly colonized after the war—the Berkshires, Massachusetts's North Shore, Cape Cod and Martha's Vineyard, the Maine and Jersey shores—are another sign of the same historical process. The building style of the postbellum summer "cottage"—the shingle style Vincent Scully has studied—is the architectural manifestation of the same social development. Howells's documentary *The*

Rise of Silas Lapham (1885) notes that in the contemporary world the hereditary upper class and industrial nouveaux riches both make it their duty to "summer," and Howells implies that such vacationing sets the social ground on which these class fractions can meet: the industrially rich Laphams first meet the Brahmin Coreys when their wives and children summer on the St. Lawrence.[12]

Evolved *at* this time, elite vacation habits also took on a heavy symbolic function *in* this time in dramatizing this group's social superiority. As Thorstein Veblen, the great theorist of post–Civil War leisure class, would argue, the upper-class vacation, with its conspicuous requirement of surplus funds and large leisure, made an especially "serviceable evidence" of a socially differentiating freedom from need. (It is worth remembering that a week's paid vaction became the norm for American white-collar employees only in the 1920s; for others it came later yet.)[13] For this reason, vacationing, like the high-cultural competences that required an equal ability to have devoted time to the training of nonproductive tastes,[14] became a piece of an upper-class *habitus* highly expressive of social distinction. When the historian of post–Civil War Hartford's gentry establishment notes that for "Hartford people of the dominant prosperous class . . . it was almost a social necessity to go to Europe every two or three years" and that "after 1875 it was a social necessity in any case to get out of the city in the summer" (practices widely shared elsewhere), his reiterated word "necessity" is fully apt. The better off of this time invested themselves in vacation travel not only because they liked to or were free to but because such travel was a chief means to establish elite social standing. Twain's *The Innocents Abroad* (1869) knows that a prime contemporary reason for going to Europe is that it marks one "select" back home.[15]

It would be wrong to assume that all readers of the "quality" journals of the Gilded Age were necessarily members of the "quality" socially. Nevertheless, these journals do address an upper-class-centered social interest. And the principal proof is that they speak so insistently to the class-signifying leisure habits I have been describing. These magazines speak to "us" on the condition that "we" are the kind of people who attach almost unlimited value to vacation travel. Typical *Harper's* illustrations show "us" to ourselves if we either actually engage in gentry vacationing or mentally identify with those who do: in *Harper's* people like "us" appear promenading at the Jersey shore, having their vacation baggage carried by servants, being paddled in canoes by ungenteelly dressed locals, interviewing a cook for the yacht. Charles Dudley Warner's *Atlantic* serial *The Adirondacks Verified* meets one of "our" needs if our needs include verifying the attractions of newly colonized vacation spots and verifying that they carry suitable social meanings: Warner assures his readers that only the cultivated will enjoy Adirondack primitivism. (The *Atlantic* article "A Cook's Tourist in Spain," by contrast, makes clear that package tours are declassé.) Warner's *Harper's* serial *Their Pilgrimage*—an almost unbelievably thorough tour of the resorts of the contemporary elite—is a valuable vademecum if our group ethic mandates ritual travel to vacationing's sacred spots.[16] The same logic holds for scores of similar features.

The writing marked as literary in the Gilded Age appeared in these journals together with the prose of vacation travel, and not just together but in virtually fixed conjunction with such prose. Murfree's celebrated "Dancin' Party at Harrison's Cove" thus ran in the same volume as Warner's *Adirondacks Verified*, Henry James's international novel *The Europeans*, and James's nonfictional "Recent Florence." Murfree's Cumberlands tale "Way Down in Lonesome Cove" ran together with Howells's Florence novel *Indian Summer* and with travel essays on Persia and "The Blue Grass Country of Kentucky." Mary Wilkins Freeman's "A Humble Romance" was originally flanked by a feature "The North Shore [of Lake Superior]"—with picturesque illustrations of the cliffs above Duluth—and another on Biarritz. Freeman's "Revolt of 'Mother'" ran together with "Across the Andes," "Mountain Passes of the Cumberland," and "The Social Side of Yachting."[17] If we take these insistent conjunctions seriously (and the list of them could be greatly lengthened), they can teach us two things. They tell us that nineteenth-century literary genres we are used to thinking of as freestanding were not autonomous in their original cultural production but formed mutually supportive parts of a concerted textual program. And they say that the literature included in this program—like the nonfictional adjuncts that give this message more overtly—must also have been produced for an elite-based reading world.

The larger point at stake here is that writing's historical publics have always been socially localized. Such publics are always established on some principle of inclusion from among those who have leisure to read and attach value to this entertainment. But the groups that have come together into literary audiences have never been grouped by their reading tastes alone: their reading interests are always bound together with the set of extraliterary interests that unite them as a group. Elsewhere I have studied one such culture of letters:[18] the antebellum domestic reading world that conjoined literary reading with other identifying cares of middle-class domesticity. Here we are witnessing the emergence of another American reading culture that gave literary writing a differently constituted social base and so enmeshed it in a different set of ancillary concerns: not childrearing and home management but the high-cultural values and vacation arts that identified the postbellum elite's more sumptuous leisure. Post–Civil War literary regionalism circulated almost exclusively within the historical reading world constituted on these terms. Accordingly, if we would understand the grounds for its demand, we need to grasp how it met imaginative needs particular to this literary-social situation.

The way forward from this point can only be opened up by speculation. Nevertheless, to see nineteenth-century regionalism within this more tightly specified social situation is to have some of its possible functions seem obvious. For one thing, its place of cultural production would clearly seem to link regionalism with an elite need for the primitive made available as leisure outlet. The "social necessity" that made European travel and countrified summering interchangeable practices established paired needs for resort to the most highly evolved contemporary civilization (as "Europe" was conceived) and to a civilization equidistantly lower, primitive, or underdeveloped. (So it is that the Loire and the Adirondacks, or Gloucester, England and Gloucester, Massachusetts could become substitutable summer alternatives.) This pairing of high-cultural-European and rustic-domestic vacation spots finds its reflection in the quality journals' nonliterary writing array: in their complementary featuring of Persia and Kentucky, northern Michigan and Biarritz, and so on. It is equally reflected in such magazines' selection of literary features: in their coproduction of International Theme novels and American regional fiction, genres that typically ran side by side. The symmetry of these categories strongly implies that regionalism worked as a literary supplement to a more general production of inhabitable backwardness, as the international novel supplemented the production of visitable "Europe." The fact that Constance Fenimore Woolson's early tale "In Search of the Picturesque" was published together with a pioneering account of the just-discovered vacation spot Mount Desert Isle,[19] a wholly characteristic conjunction, suggests that such fiction and nonfiction literally *co-operated*, in the realm of reading, to produce the unmodernized picturesque. In its first context, this genre offered freshly found primitive places for the mental resort of the sophisticated. A genteel vacationer conducts us into the country folkworld in "The Dancin' Party at Harrison's Cove."

But if regional fiction gave exercise to a sophisticate-vacationer's habits of mind, we might speculate that it also rehearsed a habit of mental acquisitiveness strongly allied with genteel reading. All reading, it may be, plays into the drive to appropriate experience vicariously, as Hawthorne and Henry James believed. But the appropriative mind appears to have been especially highly developed in the nineteenth-century leisure class (for which we could read owner class), where it was deployed along certain characteristic lines. This historical grouping is especially identified by what might be called its cultural or cross-cultural acquisitiveness. In distinction from other contemporaneous formations, the postbellum elite and its adherents made other *ways of life* the object of their admiration and desire, objects that they then felt free to annex: the upper-class vacation thus entails crossing out of one's own culture into another culture (not just place) to the end of living another way of life. Regionalism can be guessed to have ministered especially effectively to the imagination of acquisition. The paradox of this genre is that it purports to value a culture for being intactly other at the very time that it is offering outsiders the chance to inhabit it and enjoy its special "life." Twain's Hartford neighbor Charles Dudley Warner called another of his travel pieces "Our Italy"[20]—showing how the travel writing of this time both makes apparently distinctive places functionally interchangeable (*California* is our *Italy*) and textually reprocesses them into possessible property (California is *our* Italy, the Italy we own).

But if reading nineteenth-century regionalism back into its original scene of operation links it to this sort of experiential imperialism, it also ties it to deep class anxieties. The elite formation defined in part through its high-cultural affiliations and vacation practices was of course defined in other ways much more fundamentally. In the 1860s and after the elements of this coalition were brought together not just by their shared pleasures but by their shared opposition to other groups, especially to the newly antagonistic working class that postbellum industrialism also produced. That class was growingly peopled with the newly arriving immigrants capitalist development lured, so that the elite that was another byproduct of the same development found itself increasingly surrounded by foreigners in its formative years. (In Boston, the spiritual home of late-nineteenth-century high culture, 30 percent of the population was foreign-born in 1900, and 70 percent born of foreign parentage.) To this elite at this time, as many studies have shown, the Immigrant became a kind of iconic representation of the lower classes thought of as class antagonists. The Immigrant became a phobic embodiment of all imagined threats to elite superiority, from cultural mongrelization and racial dilution to political anarchism and class war.[21]

Paradoxically, then, an often-virulent nativism was another defining feature of the late-century group that loved "the foreign" in other capacities; and the components of the upper-class *habitus* assembled in the later nineteenth century served not just statically to symbolize superior status (as Veblen and his unknowing successor Bourdieu imply) but actively to manage the socially foreign's threat. The since-characteristic American elite institutions elaborated between the 1870s and the 1890s—the residential suburb, the private day school and prep school, and the country club[22]—aimed not just to mark an "exclusive" zone in status terms but actively to exclude, to shut the elite in from its social "others." The rustic vacation, similarly, served not incidentally to reconstitute a homogeneity disturbed in the larger world. E. Digby Baltzell, the principal historian of upper-class self-incorporation practices, writes with satiric glee:

> Just as the white man, symbolized by the British gentleman, was roaming round the world in search of raw materials for his factories at Manchester, Liverpool, or Leeds, so America's urban gentry and capitalists, at the turn of the century, were imperialists seeking solace

for their souls among the "natives" of Lenox, Bar Harbor, or Kennebunkport. Here they were able to forget the ugliness of the urban melting pot as they dwelt among solid Yankees (Ethan Frome), many of whom possessed more homogeneous, Colonial-stock roots than themselves. . . . All one's kind were there together. . . . When J. P. Morgan observed that "you can do business with anyone, but only sail with a gentleman," he was reflecting the fact that a secure sense of homogeneity is the essence of resort life.[23]

As a social construction, late-century high culture too served to project the aristocratically based arts of Northern and Western Europe as "Civilization" and to consign those of other classes and regions to the category of the Noncivilized. (One remembers here the turn-of-the-century high-cultural practice of having Italian opera, in the original uncomfortably popular and ethnic, performed in German.)[24] Culture so constituted could function as an apparently purely aesthetic agent of social exclusion, as the specialization of the musical repertoire to its high-classical portions specialized audiences to the educated minority acculturated in such tastes.[25] But high culture could also work as a force of coercive *in*clusion, of social management on the elite's behalf. Horace Scudder's widely successful plan to install classic American literature as mandatory reading in American public schools was overtly designed to counter the menace of the un-American. With that social ulteriority so commonly coupled with professed worship of disinterested artistic "quality" at this time, American literature as the native-born upper class selected it was here deployed as an Americanizing agent, a means to bring the immigrant young out of their hereditary ethnic cultures and into an "American" culture synonymous with elite tastes.[26]

Nineteenth-century regionalism was produced as an upper order's reading at a time of heavy immigration and the anxieties associated with such immigration. (Jewett's initial volume *Deephaven* was published in 1877, the year of the Railroad Wars, the Molly Maguires, and unprecedented industrial strife.) This conjunction invites us to consider literary regionalism as another of the leisure pastimes that dealt with the threat of the foreign from within an apparently detached entertainment realm. Regional fiction too could be considered as an exclusion mechanism or social eraser, an agency for

purging the world of immigrants to restore homogeneous community. The extremely rare appearance in such stories of any of the ethnic groups associated with contemporaneous industrialization—
Irish immigrants appear for a rarity in Jewett's "Between Matins and
Vespers"—would seem to warrant our considering regional writing
(like the summer resort or country club) a *haven* for readers, a space
of safety constructed against an excluded threat. But in a sense
regionalism's peculiarity is exactly that it did *not* exclude the foreign,
so that a more complex reading of its function is required. Perhaps
the deepest paradox of the subject I am discussing is that the late-
nineteenth-century class that saw polyglot America as a social night-
mare and that made purity of speech a premier tool of social dis-
crimination should have cherished, as one of its principal entertainment forms, the dialect or local-color tale, definable after all as the
fiction where people talk strangely.[27] Ethnically deformed speech—
what else is dialect?—is the most fundamental requirement of the
regional genre; and as a social institution this genre's action was to
immerse readers in a cacophony of almost-foreign, ethnically inflected tongues: Creole ("You t'ink it would be hanny disgrace to paint
de pigshoe of a niggah?"); New England rustic ("Thar's Mis' Bliss's
pieces in the brown kalikee bag"); backwood Hoosier ("It takes a
man to boss this deestrick. Howsumdever, ef you think you kin trust
your hide in Flat Creek school-house, I ha'n't got no 'bjection"); eastern Virginia Negro ("'Well,' sez he, 'I'm gwine to give you to yo'
young Marse Channin' to be his body-servant,' an' he put de baby
right in my arms—it's de truth I'm tellin' yo'!"); Mississippi Delta
Negro ("'Onymus Pop, you jes take keer o' dis chile while I'm gone
ter de hangin'"); Tennessee mountain ("I dunno *how* the boys would
cavort ef they kem back an' found the bar'l gone"); and so on.[28]
Through such writing, we can surmise, an audience that identified
its own nonethnic status with its social superiority could nevertheless bring itself within hearing distance of the Stranger in the Land,
so that regionalism was a means to acknowledge plural Americas. Yet
this fiction produced the foreign only to master it in imaginary
terms—first by substituting less "different" native ethnicities for the
truly foreign ones of contemporary reality: crusty Yankee fishingfolk
for southern Italians or Slavs, Appalachian hillbillies for Chinamen
or Russian Jews;[29] then by writing the heterogloss into the status of

variant on or deviant from a standard of well-bred educated speech. Nineteenth-century regional writing produced a real-sounding yet deeply fictitious America that was not homogeneous yet not radically heterogeneous either and whose diversities were ranged under one group's normative sway. Its performance of such important wishful thinking must have contributed profoundly to its historical public demand.

There is, it should be insisted, no necessary relation between the regionalist form and any of the social forces I have been discussing. This literature has been created in quite other social situations, where it has had other issues at stake in it: we would need to compose a very different description of the social life of such cognate forms as the nineteenth-century Spanish and Latin American custom sketch or *cuadro de costumbres,* or the early-twentieth-century South African *Plaasroman,* or the revived American regionalisms of the 1920s and 1930s and the 1980s. But if it has no necessary relations this literary form had certain actual relations in nineteenth-century America, relations *created for it* by the history of its cultural production—the process that sets every form the terms of its public life.

If we now recall that this genre also created roads into authorship for would-be writers, it will be clear that this statement requires emendation. Regionalism, we could now say, made places for authors but made them *in a certain position.* By virtue of its historical situation, when writers came into authorship through this genre they were placed in inevitable relation with the field of forces that structured its social place: found their literary roles bound together with the high zone in a steeply hierarchized plan of culture, with correlative class prerogatives of leisure and consumption, with a certain socially based appetite for underdevelopment, and with a related will to renew the dominance of culturally dominant groups.

The social organization of literature's public life never determines literary creation. Literature is only produced when some actual author realizes the possibilities of some historically structured literary situation; and writers have been able to realize the same situation variously, even in contradictory ways. A full social history of regional authorship would want to stress the extraordinary range of powers and interests that authors found their way to through the medium of this form. Joel Chandler Harris, author of the enduring regional work *Uncle Remus: His Songs and Sayings* (1880), was rendered almost speechless by shyness in his everday social life but spoke easily when he spoke in black vernacular dialect. In this quite literal sense Harris could be said to have found a voice through the conventions of dialect fiction.[30] To cite one more case only, George Washington Cable found his way to the politics of his liberal racial polemics of the 1880s, the important civil rights essays "The Freedman's Case in Equity" and "The Silent South," at least in part through his regional writing, through the exploration of cross-racial injury and cross-racial justice in *The Grandissimes* (1880) and other works. But if writers can make different things of the enabling conditions of their work, they become writers in circumstances not wholly of their making. And a fully history of regional authorship would show that the authors who won literary identity through this form achieved that identity in and against the particular array of forces that specified this genre's social place.

If we were considering the case of Constance Fenimore Woolson, for instance, we would be struck by the quite fundamental ways in which her personal construction of an authorial career implies the social history of the regional genre. Woolson was in the most direct of ways enabled by this form. Its emergence in the early 1870s established a literary use for the kind of places where Woolson had spent her life, and the market that developed for such work meant that this person from "nowhere" (in the word of her first book title)[31] could get her writing published. And published not just anywhere: Woolson was able to place her early work in *Harper's Monthly*, and the essential fact of her career is that her regional writing won her a specifically high-cultural literary position. The company whose fellowship sustained her in her desperately lonely life was the inner circle of American literary high culture: Thomas Bailey Aldrich, Edmund Clarence Steadman, Henry James, and the like. High-cultural status—inclusion in the world of serious writers—also gave Woolson crucial inward sustenance, the ability to take herself seriously as a writer in a life devoid of more traditional validations.[32] Had the regional form not been given this status, as it would not have had it been culturally situated on other terms, Woolson would have won such support against almost infinitely greater odds. And she could only have made with great difficulty the career move she made with relative ease, the self-transformation from a writer of country districts to literary American abroad—literary worlds apart were it not for the fact that their late-nineteenth-century cultural placement made them adjacent and complementary genres.

If we turned from Woolson (for instance) to Hamlin Garland, we would find a different model of authorship, but one achieved by working out a different relation to the same set of literary-social facts. Garland was much more heavily disadvantaged for a life in letters than the poor-but-genteel Woolson. The son of a farmer and himself a farm laborer, Garland felt set by birth and labor beneath the dignity of the cultivated classes; indeed, Garland's sense of social inferiority is as aggravated a case as American literary history has to show. Yet the market for literary regionalism in the late nineteenth century made a place for Garland too in letters—but this time at the price of more painful psychic dislocations. As *A Son of the Middle Border* records, Garland desperately desired to acquire mental culture to lift himself from the disparagement of manual labor into the higher ranks of mind-workers. Given the organization of culture in his time, this meant in practice that Garland tore up his roots in Iowa and South Dakota to transplant himself to the east of high culture: his autobiography, a kind of nonfiction *Jude the Obscure*, shows him in his mid-twenties, virtually starving and freezing in order to keep reading in the Boston Public Library. Garland's first literary dream had been to write short stories in the manner of Hawthorne. But in this different cultural world he became acquainted with a different target for his aspiration, the regionalist form. Armed with this form, he returned to the upper midwest in the late 1880s and "discovered" both its literary potential and the subject matter of his own future art, the hard-bitten farm stories that became *Main-Travelled Roads* (1891).[33]

Garland too was enabled by the regionalist genre. Garland too found a chance to exploit his outsider's social knowledge through the workings of this form. And Garland too (if a little less securely than Woolson) won a prized "insider" status through this mode of work. When editors like Howells of *Harper's Monthly* or Richard Watson Gilder of *The Century* approved of his stories of rural life this parvenu of letters won the feeling of election into the culture of his dreams.[34] But Garland could only win the literary status that attached to regionalism in his time at the cost of more or less violently estranging himself from the culture of his origin; and the violations his authorship entailed put their distinctive mark on his work. In his most powerful early story, "Up the Coulee," the impoverished midwestern farm world is revisited by a prodigal son who has become a member of the eastern art world and leisure-vacationing class (this character was yachting abroad when he missed the news that the family farm was about to be lost). Not Garland's own condition except in his wishes—leisure-class life is the only thing this story describes unconvincingly—this social position is the one Garland feels himself to have become aligned with in taking up his literary career. The cultural relocation attached to his choice of genre has its triple yield in a gloating desire for the life of prestige; a corresponding guilt toward the home world he has so willingly escaped; and a rage against the system of social difference that makes elite pleasures be purchased at country people's expense. Garland's farm stories find their sequel, accordingly, in his rampant 1890s populism and his rage against literary centers in the screeds of *Crumbling Idols*—a conjunction that makes no sense except in a situation where literary regionalism, class privilege, and high-cultural hierarchy have been bound together.

Other regionalist careers display other permutations; but by now I hope a general point has been established. Literary forms, I have been contending, create different sorts of literary access; but no form creates access unconditionally. Such forms are always placed in some determinate set of literary-cultural relations, and the place they create for authors is inevitably a place *within* this specification of their work's life and use. But how the conditions of literary practice actually condition literary production—how such apparent externalities mediate the will to write—is a question still largely unanswered. This question will need to be asked in another place.[35]

NOTES

1. Edward Eggleston, *The Hoosier Schoolmaster* (1871; rpt. New York: Hart Publishing Co., 1976), 6; Thomas Nelson Page, *In Ole Virginia* (New York: Charles Scrib-

ner's Sons, 1887), front page. Compare the notice on dialects at the start of *Adventures of Huckleberry Finn*, the best-known example of this prefatory move.

2. See Ann Douglas [Wood]'s bracingly opinioned "The Literature of Impoverishment: The Women Local Colorists in America, 1865–1914," *Women's Studies* 1 (1972):3–40.

3. The 1896 edition of *Deephaven* (Boston: Houghton Mifflin) lists itself as the twenty-third edition. On Murfree's circulation figures, see Nathalia Wright's introduction to *In the Tennessee Mountains* (Knoxville: University of Tennessee Press, 1970), xiii. Harte's contract with the *Atlantic Monthly* is detailed in William Dean Howells, *Literary Friends and Acquaintance*, 252. On Sherwood Bonner, see H. H. McAlexander, *The Prodigal Daughter: A Biography of Sherwood Bonner* (Baton Rouge: Louisiana State University Press, 1981), especially 150–65.

4. Of the many histories of the incursion of translocal social structures on previously more isolated local cultural economies the most influential has been Robert H. Wiebe's story of the erosion of "island communities" in *The Search for Order, 1877–1920* (New York: Hill and Wang, 1977). The association of regionalism with the decline of local communities, a long-standing critical commonplace, is voiced especially eloquently in Warner Berthoff, "The Art of Jewett's *Pointed Firs*," *New England Quarterly* 32 (1959):49–53.

5. See Harriet Beecher Stowe, *Oldtown Folks* (1869; rpt. New York: Library of America, 1982), 885, and Wright, "Introduction," xi.

6. For important arguments to this effect, see Steven Hahn and Jonathan Prude, eds., *The Countryside in the Age of Capitalist Transformation: Essays in the Social History of Rural America* (Chapel Hill: University of North Carolina Press, 1985), especially the essays by Steven Hahn and John Scott Strickland; and Hal S. Barron, *Those Who Stayed Behind: Rural Society in Nineteenth-Century New England* (New York: Cambridge University Press, 1984). For a related critique of the homogenizing local-to-federal historiography associated with the regional form, see Louis A. Renza, *"A White Heron" and the Question of Minor Literature* (Madison: University of Wisconsin Press, 1984), 43–56.

7. See especially James Clifford, *The Predicament of Culture: Twentieth-Century Ethnography, Literature, and Art* (Cambridge, Mass.: Harvard University Press, 1988), 215–51.

8. On the institutionalization of a self-conscious high culture in the United States, see Lawrence Levine, *Highbrow/Lowbrow: The Emergence of Cultural Hierarchy* (Cambridge, Mass.: Harvard University Press, 1988), and Paul DiMaggio's essays "Cultural Entrepreneurship in Nineteenth-Century Boston: The Creation of an Organizational Base for High Culture in America" and "Cultural Entrepreneurship in Nineteenth-Century Boston, Part II: The Classification and Framing of American Art," *Media, Culture, and Society* 4 (1982):33–50 and 303–22. I discuss the correlative establishment of a high literary culture in *The School of Hawthorne* (New York: Oxford University Press, 1990), especially chaps. 3 and 4.

9. There is no comprehensive history of this development. For important partial accounts the following are especially helpful: Ronald Story, *The Forging of an Aristocracy: Harvard and the Boston Upper Class, 1800–1870* (Middletown, Conn.: Wesleyan University Press, 1980); E. Digby Baltzell, *The Protestant Establishment: Aristocracy and*

Caste in America (1964; rpt. New York: Vintage, 1966), 109–42; Wiebe, *Search for Order*, 111–32; John Sproat, *"The Best Men": Liberal Reformers in the Gilded Age* (New York: Oxford University Press, 1968); and Burton Bledstein, *The Culture of Professionalism: The Middle Class and the Development of Higher Education in America* (New York: W. W. Norton, 1976). The Story quotation comes from *Forging of an Aristocracy*, 165.

10. For disaggregations of the social support for high culture in the Gilded Age, see Levine, *Highbrow/Lowbrow*, 227 and *passim*, and DiMaggio, "Cultural Entrepreneurship, Part II," 308. See also Roger Stein, "Artifact as Ideology: The Aesthetic Movement and its American Cultural Context," in *In Pursuit of Beauty: Americans and the Aesthetic Movement* (New York: Metropolitan Museum of Art/Rizzoli, 1986), 22–51. Jane Addams recounts her self-depleting devotion to what she calls "the feverish search after culture" in the magnificent chapter "The Snare of Preparation" in her *Twenty Years at Hull-House* (1910; rpt. New York: New American Library, 1961), 60–74. On the nineteenth-century library as scene of genteel social engineering, see Dee Garrison, *Apostles of Culture: The Public Librarian and American Society 1876–1920* (New York: Macmillan, 1979), 35–50. For a parallel theory of the art museum as instrument of reacculturation, see Joseph Choate as cited in Levine, *Highbrow/Lowbrow*, 201.

11. J. B. Harrison, "Three Typical Workingmen," *Atlantic Monthly* 42 (December 1878):725.

12. The social history of American vacationing is a great book that remains to be written. This paragraph draws on two useful contributions to that history: Baltzell, *Protestant Establishment*, 116–21, and Vincent J. Scully, Jr., *The Shingle Style and the Stick Style*, rev. ed. (New Haven: Yale University Press, 1971), 24–33 (and see all of the plates). Other brief but useful contributions to the nineteenth-century phase of this subject include Foster R. Dulles, *A History of Recreation*, 2d ed. (New York: Appleton-Century-Crofts, 1965), 148–53, and Daniel T. Rodgers, *Work Ethic in Industrial America: 1850–1920* (Chicago: University of Chicago Press, 1978), 95–96 and 105–7.

13. See Thorstein Veblen, *The Theory of the Leisure Class* (1899; rpt. New York: New American Library, 1953), 47, as well as the whole chapter "Conspicuous Leisure," 41–60. Veblen's theory of how leisure activities or "lifestyle" choices function symbolically to enact social status is revived and elaborated in Pierre Bourdieu's *Distinction: A Social Critique of the Judgment of Taste*, trans. Richard Nice (Cambridge, Mass.: Harvard University Press, 1984). In Bourdieu's terms the postbellum leisure-class vacation would be an example of "the latest difference" (247), the most recently acquired group exemption from material necessity, which functions with special salience in establishing distinction. Rodgers supplies the information about white-collar vacations in *Work Ethic*, 106.

14. On cultural competence as a sign of privileged access to leisure, see the devastating chapter "The Higher Learning as an Expression of the Pecuniary Culture," in Veblen, *Theory of the Leisure Class*. According to Bourdieu's *Distinction*:

> If, among all these fields of possibles, none is more obviously predisposed to express social differences than the world of luxury goods, and, more particularly, cultural goods, this is because the relationship of distinction is inscribed within it, and is reactivated, intentionally or not, in each act of consumption, through the instruments of economic and cultural appropriation which it requires. (226)

15. Kenneth R. Andrews, *Nook Farm: Mark Twain's Hartford Circle* (Cambridge, Mass.: Harvard University Press, 1950), 96–97. Mark Twain, *The Innocents Abroad* (1869; rpt. New York: New American Library, 1966), 22.

16. Warner writes in part VI of *The Adirondacks Verified*: "The instinct of barbarism that leads people periodically to throw aside the habits of civilization and seek the freedom and discomfort of the woods is explicable enough. But it is not so easy to understand why this passion should be strongest in those who are most refined and most trained in social and intellectual fastidiousness. Philistinism and shoddy do not like the woods" (*Atlantic Monthly* 41 [June 1878]:755–56). "A Cook's Tourist in Spain" ran in *Atlantic* 54 (July 1884):33–51. Warner's *Their Pilgrimage* was serialized in several installments in *Harper's Monthly* 72 (1885–86).

17. "Dancin' Party" and the other works cited ran in *Atlantic Monthly* 41 and 42 (1878); "Lonesome Cove" and the rest ran in *Harper's Monthly* 72 (1885); "A Humble Romance" and the rest in *Harper's* 69 (1884); and "The Revolt of 'Mother'" et al. in *Harper's* 81 (1890). Such conjunctions can be found for virtually all regional works: Woolson's "Rodman the Keeper" ran with James's *The American*, Wilkins Freeman's exquisite "A Poetess" with "Texan Types and Contrasts" and "Social Life in Oxford," and so on.

18. See my *Cultures of Letters: Scenes of Reading and Writing in Nineteenth-Century America* (Chicago: University of Chicago Press, 1993), chaps. 1–3.

19. See *Harper's* 45 (July and August 1872):161–68 and 321–41.

20. See *Harper's Monthly* 81 (November 1890):813–29.

21. The Boston population figure is cited in DiMaggio, "Cultural Entrepreneurship," 30. For extensive discussions of the anti-immigrant bias of the late-nineteenth-century American elite, see Baltzell, *Protestant Establishment*, 109–42, and Sproat, *"The Best Men,"* 250–57. John Higham's *Strangers in the Land: Patterns of American Nativism 1860–1925*, 2d ed. (New Brunswick, N.J.: Rutgers University Press, 1988) is the standard history of the American response to immigration.

22. For a full account of these developments, see Baltzell, *Protestant Establishment*, 114–42.

23. Ibid., 118–19.

24. Levine cites this amazing fact in *Highbrow/Lowbrow*, 220. Levine writes eloquently about high culture as a mechanism deployed "to identify, distinguish, and order this new universe of strangers" (177); see particularly the chapter "Order, Hierarchy, and Culture."

25. Ibid., 119.

26. See Horace Scudder, "American Classics in School," *Atlantic Monthly* 60 (July 1887), and my *School of Hawthorne*, 59–61. The Scudder polemic ran in the same volume with Chesnutt's dialect tale "Po' Sandy" and James's *The Aspern Papers*.

27. Veblen comments on correct speech's function as a class marker: "Elegant diction, whether in writing or speaking, is an effective means of reputability. . . . Great purity of speech is presumptive evidence of several successive lives spent in other than vulgarly useful occupations" (*Theory of the Leisure Class*, 257). Story's *Forging of an Aristocracy* notes the demarcation of a high-status style of speaking in the earlier nineteenth century at Harvard, a premier site of elite class formation. He also notes that at that earlier time the effort of the genteel was to differentiate themselves from countryfolk or

the "rural element"—a group that has ceased to be a threatening adjacency, and so that can become an object of nostalgic appreciation, in late-nineteenth-century regional fiction. See 112–13 and 120–21.

28. My polyglot patchwork is taken from Cable's *The Grandissimes*, Wilkins Freeman's "An Honest Soul," Eggleston's *Hoosier Schoolmaster*, Page's "Marse Chan," Bonner [MacDowell]'s "Hieronymus Pop and the Baby," and Murfree's *The Prophet of the Great Smoky Mountains*, though a hundred other sources would do as well. Such quotation reveals how much, in dialect fiction, the apparently faithful record of different local speechways actually involves standard deformations of standard written English: the heavy use of the apostrophe, the picturesque misspelling of common pronouns and conjunctions, and so on.

29. The Anglo-Saxonism of the regional Other is sometimes an explicit part of its appeal: in Rose Terry Cooke's "Hopson's Choice," the folksy Hopsons live in a pastoral or nonindustrial New England valley first settled by "Andrew Hopson, yeoman, from Kent, Old England" (*Harper's Monthly* 69 [September 1884]:607). Appalachia has always been mythically associated with a preserved remnant of pure English origins. A subject for further study is why American blacks should have become desirable objects of regionalist contemplation in the decade of steeply increased immigration from Southern and Eastern Europe—as if blacks became an honorary extension of "our" family in face of this more foreign threat.

30. On Harris's impeded speech, see Robert Hemenway's introduction to *Uncle Remus: His Songs and His Sayings* (New York: Penguin, 1982), 16–18.

31. The full title of this volume is *Castle Nowhere: Lake-Country Sketches* (New York: Harper and Brothers, 1875).

32. For material on Woolson, see Joan Myers Weimer's introduction to her selection of Woolson stories, *Women Artists, Women Exiles: "Miss Grief" and Other Stories* (New Brunswick, N.J.: Rutgers University Press, 1988), and Rayburn S. Moore, *Constance Fenimore Woolson* (New York: Twayne, 1963).

33. See *Son of the Middle Border* (1917; rpt. New York: Reprint Services, 1988), 318–76.

34. Garland, like many of his contemporaries in the 1880s, virtually equated the *Century* and *Harper's* with Literature and (in the words of his memoirs) "resolved upon being printed by the best periodicals." The extraordinary power of the literary establishment of this time to control the precinct of literary honor is revealed in Garland's self-abasing awe before the administrators of the "high": Howells's words of praise "were like gold medals" to Garland, and Gilder's praise "equivalent to a diploma" (*Son of the Middle Border*, 376, 387, and 412). Garland's love-hate relation to nineteenth-century high culture is well discussed in Larzer Ziff, *The American 1890s* (New York: Viking, 1966), 93–180.

35. See my *Cultures of Letters*, chaps. 5 and 6, which extend this study into the career histories of two regional authors: Sarah Orne Jewett and Charles W. Chesnutt.

5 WHITE KIDS AND NO KIDS AT ALL

LANGUAGES OF RACE IN ANTEBELLUM U.S. WORKING-CLASS CULTURE

Eric Lott

In the late 1820s, a new "popular" sphere of urban, commercial working-class culture began to emerge in the northeastern United States. Historians have recently explored the way this largely masculine arena developed alongside but independently of both bourgeois culture and that of the trade unions. Sean Wilentz has read this culture's allegiances and predilections as a sensational, street version of radical artisans' emphases on liberty, egalitarianism, and cultural independence, in its own way connecting "workingmen's pride, resentments, and simple pleasures to the language of republican politics."[1] I want to pursue further the notion that the class character of this culture adamantly politicized it, but in doing so I stress the way working-class cultural politics was rooted in and communicated through languages of race.[2] The uses of race in this "anti-authoritarian" culture have not been properly examined; labor historians have done little to clarify the affective results of American "freedom's" dependency on American slavery and racism.[3] Typically, writers throw up their hands and apologize for the racial attitudes of white workers then and now or, more recently, indict the working class for a thoroughgoing racism that prevented the development of a labor abolitionism in America.[4] I believe the reality was a good deal more contradictory than either of these views, as a look at the new amusements in antebellum working-class cultural life will show. This realm was a primary site of antebellum "racial" production, inventing or at least maintaining the working-class languages of race that appear to have been crucial to the self-understanding of the popular classes—and to others' understanding of them as well. In blackface acts and other forms of "black" representation, racial imagery was typically used to soothe class fears through the derision of black people, but it also often became a kind of metonym for class. Even then it usually referenced only a cherished working-class relationship to its objects of fun; yet one occasionally finds in this imagery the tones of racial sympathy. Indeed the popular theater, the saloon, the museum, and the penny press—to name the institutions I will look at here—prominently displayed the uneven and ambiguous racial feelings that resulted from the grounding of much racial discourse in working-class culture.

The centerpiece of this discourse, as I have hinted, was blackface minstrelsy, and it will be my focus as well. The disparate meanings of blackface found their material basis in the various concrete ways "popular" domains engaged black culture, in the physical spaces and cultural institutions where it was produced and greeted by predominantly working-class audiences. Accordingly, in minstrel shows as elsewhere, accents of class and of race became confused, on many occasions even substituting for one another, which unsettled the stable outlines of both. I will argue that in its representations of "blackness" this culture reproduced and revitalized a set of class values. It was the way it *staged* class that was most often the gripe; the way the stale patter and bad puns and achieved grotesquerie kept sliding from racial burlesque into class affiliation, or affirmation. This in turn had the unintended effect of highlighting the collective vehemence of black culture that minstrelsy and other forms had originally set out to restrain. It was through "blackness" that class was staged, in a working-class orbit that encouraged the excesses of "blackness." To many observers the combination could not have been more irksome.

THE GREAT DIVIDE

The minstrel show, eclectic in origin, primitive in execution, and raucous in effect, virtually announced itself as one of our first popular institutions. The nineteenth-century debate about it perhaps seems familiar because minstrelsy helped constitute a break between elite, genteel, and low cultures (and thus an anxious discourse about that break) which would be fundamental by our century. In fact the double emergence of the first remarkable body of (black and white) U.S. imaginative literature and such notable popular phenomena as minstrelsy, melodrama, and the dime novel neatly demonstrates Fredric Jameson's point about the dialectical interrelatedness and opposition of high and low cultural forms; in capitalist societies they presuppose and depend on each other, are twin responses to a common, class-divided history. Many writers (such as dime novelist George Lippard) themselves put a broadly class face on the opposition in terminologies of the scandalous "upper ten" and the abused "lower million." Indeed by the early 1840s, minstrelsy, alongside lower-million amusements such as the public lecture, the public museum, and melodrama, was ranged explicitly against the opera, the "legitimate" theater, and the concert hall—the American beginnings of what Andreas Huyssen has called the "great divide."[5] In this sense, minstrel shows actually resembled the nineteenth-century dime museum, as George Rehin has observed. On one hand, they constantly deflated the pretensions of an emerging middle-class culture of science, reform, education, and professionalism; while on the other, they disseminated information about technology and urban life for working people very often new to the city: "minstrel 'darkies' were conned and swindled, run down by trolleys, shocked by batteries, and jailed for violating laws they didn't understand."[6] They ultimately assuaged an acute sense of class insecurity by indulging feelings of racial superiority.

Yet minstrel companies unquestionably had a defiant sense of both their own and their audiences' compromised cultural position. Part of a general emergence of artisan culture into national view, the minstrel vogue, along with mass political parties and the penny press, helped to create or organize a new public whose tastes the popular amusements now represented for the first time:

Music now is all de rage;
De Minstrel Bands am all engaged;
Both far and near de people talk
'Bout Nigger Singing in New York.

Barnum's Museum can't be beat:
De Fat Boys dar am quite a treat.
Dar's a Big Snake too, wid a rousing stinger;
Likewise Pete Morris, de Comic Singer.

De Chatham keeps among de rest—
Entertainments ob de best.
In public favor dis place grows,
'Specially on account ob *Mose.*

De Astor Opera is anoder nice place;
If *you* go thar, jest wash your face!
Put on your "kids," an fix up neat,
For dis am de spot of de *eliteet!*[7]

By the time this song was published in 1849 (it was probably performed somewhat earlier), the minstrel show had long found its urban
northeastern audience: the Bowery milieu whose more vehement representatives rioted at the Astor Place Opera later in the year. We might
in fact take this variety of song as a rallying cry for that event, inasmuch as both riot and songs marked the end of an earlier fluidity and
intermixture of class entertainments and institutional sites.

One does not quite yet find this song's sentiments consolidated
in, for instance, the early 1830s (though of course blackface always
bore a fiercely popular stamp). First performed in those years
between the acts at "respectable" theaters, minstrelsy in New York
steadily retreated over the next decade to lower-Broadway, and
lower-class, houses. The long-accepted (and somewhat permeable)
internal division of theater audiences into cheap gallery, fashionable
box, and middling pit seats—the so-called gods, gentlemen, and
groundlings—gradually became rough external divisions between
class-specific theaters. In 1820 the "internal situation" of a Boston
house still looked this way to one patron:

It appeared that the gallery was the resort of the particoloured race
of Africans, the descendants of Africans, and the vindicators of the

abolition of the slave trade; that the tier of boxes below it in the center was occupied by single gentlewomen who had lodgings to let, and who were equally famous for their delicacy and taciturn disposition. The remainder of the boxes, I was given to understand, were visited by none but the dandies, and people of the first respectability and fashion; while the pit presented a mixed multitude of the lower orders of all sorts, sizes, ages, and deportments.[8]

"Africans," "vindicators of abolition," and "mixed multitude," one surmises, are shorthand for the rabble; but the rabble (at least its white members) soon had its own playhouses, and made its triumphant mark on existing ones. This was not a simple matter of newly specialized theaters, as Raymond Williams has reminded us; the specialization itself was produced by, and in a range of ways mirrored, the social structures and tensions in metropolizing northeastern cities.[9] Exemplars of a new cultural sphere, minstrel shows were unrelentingly self-conscious about it, continually inscribing audiences' allegiances in the form of the show: *you* would never go to the Astor Opera because you came here. The effect of this, however, was in one sense to equate "low" audiences with the racial ritual that defined their cultural position, to implicitly identify the Bowery constituency with the blackness they "put on."

They were in any case understood to inhabit the bottom. The *Philadelphia Public Ledger* conceded the class character of the audience for minstrelsy and melodrama in its response to the Astor Place riot:

> It leaves behind a feeling to which this community has hitherto been a stranger—an opposition of classes—the rich and poor—white kids and no kids at all; in fact, to speak right out, a feeling that there is now in our country, in New York City, what every good patriot has hitherto considered it his duty to deny—a *high* class and a *low* class.

If this is vague sociology it is better cultural geography. For not only in the theater but in the public sphere generally, as Peter Buckley has shown, a bifurcation had indeed occurred between the 1830s and 1850. From the late 1820s, when audiences and entertainments were still broadly representative of the social totality, northern urban culture had begun to develop along two lines—in New York, one following Chatham Street and then up the Bowery, the other march-ing fashionably up Broadway to the Astor Opera House. "These two cultural axes were not initially in opposition," Buckley writes, "yet gradually there developed, especially after 1837, two distinct idioms, two audiences and two versions of what constituted the 'public' sphere of communication and amusement."[10] In 1849 the cultures clashed where the axes nearly met, at Astor Place.

The Astor Place riot proved a full-scale eruption of national and class tensions into the sphere of culture. With some help from the press, and from nativist Bowery agitators like dime novelist Ned Buntline (E. Z. C. Judson)—himself a direct link between the new culture of amusements and growing social fissures—a lengthy rival-ry between the British "legitimate" Shakespearean actor Charles Macready and the air-sawing American Edwin Forrest entered a new register as the two actors played *Macbeth* in concurrent New York productions. To their respective constituencies, this was a struggle for political legitimation fought out in cultural terms the "great divide" had made available. If Forrest had for more than twenty years created various incarnations of a Jacksonian hero (Metamora, Jack Cade, Spartacus),[11] Macready, as the feud developed, came to signify an aristocracy of "taste," the upper ten, the Dickens of *Amer-ican Notes*. On May 7, Macready's New York opening at the Astor Opera House was interrupted by boos, rotten lemons, and ulti-mately a row of chairs from a conspiratorial claque of Forrest's Bow-ery "b'hoys." A published list of signatories (including Washington Irving and Herman Melville) quickly responded, vowing order and urging Macready to continue his performances. Three nights later, similar demonstrations plagued Macready's *Macbeth*; refusing to be bullied, however, and buttressed by some well-placed police, Macready pressed on. A crowd of over five thousand, further angered by admission restrictions and the show of police force, now gathered outside the Opera House, assaulting the structure with paving stones and yelling such slogans as "Burn the damned den of the aristocracy!" and "You can't go in there without kid gloves on!" The militia, two hundred anxious troops, readied themselves for this assault, which was soon turned on the troops themselves. First they fired over the heads of the crowd, and then directly into it; twenty-two were killed, over one hundred and fifty wounded. As Buckley puts it, "The Astor Place riot appeared to be a moment when the mob became a class and when the classes seemed in irreconcilable opposition."[12] The minstrel show, in other words, inhabited—and began actually to signify—not an undifferentiated "mass" culture but a class-defined, often class-conscious, cultural sphere.

But while the broadest structural outlines of minstrelsy's class character are sharp enough, the rest is rather less so. We should note, for instance, that its audience's class make-up was often contradictory; while the audience was comprised predominantly of young male workers, there were also a fair number of men and women from other classes, not only in the more mixed audiences of the 1830s but later as well. The journeyman craftsmen and semi- or unskilled workers (teamsters, boatmen, barbers, etc.) who increasingly constituted the minstrel show's audience when theater prices plummeted after the 1837 Panic were often joined by people from "contradictory class locations," to use Erik Olin Wright's term: shopkeepers, clerks, small master artisans.[13] Regarding even the class-bound audiences of the 1840s there was some confusion among commentators about just who was out there in the pit and gallery; one of minstrelsy's functions was indeed to bring various class fractions into contact with each other, to mediate their relations, finally to aid in the construction of class identities over the bodies of black people.[14] Emerging splits within the working class (between artisans and proletarianized workers, for instance, or between "natives" and immigrant Irish) were often made manifest in terms of these groups' differential relations to racial privilege, even as the formation of a northern working class depended on a common sense of whiteness. In short, the new milieu blackface occupied was brought unevenly into being, cutting across the popular classes and constituting in itself a field of conflict over which "public" would in fact turn out to define it. Nor was it simply created out of nowhere; consisting partly of appropriations of extant institutions, partly of new inventions, it grew up right alongside the more respectable entertainments.[15]

These unevennesses were enough to tilt the "lower million's" rhetoric of class in the direction of a populist sensibility, as the phrase itself suggests, but they hardly mitigated the minstrel show's class basis. As David Montgomery has observed of the people who were minstrelsy's adherents: "The praise they bestowed on the 'honest mechanics' of their communities echoed through the popular songs and dime-novel literature of the day. . . . Although this culture was infused with a populist, rather than a strictly class consciousness, it clearly separated the nation into 'the producers' and 'the exploiters.'" Ideologically the minstrel show was a "popular" or "producer's" form, mightily class-inflected but unstable in its class ideologies and shifting in its class make-up; structurally it was a working-class form, firmly grounded in the institutional spaces and cultural predispositions of workers.[16] Christy's Minstrels had their longest New York run at a theater named Mechanics' Hall. Working-class values and desires were aired and secured in the minstrel show. Its racial "narrative" dovetailed with its class sources in surprising and sometimes confusing ways. Theatrical displays of "blackness" seemingly guaranteed the atmosphere of license so central to working-class entertainment forms in this period. And blackface provided a convenient mask through which to voice class resentments of all kinds—resentments directed as readily toward black people as toward upper-class enemies. But there was also a historical logic in glossing working-class whites as black, given the degree to which large sections of these groups shared a common culture in many parts of the North. Certain minstrel forms attested to this fact; moreover, as David Roediger has shown, many popular racial slurs both onstage and off ("coon," "buck") also referred to whites.[17] Occasionally these facts resulted in potential identifications between black and white, however quick the minstrel show usually was to forestall them.

All of which may begin to suggest that blackface, in a real if partial sense, *figured* class—that its languages of race so invoked ideas about class as to provide displaced maps or representations of working-classness. Thus, it was said of T. D. Rice's English tour that his blackface skits were "vulgar even to grossness," and captivated "the chimney sweeps and apprentice boys of London, who wheeled about and turned about and jumped Jim Crow, from morning until night, to the annoyance of their masters, but the great delight of the cockneys."[18] The submerged equation here of slaves and white workers (apprentices and perennially blackened sweeps ranged against their "masters") was not at all unusual—it was popularized in radical artisans' rhetoric of "wage slavery." Nor was the implicit (and opposing) claim that caricatures of blacks culturally represented workers above all. Blackface quickly became a sort of useful shorthand in referring to workingmen. New York's Castle Garden, noted the *Journal of Music*, nightly featured a variety of distinguished musical offerings, "and two or three songs by ANNA ZERR, who (shame to say) stooped to pick up one night and sing 'Old folks at home,' for the b'hoys; one would as soon think of picking up an apple-core in the street."[19] Indeed, the overlapping of racial and class codes probably made the minstrel show's audiences seem more homogeneously working-class than they actually were; in this way as in others, minstrelsy helped resolve internal differences within plebeian culture, creating notions of white working-classness and blackness at one and the same time.[20]

Certainly this rhetorical situation only hardened observers of the theater against blackface's constituency. "There must be some . . . place for a certain class of people to effervesce in their excitements of pleasure," said one wit of the Chatham Theatre, a primary site of minstrelsy and by all accounts the "lowest." "It has been useful as a kind of sewer for the drainage of other establishments." The sporting paper *Spirit of the Times* produced a clipped taxonomy: "Firemen, butcher-boys, cab and omnibus drivers, 'fancy' men, and b'hoys, generally." Yet while the minstrel show was too mediated or overdetermined a form to have been simply the creation of a workers' culture, or enjoyed solely by it, the "sheer weight of numbers," as Gareth Stedman Jones has argued of the English music hall, "the preoccupations and predilections of workers" did impose a "discernible imprint" upon minstrelsy's racial imagery.[21] Conversely, racial rhetoric became instrumental to ideas about working people themselves. How, exactly, did this situation come about?

Historians agree that American culture in the northeast underwent profound changes between 1825 and 1835. Among other things, a bourgeoisie worthy of the name came into being. As many recent historians have in different ways constructed this history, an unprecedented separation and discrete self-definition of classes occurred after the middle 1820s. For Burton Bledstein, an emerging "professionalism" constituted the "cultural process by which the middle class in America matured and defined itself"; for Karen Halttunen, antebellum sentimentalism was "central to the self-conscious self-definition of middle-class culture." Mary Ryan's account places the family at the center of middle-class formation—the child-rearing practices, familial values, and domestic ideologies that became, in her striking phrase, the "cradle of the middle class." Paul Johnson and Paul Boyer, like David Brion Davis before them, both see a culture of moral reform as crucial to the middle class's self-making; as Boyer has it, a phalanx of temperance reformers, advocates of industrial morality, and the like, concerned to instill good Christian principles in an undisciplined work force, in fact helped "an embryonic urban middle class define itself." This work undoes an earlier historiographical tradition (the "consensus school"), still alive in the writing of scholars such as Sacvan Bercovitch, which saw a hegemonic culture of liberalism at work in all walks of American life—summed up in Louis Hartz's remark that America is "a kind of national embodiment of the concept of the bourgeoisie." As Stuart Blumin has argued, "However broad the bourgeois consensus may have been in comparison to European societies, it was not so broad that it precluded the formation of distinct classes within American society." For what is implied in the notion of middle-class formation is precisely the formation of a distinctive working-class culture or way of life—though of course the development of each class (and their class fractions) was uneven, halting, not necessarily synchronous with the others.[22]

The broadest social effects of working-class formation in a new free-labor economy may be briefly noted. The crafts were fairly quickly proletarianized, splitting formerly self-sufficient artisans into masses of wage workers on one hand and select groups of industrious mechanics and industrial entrepreneurs on the other; control over the trades went to merchant capitalists who had in some cases been artisans themselves. The word "boss" was coined in these years, Paul Johnson observes, a sign that the interests of master and worker were now different and opposed. In many trades, deskilling accompanied this keener sense of social hierarchization, and increasingly rigid practices of industrial discipline were instituted. Making and selling for the first time became distinct activities; employees in the front rooms of, say, shoemakers' shops were separated off from— and as "clerks" came eventually to occupy a higher class than—the artisans who made the shoes. Housing practices mimicked these new divisions. Master craftsmen, men on the way up, moved away from their places of business and into residential neighborhoods, while workers moved themselves and their families out of their masters' homes—if, that is, they had been lucky enough to live in them in the first place. In a host of new journeymen's societies and more informal collectives, workingmen implicitly set themselves off from a supposedly harmonious community of "the Trade." Massive Irish and German immigration soon segmented that community even further, transforming the American working class, by the mid-1850s, into a largely foreign-born population.[23]

The minstrel show's cognitive equation of black and white working class had its origins here. In *Policing the Crisis*, Stuart Hall and colleagues argue that disarticulations of hegemony accompany periods of extreme capitalist crisis, generating fresh repertoires of domination. The strained class relations that resulted from the explosion of capitalist energies in early nineteenth-century America produced various such languages and practices. A new discourse of crime and lower-class criminality in these years was one example, although journals like the *Police Gazette* also admitted of more populist, "republican" accents—resulting in a war of definition between, as Dan Schiller puts it, "rogues" and the "rights of men." Similarly, a new discourse of race, employed largely by workers themselves, also helped mute newly created class conflicts, particularly in the post-depression 1840s. The insecurity that attended class stratification produced a whole series of working-class fears about the status of whiteness; working-class white men, Richard Slotkin points out, began to perceive "the form of labor degradation in racial and sexual terms," rejecting such degradation by affirming positions of white male superiority.[24]

Sandwiched between bourgeois above and black below, respectable artisans feared they were becoming "blacker" with every increment of industrial advance, and countered with the language and violence of white supremacy. But the very vehemence of their response indicated the increasing functional and discursive interchangeability of blacks and working-class whites. The neighborhoods to which white workers moved, for example, were often racially integrated, effectively negating the cushion of difference, and this condition, along with workers' fears of being displaced by blacks from work, seems to have given rise to much of the racist violence in the antebellum U.S.[25] Likewise, the term "blackleg" was used to describe what later strikers would call a "scab," its racial overtones further evidence of black and white working-class competitiveness and interchangeability—blacklegs *were*, in some cases, black. An extreme instance of working-class "blackening" was that of the immigrant Irish, whom antebellum whites widely equated with blacks as an alien, subhuman, and brutal species.[26] The rhetoric of race that was a specific product of antebellum America's capitalist crisis thus *equated* working-classness and blackness as often as it differentiated them—an antinomy with properly equivocal results. For while it gave "the cutting edge of racial feeling," Slotkin writes, to working-class disdain for both Lords of the Loom and Lords of the Lash, it also produced "artificial and ultimately destructive distinctions within the working classes."[27] Blackface minstrelsy, I would argue, was founded on this antinomy, reinstituting with ridicule the gap between black and white working class even as it reveled in their (sometimes liberatory) identification.

This dynamic surfaced not only in the minstrel show but in a variety of popular domains of discourse[28]—largely because they constituted one major way in which working people resisted the constricting demands of metropolitan industrialization. It should come as no surprise that social conflicts in which race and class interpenetrated and contradicted one another were acutely registered in the cultural forms and spaces that arose to ease them.

DOMAINS OF DISCOURSE

In the early 1830s, changes in the northern American class structure urged the need for a discrete sphere of working-class sociability just as an urban culture industry began to emerge. The classes began to forge social lives independent of each other; drinking became a staple of working-class boardinghouses as abjuring drink became a badge of respectability. Goaded by these developments and accelerating them in turn, amusements of all kinds began to spring up in New York's Bowery. Unsympathetic observers noted the connection, and one blamed boardinghouse life itself for the upsurge in New York amusements. "There is no bond of union among the lodgers of a boardinghouse," wrote popular playwright William K. Northall; in the absence of fireside enjoyments boarders were forced upon their own resources, and "public places of entertainment offer the readiest means to these poor undomesticated animals." At least the animals appear to have gotten what they wanted. Although the city had decided in 1823 to regulate an already alarming undergrowth of novelties in the summer gardens, Peter Buckley speculates that this only drove such "minor" amusements onto the commercial stage. The Bowery Theatre opened in 1826; and while it had begun with "legitimate" fare, by 1830 innovative theater manager Thomas Hamblin was booking melodrama, performing animals, jugglers, minstrelsy, and more—that theater's contribution to a whole new downtown milieu. Scores of cheap dancehalls, billiard rooms, saloons, and amphitheaters for bare-knuckle prizefights and cockfights, as well as such prime minstrel-show sites as the Olympic, Franklin, and Chatham theaters, had all established themselves by the late 1830s, more or less in spite of the Panic. Not only theater managers like Hamblin, but entrepreneurs such as P. T. Barnum revolutionized commercial forms of leisure, Barnum developing in his museum the variety acts that were coming to characterize many downtown "vaudevilles." The first organized minstrel troupe, Dan Emmett's Virginia Minstrels, grew out of this context in 1843; while the accounts conflict, the troupe was probably born in a hotel across from the Bowery Theatre.[29]

It is difficult to capture both the unevenness and peculiar coherence of this popular sphere in the antebellum years. The character of the minstrel show, in particular, appears to have shifted slightly at least once in each of the three decades under consideration—shifts that refer us not only to changing historical formations or conventions of racial representation, but also to the earliest development of the culture industry itself. Beginning as an *entr'acte* affair of solo songs and dances in legitimate theaters and certain popular sites, minstrelsy remained an art of short burlesque and comic relief throughout much of the 1830s. But from its development into a full-fledged show in the post-Panic early 1840s until its partial absorption into the *Uncle Tom's Cabin* melodramas in the early and middle 1850s, minstrelsy formed one major part of urban popular culture, settling into a rather lifeless, and enormously profitable, institutionalization in the late 1850s.

Produced in theaters that hosted the whole range of popular amusements, blackface performance was marked by the new styles of staging and commercial organization that were only one example of this theatrical culture's internal continuity. In 1839 Mitchell's Olympic Theatre, mid-Panic, halved its admission prices; and it focused almost exclusively on what William Mitchell described as "tragico-comico-illegitimate" productions—essentially travesties of local events and amusements. These innovations sustained minstrel companies as well. Their topical commentary, Shakespearean or operatic burlesques, and stock companies (useful in generating familiarity between popular actors and audiences) resulted in extended runs. Shakespearean burlesque proved particularly long-lived, so intimate were even popular audiences in the antebellum years with what one minstrel parody called "de Bird of Avon." Shakespeare's plays became *Hamlet the Dainty*, "Bad Breath, the Crane of Chowder," *Julius Sneezer*, "Dars-de-Money"; while, as Lawrence Levine has shown, Shakespeare was truly an author for the million, such travesties defined even more clearly this culture's difference from that of the upper ten. One *Hamlet* parody refused to distinguish between hawk and handsaw:

Oh! tis consummation
Devoutly to be wished,
To end your heartache by a sleep;
When likely to be dished,
Shuffle off your mortal coil,
Do just so,
Wheel about and turn about
And jump Jim Crow.

Due to the popularity of such fare, theaters devoted solely to blackface began to appear by the late 1840s, and many troupes eventually, if briefly, supported their own "Ethiopian Opera Houses."[30]

The coherence of this class culture, I have noted, was also to be found in its self-conscious relationship to its own amusements. Many minstrel songs amount to little more than narratives of the audience's preferred entertainments, and much of the playing time of productions such as Benjamin Baker's wildly popular *A Glance at New York in 1848* (1848) was taken up, Peter Buckley notes, with the "vigorous consumption of popular amusement and commodities—the popular fiction, the 'waudevilles,' . . . corner rolls and fried liver" that defined this culture's everyday life. Like other popular plays in this period, for instance, *New York As It Is* (1848), an updated version of *A Glance at New York*, features scenes set at the Chatham Theatre itself, as well as a bout of "nigger" dancing. This commercial self-consciousness was, like minstrelsy, one result of an aesthetic of local travesty; it was also an obvious product of culture-industry cunning, a self-serving roll call of brand names. But it served, again, to equate working-class audiences with the arts, notably blackface, that they patronized—the most immediate reason, perhaps, for the overlay of racial and class imagery. As Young America writer Cornelius Mathews was one of the last to point out, the more popular pleasures and their characteristic audiences were something like interchangeable metaphors for one another. In *A Pen-and-Ink Panorama of New York City* (1853), Mathews boards a Hudson River steamer and is soon surrounded by "a group of Bowery pit inhabitants" who "begin to dance to the banjo and triangle."[31] (A plantation frolic on the Hudson!) By 1853, the signifying chain linking workingmen to Bowery amusements and through these to blackface performance was little more than a cliché of social observation. What concerns us here are the chain's uncertain racial outcomes.

Perhaps its strongest link, in these times of temperance, was alcohol. As early as the 1820s, saloons and grocery-grog shops had become the mainstay of an emergent culture, despite the attempts of proto-industrialists and other elites to police working-class habits and amusements through the revival, the Sunday school, and the temperance society—that "middle-class obsession," Paul Johnson calls it. It is true that drinking was so central to this culture that journeymen and laborers hardly needed a separate place to indulge the pastime. E. P. Thompson remarked the "alternate bouts of intense labour and of idleness, wherever men were in control of their own working lives," and although employers were increasingly in a position to insist on abstemious codes of industrial behavior, shop-floor traditions such as brandy-tippling and hangover-induced, inoperative "Blue Mondays" provided the readiest means of workers' control. Yet saloons were not simply more and better spaces for saturnalia; they were semi-official working-class institutions. Their function was often proclaimed in various sorts of bold inscription hung above entrance doors:

1. *King*—I govern all.
2. *General*—I fight for all.
3. *Minister*—I pray for all.
4. *Laborer*—And I pay for all.

Custodians of a sometimes overtly politicized cultural style, tavern-keepers nourished camaraderie, mutuality, and solidarity among their patrons. For immigrant workers especially, friendly saloons were upholders of traditional customs and rituals, or political halfway houses, Irish nationalist Daniel O'Connell a regular toastee. Major figures of immigrant life, among them prizefighter Yankee Sullivan and politician David Broderick, organized constituencies and maintained positions by tending saloons. Broderick actually named his saloon The Subterranean after the radical newssheet of his friend, firebrand Mike Walsh.[32]

A wide variety of amusements was to be found in the saloon, from cockfights to minstrel acts; for every T. D. Rice making his fortune on the stage, we might suppose several or even dozens of imitators to have worked local taverns. Some of these, like the men who formed the Virginia Minstrels in 1843, went on to fame of their own; and many of the taverns themselves began an upgrading to the status of "concert saloon" by the late 1840s. Yet the presence in this particular milieu of someone like Mike Walsh—who, however radical in his class sympathies, went so far as to form an alliance with pro-slavery Calhoun Democrats in the early 1840s—perhaps affirms the racist intentions of blackface's casual presence in the saloon. It is nevertheless clear that Repealer O'Connell and Liberator William Lloyd Garrison frequently corresponded in the 1840s, attempting for a time an "internationalist" labor abolitionism that could not have left many Irish-American saloon-goers untouched though it ultimately failed in its project. Indeed, one tavern in Philadelphia, writes Bruce Laurie, sported a placard with a bust of O'Connell and a snippet from Byron's *Childe Harold* that may have permitted a variety of political investments: "Hereditary bondsmen! who would be free, / Themselves must strike the blow"—instancing again the potentially positive equation of white working class and black. (Significantly, Frederick Douglass appended this couplet to the end of the Covey chapter [XVII] of *My Bondage and My Freedom* [1855]; he also used it to argue in favor of black enlistment in the Civil War.) The conflicted intimacy American racial cultures shared is certainly there in a detailed account of saloon life later in the century, in which a black man, said an observer, sang songs "of many kinds, comic, sentimental, pathetic, and silly," inducing tears and a respectful hush with his "strange, wailing refrain."[33] This was of course only another kind of condescension, and it set the terms of interracial association, but in the mid-nineteenth century productive working-class political ties across racial boundaries usually had no other base of support.

If the saloon was a more "organic" component of this culture, the museum marked the extent of early American "cultural industrialization." Future University of Michigan president Henry Tappan in 1851 delineated the difference between its British and American versions: "*Museums—a place for the Muses*," he wrote, "fit appellation" for such an institution as the British Museum. In New York, however, the word denoted only "a place for some stuffed birds and animals, for the exhibition of monsters, and for vulgar dramatic performances—a mere place of popular amusement." Although we should be much more careful in assessing the attraction of landmarks like Barnum's American Museum, this remark indicates, from the point of view of the educated classes, the adjectives they called forth. Yet they were of no slight lineage. Historians have emphasized the importance of such plebeian places of learning to Revolutionary-era artisans, rationalist Painites whose thirst for knowledge was slaked by scientific exhibits and astronomical lectures. From a certain angle, indeed, the story of the museum is one of declension, Jeffersonian republicanism vulgarized into Jacksonian democracy. Neil Harris, however, has argued that Barnum's relation to his audiences was underwritten by an "operational aesthetic," an active, intellectual responsiveness on the part of patrons who were delighted with issues of truth and falsity and as ready to be fooled by an ingenious humbug as thrilled by a genuine curiosity. Yet as Peter Buckley argues, this more sympathetic view still tends toward an ahistorical idea of undifferentiated cultural predisposition. "Barnum's pieces of management," rather, "were concrete responses to the need to create a paying reliable public at a time when this 'public' was a contested political category and when the market for popular amusement was typed by its plebeian origins and attitudes." Barnum was helping this popular sphere define itself, that is to say, by putting it in his pocket. A new public was being won over in every sense by the culture-industry innovations it was beckoning into existence.[34]

Race figured prominently in the spate of amusements the museum offered, most obviously in blackface acts but in other productions as well. One way to evade the genteel prejudice against theatrical vice was to provide the same entertainments under the roof of a seemingly more respectable institution; Henry James, one of Barnum's early customers, later wrote that Barnum's "'lecture room,' attached to the Great American Museum, overflowed into posters of all the theatrical bravery disavowed by its title." Barnum, whose early enterprises (dwarfs, minstrel dancers, foreign jugglers) planted him firmly within the Bowery setting, was himself a sometime blackface performer, "and to my surprise was much applauded," he wrote. The showman's first major success was the exhibition of a blind, paralytic black woman named Joice Heth, a slave Barnum purchased in 1835—a particularly gruesome instance of the economics of minstrelization. Barnum claimed Joice Heth to be one hundred and sixty-one years old, and to have been the nurse of George Washington. "She was apparently in good health and spirits, but from age or disease, or both, was unable to change her position; she could move one arm at will, but her lower limbs could not be straightened; her left arm lay across her breast and she could not remove it." Yet she was "pert and sociable," Barnum wrote, often breaking suddenly into hymn. His display at New York's Niblo's Garden of the gnarled old woman, who combined patriotic appeal (she spoke of dressing "dear little George") with circus monstrosity, brought Barnum an estimated fifteen hundred dollars a week.[35] It was in Barnum's use of such appalling spectacles that the tastes of his plebeian audiences were "represented"—in the sense both of satisfying their desires and of raising them to public view.

Joice Heth was only the beginning of Barnum's intrigues with "blackness." He exhibited a skillfully constructed mass of animal parts as the "Fejee Mermaid" in 1842; he hosted blackface acts all through the antebellum years; and in the 1850s the American Museum ran stage productions of Harriet Beecher Stowe's *Uncle Tom's Cabin* and *Dred*. Like his audiences, Barnum seems to have been fascinated with the mystery of color. In 1850 he hired a black man who claimed to have discovered a weed that would turn Negroes white. True to form, Barnum the future Republican trumpeted this discovery as the solution to the slavery problem, while newspapers daily reported any changes in the black man's hue. Barnum takes obvious relish in mimicking this very process in his enlarged autobiography, *Struggles and Triumphs* (1869). Someone mistakes the young Barnum for a querulous black man after one of his blackface performances, and makes a move for his revolver; nothing daunted, Barnum, as he wrote, "rolled my sleeve up, showed my skin, and said, 'I am as white as you are, sir.' [The man] dropped his pistol in positive fright and begged my pardon." These instances of imaginary racial transmutation literalize one train of thought responsible for the minstrel show. They are less articulations of difference than speculations about it. They imagine race mutable; very briefly, they throw off the burden of its construction, blurring the line between self and other, white workingman and black. (In this, blackface actors approached certain fictional uses of the mulatto figure.) They obviously devalue blackness, canceling only to (triumphantly) reinstitute racial boundaries: through biology with the weed, through make-up with blackface. But they perform this whole operation with a kind of ludic, transgressive glee.[36] One also finds this, for instance, in minstrel-show stump speeches, themselves a species of inflated Barnum-speak. Indeed, stump speeches occasionally parodied certain popular practices devoted to the fixing and classifying of racial boundaries—phrenology, for instance, or the midcentury "science" of racial ethnology.

There was indeed a revealing continuity among these discourses. Egyptologist George Gliddon, who in *Ancient Egypt* (1844) argued that the greatness of the Egyptians owed to their Caucasian, not Negro, origins, did lecture tours carrying an extensive collection of Barnum-like artifacts; Samuel Morton's *Crania Americana* (1839), which gauged the mental capacity of different races by skull size, was at least as indebted to phrenological cabinets as to controlled experiment. The class character of blackface performance went some way toward making these discourses seem absurdly similar, or just plain absurd. "On dis side ob me, you may obserb, I hab a cast ob de head ob a gemman ob color; on de udder side, I hab a cast ob de head ob a common white feller," goes a "lecture" on phrenology. A series of perambulatory speculations follow, coming to rest in the observation that all great men are "brack": blacklegs, blackguards, etc. As to the difference, finally, between the two specimens, "Julycum Cezar Pompy Dan Tucker" and the "dam white rascal": "You see den, dat clebber man an dam rascal means de same in dutch, when dey boph white; but when one white an de udder's brack 'dat's a grey hoss ob anoder color.' "[37] It is no doubt remarkable to discover in a minstrel act an inquiry into the construction—by language, no less—of racial difference; but this speech and the minstrel show generally share with Barnum's antics an urge, no less real for its derisive humor, to investigate the boundaries of race established by "respectable" science, to play with, even momentarily overturn, their placement. This was so even when there was fundamental accord as to that placement: lower-million impatience with the discourses of learned authority, not to mention the complexities of working people's everyday negotiations with race, might result in assaults on the color line itself.

Class prickliness usefully inflected the production of "race" also in the penny press, which was sometimes capable of outright contradiction; New York newspapers like the *Transcript* and the *Sun*, for instance, often printed both self-consciously egalitarian antislavery material and lurid accounts of white assaults on blacks.[38] Perhaps the most interesting product of this culture's racial paradoxes was urban journalist "Walter" Whitman. As a reporter for the *New York Aurora* in the early 1840s (where he was, in fact, a colleague of Mike Walsh); the author of a temperance dime novel, *Franklin Evans; or, The Inebriate* (1842); a columnist at the *Brooklyn Star* in the mid-1840s; and, shortly after, a many-hatted editor at the *Brooklyn Daily Eagle*, Whitman stands out in his attention to the various modes and media of "racial" representation, from minstrelsy to painting to politics itself. He too registered the contradiction between white supremacy and staunch egalitarianism, and while it can scarcely be said that Whitman always found himself on the better side of this problem, he at least has the virtue of having wrestled with it. There were surely complacent moments, such as *Franklin Evans's* racialist-gothic subplot, in which the protagonist, after a drunken binge, finds himself married to a Creole woman—herself a figure for his profligacy. Worse than this: "Is not America for the Whites?" Whitman wrote in 1858. "And is it not better so?" On the other side were Whitman's anti-slavery views, his celebrations of black English, or his praise of William Sidney Mount's paintings of black life—which, he wrote in William Cullen Bryant's *New York Evening Post*, "may be said to have a character of Americanism."[39] Falling somewhere between these instances was Whitman's interest in blackface minstrelsy.

Whitman was a great lover of the minstrel show, seeing in it an American example of what he had found in opera, but he could never quite decide whether it represented the best or the worst America had to offer in the way of a national art. He avidly attended blackface performances, as he did many Bowery productions, and he praised them in print. One troupe, the Harmoneons, said Whitman in 1846, proved that much could be done with "low" material: "'Nigger' singing with them is a subject from obscure life in the hands of a divine painter: rags, patches and coarseness are imbued with the great genius of the artist." One is struck by the notion of our democratic poet feeding on blackface coarseness and obscurity; he certainly seems to have taken them for a people's culture, representative not only of black life but of the Bowery pit as well. However, Whitman later excoriated minstrelsy, not for its racism but for its vulgarity—"I must be pardoned for saying, that I never could, and never will, admire the exemplifying of our national attributes with Ethiopian minstrelsy"—a judgment whose evident distaste for black people themselves indicates a somewhat common split in working-class culture between anti-slavery beliefs and personal abhorrence of blacks, not to mention abolitionism as a movement. (There were also, of course, other sorts of disjunctions and contradictions.) We do know that at the time of Whitman's greatest enthusiasm for the minstrel show he was extensively engaged in Free Soil politics, that late-1840s challenge to the pro-southern Democracy that would shortly grow into the Republican party. But the ambiguities of Whitman's culture inhered even in the relatively egalitarian Free Soil movement, for it was ideologically broad enough, Eric Foner observes, to encompass those opposed to slavery on moral grounds as well as those against the presence of Negro slaves in newly acquired territories and those worried about more fugitive slaves fleeing north—in short, "the most vulgar racists and the most determined supporters of Negro rights, as well as all shades of opinion between these extremes." Whitman is a salutary reminder that there are no simple correspondences between individual racial feeling, cultural predisposition, and political ideology; in this, he is perhaps a representative case; and he is representative as well in demonstrating both the potential and the real limits of class egalitarianism as a wellspring for anti-racism.[40]

It is an ambiguity one finds even in such working-class forms as the dime novel. Although black characters (and black writers) were seldom featured in such fiction, Michael Denning has argued that certain of its favorite class plots could result in surprisingly radical racial stories. George Lippard's *New York: Its Upper Ten and Lower Million* (1853) uses the familiar trope of a lowly mechanic's inheritance to narrate the fortunes of one of its black protagonists, Randolph Royalton. Born of a black slave mother, Randolph is the half-brother of the white Harry Royalton. Both have a claim on the Van Huyden inheritance; seeking it for himself, Harry hires a slave catcher to abduct Randolph and his sister into slavery. The inheritance takes on symbolic weight when Lippard reveals that Randolph's mother was the daughter of a great "leader of the American people"—Thomas Jefferson, perhaps, since stories of his purported slave children were well known. (William Wells Brown called on them the same year in *Clotel*.) The story thus becomes, writes Denning, "an allegorical assertion of the Black Randolph's rightful share in the inheritance of the Republic"; derived from stories of noble white mechanics, the plot suddenly accommodates a sympathetic tale of black people's fate in America.[41] (Neither Randolph the black hero nor Arthur Dermoyne the white mechanic receives his inheritance.) Lippard certainly shared the racism of much of the antebellum labor movement, and in his *The Quaker City; or, Monks of Monk Hall* (1844) uses race as a metaphor for corruption: the swindling, pretended southern aristocrat, Colonel Fitz-Cowles, turns out to be the son of a Creole slave. But the lineaments of Randolph's story reveal that when structured along acceptable class lines, when, that is, there was an implicit twinning of blacks and working-class whites, black characters in such writing, as in popular culture at large, could be portrayed in liberatory ways.

As it turned out, the converse was equally true: more than once, and increasingly as the 1840s went on, the presence of "blackness" in this culture would pose a significant class threat.

"NO DAINTY KID-GLOVE BUSINESS"

It was, most of all, as a "culturalist" class ideology, a manifestation of class values in audience rites and cultural self-presentation, that blackface sponsored a sense of incipient class trouble. The social tenor of the new amusements very quickly became fodder for the critics, who began to light on the defining—ideological—behavior of this emergent "public." Even as early as the 1830s, T. D. Rice's performances of "Jim Crow" at the Bowery Theatre routinely brought crowds onto the stage:

> When Mr. Rice came on the stage to sing his celebrated song of Jim Crow, they not only made him repeat it some twenty times, but hemmed him in so that he actually had no room to perform the little dancing or turning about appertaining to the song; and in the afterpiece, where a supper-table is spread, some among the most hungry very leisurely helped themselves to the viands. It was a rare treat, indeed, to the audience.

Now this was theater for the million. Even when they did not partake of stage viands, audiences yet made their demands plain. The *New York Mirror* noted of one 1833 Bowery performance:

> A few evenings since [the orchestra] were performing an overture, which did not exactly suit the cultivated taste of some worthies in the pit. "Yankee Doodle," being more in unison with the patriotic ideas of propriety, was loudly called for, and its melting tones forthwith breathed forth in mellifluous harmony. The pit were gratified, and evinced their satisfaction by a gentle roar.[42]

This is by no means the last we will see of such demonstrations; nor is it the last of stage reports whose irony, in a kind of homeopathic reaction to the events they describe, is barely under control.

Yet as many have pointed out, it is at first baffling that such audience activities should in the 1830s have taken on class signification. For they had marked the experience of theatergoing as early as the turn of the nineteenth century. In 1802 Washington Irving (as "Jonathan Oldstyle") was assailed by "thunderbolts" from the gods in the gallery:

> Some how or another the anger of the gods seemed to be aroused all of a sudden, and they commenced a discharge of apples, nuts & gingerbread, on the heads of the honest folks in the pit. . . . I can't say but I was a little irritated at being saluted aside of my head with a rotten pippin, and was going to shake my cane at them; but was prevented by a decent looking man behind me, who informed me it was useless to threaten or expostulate. They are only *amusing themselves* a little at our expence, said he, sit down quietly and bend your back to it. My kind neighbour was interrupted by a hard green apple that hit him between the shoulders—he made a wry face, but knowing it was all in joke, bore the blow like a philosopher.

No: nothing especially new about the "gentle roar" of later years. Why then the access of irony in accounts of 1830s theater? As in so many instances, the irony says less about theatrical events than about the ironists themselves—particularly their increasing social distance, both within the theater and without, from an emerging self-conscious class culture unheedful of the vulgarity of racial display. Theater audiences and performances were becoming more *differentiated*, not more rowdy.[43]

By the 1840s, rowdiness had begun to seem a class style. If "legitimate" productions in this period aspired to a new restraint, popular amusements cultivated a sort of demonstrative excess through which cultural allegiances were formed or class values negotiated. This ethos was briefly crystallized in the post-Panic street and stage appearance of the Bowery b'hoy, that "compound of East Side swell, gutter bum, and volunteer fire laddie," in Richard Dorson's words, who parodied the styles of the "upper ten" and posed the greatest cultural challenge to uptown mandarins.[44] Termed "Mose" after the stage character that set forth his popular image, the b'hoy affected a brusque manner, peculiar lingo, and extravagant costume, often capped by hair in "soap-locks" plastered to the temple and a shiny stovepipe hat. In many ways he exemplified the U.S.'s first working-class subculture—volunteer fireman bent on class travesty, butcher wise in the ways of cultural *bricolage*. Although the b'hoy's rubric invoked Irishness, no single ethnic profile defined him, nor was he (contrary to later myth) a partisan of nativism. As one member of the subculture later recalled:

> I was at that time what was known as a "Bowery Boy," a distinct "gang" from either the "know-nothing" or "Native American" parties. The gang had no regular organization, but were a crowd of young men of different nationalities, mostly American born, who were always ready for excitement, generally of an innocent nature.[45]

"Generally," of course, makes room for the Astor Place riot—a phenomenon not only concurrent with the emergence of the b'hoys but in great part a result of their conscious cultural self-definition. By about 1847 their arrival was being announced in various fictional forms, but it was secured by *A Glance at New York in 1848*, one of the greatest melodramatic successes of the nineteenth-century New York stage.

"Mose's" reception on opening night made it clear that the b'hoys' time had come. As a near-contemporary wrote:

> He stood there in his red shirt, with his fire coat thrown over his arm, the stove-pipe hat . . . drawn down over one eye, his trousers tucked into his boots, a stump of a cigar pointing up from his lips to his eye, the soap locks plastered flat on his temples, and his jaw protruded into a half-beastly, half-human expression of contemptuous ferocity. . . . Taking the cigar stump from his mouth and turning half-way round to spit, he said:
> "I ain't a goin' to run wid dat mercheen no more!"
> Instantly there arose such a yell of recognition as had never been heard in the little house before. . . . Every man, woman, and child recognized in the character all the distinctive external characteristics of the class.[46]

A Glance at New York and sketches like it were riotously egalitarian, offering a kind of plebeian heroism against the dangers of downtown New York. As with Davy Crockett, one of Mose's frontier antecedents, pugilism was his avocation: "I'm bilein' over for a rousin' good fight with some one somewhere. . . . If I don't have a muss soon, I'll spile."[47] But the urban (and often pugilistic) business of fire fighting was his central preoccupation:[48]

> Seys I, "What's de matter, good woman?" Seys she, "My baby's in de house, and it's burnin'!" Seys I, "What!"—I turned my cap hindside afore, and buttoned my old fire-coat, and I went in and fetched out dat baby. . . . Ever since dat time I've had a great partiality for little babies. The fire-boys may be a little rough outside, but they're all right here. (*Touches breast.*) It never shall be said dat one of de New York boys deserted a baby in distress.

The figure of Mose, with his "g'hal" Lize or his partner Sykesy, focused an urban style that gave visible, class-resistant expression to the Bowery milieu.[49]

Whitman, whose early journalism, if not his early poetry, is in the b'hoy manner, late in his life captured this sensibility of the 1830s Bowery Theatre:

> Pack'd from ceiling to pit with its audience mainly of alert, well dress'd, full blooded young and middle-aged men, the best average of American-born mechanics . . . the whole crowded auditorium, and what seeth'd in it, and flush'd from its faces and eyes, to me as much a part of the show as any—bursting forth in one of those long-kept-up tempests of hand-clapping peculiar to the Bowery—no dainty kid-glove business, but electric force and muscle from perhaps 2000 full-sinew'd men.

Even more urgently did the *Spirit of the Times* in 1847 observe

> a vast sea of upturned faces and red flannel shirts, extending its roaring and turbid waves close up to the foot-lights on either side, clipping in the orchestra and dashing furiously against the boxes—while a row of luckier and stronger-shouldered amateurs have pushed, pulled and trampled their way far in advance of the rest, and actually stand with their chins resting on the lamp board, chanking peanuts and squirting tobacco juice upon the stage.[50]

Such talk kept the class ardor of this plebeian culture in full view, even before the Astor Place riot. Though the standard account of Bowery patrons usually repeated the familiar metaphors, which very quickly assumed the status of narrative convention, those metaphors lost little of their power to disturb.

Yet few have noted how much this working-class cultural expression owed to the accents of race. I have mentioned that productions like *A Glance at New York* did not stint on narratives of leisure time. One scene finds Lize on her way to work; she and Mose meet, and the two plot that evening's fun:

> *Mose.* Say, Lize, you're a gallus gal, anyhow.
>
> *Lize.* I ain't nothin' else.
>
> *Mose.* What do yer say for Waxhall [the Vauxhall] to-night?
>
> *Lize.* What's a-goin' on?—is de wawdeville plays there?
>
> *Mose.* No—there's goin' to be a first-rate shindig; some of our boys will be there.
>
> *Lize.* . . . .I'd rather go to Christy's. Did you ever see George Christy play the bones? ain't he one of 'em?
>
> *Mose.* Yes, he's some.[51]

Lize proceeds to sing one of the Christy's Minstrels' songs, to Mose's demotic approval. This attests again to the frequency with which blackface was used in nineteenth-century discourse to locate white working people. And it is almost predictable that minstrel acts would appropriate Mose himself—one of the many figures of white American humor that underwent a telling sea change on the minstrel stage.[52] The b'hoy appears not to have been compromised by this disguise. Mose's mechanic accents already tend toward the dialect represented as black on the popular stage; some minstrel songs merely blackened a Mose conforming in all other respects to the outlines of the stage b'hoy:

> Wake up, Mose! De Fire am burning;
> Round de corner de smoke am curling.
> Wake up, Mose! the engine's coming;
> Take de rope and keep a running!

"Fire, Fire, Fire" (1848) moves the titular conflagration to the plantation for heroism in black; "Work! Niggers, work!" (1849) celebrates b'hoy culture in sepia tones:

I like to see de engines fly
Through streets and ober ditches;
And when de b'hoys get in a row,
Dey fight like sons of—Freedom![53]

Such were the ready class associations of "blackness" that even this transmutation came with little effort. As the *Journal of Music* wrote, "What magnificent basses and tenors may be heard among our firemen, when making merry together and singing [such blackface songs as] "Uncle Ned," "Old Dan Tucker," or "Lovely May!"[54] To be sure, the rowdiness that enabled chants of freedom was achieved by way of oppressive racial caricature, and in this the minstrel show mimicked Jacksonian social relations all around. What is surprising is the degree to which the blackness of the oppressed could itself become an idiom of class dissent—a fact, I am arguing, that implied some sense of cross-racial identification. The danger was of course that the b'hoys' blackface conquest of the theater foretold greater disasters than those at Astor Place.

An indication that "black" practices routinely conveyed this kind of danger appears in an 1849 account of saloon dancing by George Foster, the most famous urban chronicler of nightlife and amusements in this period. Retracing Dickens's steps (in *American Notes*) on a Saturday night slumming trip to New York's depressed Five Points section, Foster describes the entertainment at Pete Williams's saloon, now renamed Dickens's Place. The performers are black, not blackfaced; they number a fiddler, a trumpeter, and a bass drummer. The dancers are racially mixed: "Thieves, loafers, prostitutes and rowdies, as well as . . . honest, hard-working people." The orchestra strikes up a blackface minstrel tune, "Cooney in de Holler":

The dancers begin contorting their bodies and accelerating their movements, accompanied with shouts of laughter and yells of encouragement and applause, until all observance of the figure is forgotten and every one leaps, stamps, screams and hurras on his or her own hook. Affairs are now at their hight [sic]. The black leader of the orchestra increases the momentum of his elbow and calls out the figure in convulsive efforts to be heard, until shining streams of perspiration roll in cascades down his ebony face; the dancers, now wild with excitement, like Ned Buntline at Astor Place, leap frantically about like howling dervishes, clasp their partners in their arms, and at length conclude the dance in hot confusion and disorder.[55]

The point here is not merely that black cultural forms and their minstrel counterfeits evoked the riotousness that had lately riven the city. It is also that the language of revolt and the language of amusement were impossible to separate; they bled into one another, the same words referring effortlessly to two, now necessarily related, phenomena. What Foster is describing is in fact the riot—a fling beginning merrily enough and descending, urged on by the leader, into hot confusion and disorder. If the Astor Place riot had itself manifested social divisions in the sphere of culture, it now made a language of eruption available for revolutionary cultural events. The inference that blackface forms despite all appearances might have been included among these is hard to resist, given that the revolution then brewing under the name of William Lloyd Garrison's "No Compromise With Slaveholders" was adding a racial component to the threat of social breakup. Fervid cultural forms, often "black" ones, sustained the sense of blood and revolution that came to be associated with Astor Place.

No wonder high-toned commentators directed a broad vocabulary of distaste at these developments. Following the riot, the *Home Journal* wrote that if Macready wished to see those he had offended, he had only to "follow a well-dressed idler down Broadway and observe the looks he gets from *Mose* and the soap-lock-ery as he goes along":

> Let but the more passive aristocratic party clearly select a favorite . . . and let there be but a symptom of a handle for the B'hoys to express their dissent, and the undercurrent breaks forth like an uncapped hydrant.

But the b'hoys themselves found the "aristocratic party" far from "passive." Said one speechmaker at a rally the day after the riot, "For what—for whom was this murder committed? . . . To please the aristocracy of the city, at the expense of the lives of inoffending citizens . . . to revenge the aristocrats of this city against the working classes."[56] These were, perhaps, the same "sons of freedom" that blackface acts were so apt to celebrate. Certainly those acts were fluent in such a language of class. The dictates of autonomy readily enough produced blackface butts of derision for white men on the bottom; yet, perhaps as a result of minstrel figures' sexual or sentimental power, they were occasionally objects of white male envy as well, even figures of interracial identification—providing in imaginary ways the labor abolitionism that failed to materialize in the northeast before the Civil War. Minstrelsy's use of racial license to map class revolt was one gesture in the sphere of culture toward what remained undone in the realm of politics.

With the eruption of class into the cultural arena—*in the modality of race*—the lower million had certainly shattered the mirror held up to nature, the universally representative character of "the" theater. Actor William Davidge complained in 1866 (in a ritual mode by then at least twenty years old) that "the rapid increase in the population in newly formed cities, produces a style of patrons whose habits and associations afford no opportunity for the cultivation of the arts."[57] In 1850 that would have been far the best face to put on it. By then the minstrel show was offering class turbulence with a racial accent—one element of a cultural revolution that made correlate use of grave racial conflicts. It was a prime example of the sometimes contestatory character of plebeian culture, articulating class difference, intentionally or not, by calling on the insurrectionary resonances of black culture. To put it another way, popular entertainments in which race was foregrounded yielded up a sense of unrest waiting to be tapped at its class source. For a brief time in the nineteenth century it seemed that the blackface impulse, based so firmly on the association of "blackness" with the white working class, was backfiring. As certain traditions of racial appropriation were "elevated" into an art of black humiliation, that art fed in turn off of class energies that resisted containment—and that had the unintended consequence of marking the public threat of black culture.

NOTES

1. Sean Wilentz, *Chants Democratic: New York City and the Rise of the American Working Class, 1788–1850* (New York: Oxford University Press, 1984), 263. Recent

labor historians have elaborated the ways in which the American working class reworked republican principles, descended from Enlightenment figures such as Tom Paine, into an "artisan republican" rhetoric designed to resist the emerging capitalist order.

2. I am relying here on the example of Gareth Stedman Jones's *Languages of Class: Studies in English Working Class History, 1832–1982* (New York: Cambridge University Press, 1983), 8.

3. I am, of course, invoking one of the central ideas of Edmund Morgan's *American Slavery—American Freedom: The Ordeal of Colonial Virginia* (New York: Norton, 1975), a profound work of paramount importance to my own. David Roediger, "'Labor in White Skin': Labor and Working-Class History" in Mike Davis and Michael Sprinker, eds., *Reshaping the U.S. Left* (London: Verso, 1988), 287–308; and Stanley Aronowitz, "Writing Labor's History," *Social Text* 25/26 (1990):171–95 offer useful sustained critiques of the new labor history; both argue the inextricability of working white men's freedom and American slavery and racism.

4. The former tendency occurs in much of the writing of recent social historians; for an example concerning post–World War II history, see Thomas B. and Mary Edsall, *Chain Reaction: The Influence of Race, Rights, and Taxes on American Politics* (New York: Norton, 1991). The latter tendency is evident in Mike Davis, *Prisoners of the American Dream: Politics and Economy in the History of the U.S. Working Class* (London: Verso, 1986); Alexander Saxton, *The Rise and Fall of the White Republic: Class Politics and Mass Culture in Nineteenth-Century America* (London: Verso, 1990); and David Roediger, *The Wages of Whiteness: Race and the Making of the American Working Class* (London: Verso, 1991)—excellent works to which I am extensively indebted but with whose emphases I disagree.

5. Fredric Jameson, "Reification and Utopia in Mass Culture," *Social Text* 1 (1979):133–34. The title of Lippard's last novel was *New York: Its Upper Ten and Lower Million* (1853). Huyssen's term comes from his *After the Great Divide: Modernism, Mass Culture, Postmodernism* (Bloomington and Indianapolis: Indiana University Press, 1986).

6. George Rehin, "The Darker Image: American Negro Minstrelsy through the Historian's Lens," *Journal of American Studies* 9(3) (1975):371. Other important work on minstrelsy includes Ralph Ellison, "Change the Joke and Slip the Yoke," in *Shadow and Act* (1964; rpt. New York: Vintage, 1972), 45–59; Hans Nathan, *Dan Emmett and the Rise of Early Negro Minstrelsy* (1962; rpt. Norman: University of Oklahoma Press, 1977); Leroi Jones [Amiri Baraka], *Blues People: Negro Music in White America* (New York: Morrow, 1963), 82–86; James H. Dorman, "The Strange Career of Jim Crow Rice," *Journal of Social History* 3(2) (1969–70):109–22; Nathan Irvin Huggins, *Harlem Renaissance* (New York: Oxford University Press, 1971), 244–301; Robert C. Toll, *Blacking Up: The Minstrel Show in Nineteenth-Century America* (New York: Oxford University Press, 1974); Alexander Saxton, "Blackface Minstrelsy and Jacksonian Ideology," *American Quarterly* 27(1) (1975):3–28; Sylvia Wynter, "Sambos and Minstrels," *Social Text* 1 (1979):149–56; Joseph Boskin, *Sambo: The Rise and Demise of an American Jester* (New York: Oxford University Press, 1986), 65–94; and Roediger, *The Wages of Whiteness*, 95–131. Much of this work revises older standard studies such as Carl Wittke, *Tambo and Bones: A History of the American Minstrel Stage* (Durham, N.C.: Duke University Press, 1930) and Constance Rourke, *American Humor: A Study*

of the American National Character (New York: Harcourt Brace Jovanovich, 1931), 77–104.

7. "Pompey's Rambles," in *White's New Book of Plantation Melodies* (Philadelphia: T. B. Peterson, 1849), 15–16; see also "Broadway Song," in *Buckley's Song Book for the Parlor* (New York: P. J. Cozans, 1855), 43, and "Coney Island," in *Budsworth's New Comic Ethiopian Songster* (New York: F. A. Brady, 1861), 54.

8. Quoted in David Grimsted, *Melodrama Unveiled: American Theater and Culture, 1800–1850* (Chicago: University of Chicago Press, 1968), 52–53.

9. Raymond Williams, "Social Environment and Theatrical Environment," in his *Problems in Materialism and Culture* (London: New Left Books, 1980), 131.

10. *Philadelphia Public Ledger,* May 16, 1849; Peter Buckley, "To the Opera House: Culture and Society in New York City, 1820–1860," Ph.D. dissertation, State University of New York-Stony Brook, 1984, 31.

11. See Bruce McConachie, "The Theatre of Edwin Forrest and Jacksonian Hero Worship," in Judith L. Fisher and Stephen Watt, eds., *When They Weren't Doing Shakespeare: Essays on Nineteenth-Century British and American Theatre* (Athens: University of Georgia Press, 1989), 3–18. Forrest, a great fan of minstrelsy, was also certainly one of the first to "black up"—as "Cuff, a Kentucky negro," in Cincinnati in 1823. See E. L. Rice, *Monarchs of Minstrelsy* (New York: Kenny, 1911), 23.

12. For accounts of the Astor Place rioting, see the *New York Herald,* May 11, 1849; "Opinions of the Press on the Late Occurrences in Astor Place," *New York Herald,* May 16, 1849; William K. Northall, *Before and Behind the Curtain* (New York: Burgess, 1851), 123–51; Alvin Harlow, *Old Bowery Days: The Chronicles of a Famous Street* (New York: Appleton, 1931), 323–32; Richard Moody, *The Astor Place Riot* (Bloomington and Indianapolis: Indiana University Press, 1958); Grimsted, *Melodrama Unveiled,* 68–74; Buckley, "To the Opera House," 20; and Lawrence Levine, *Highbrow/Lowbrow: The Emergence of Cultural Hierarchy in America* (Cambridge, Mass.: Harvard University Press, 1988), 63–68.

13. Erik Olin Wright, *Classes* (London: Verso, 1985), 19–63.

14. See Eric Lott, *Love and Theft: Blackface Minstrelsy and the American Working Class* (New York: Oxford University Press, 1993), chap. 6.

15. For this diversity, see, among others, Richard Stott, *Workers in the Metropolis: Class, Ethnicity, and Youth in Antebellum New York City* (Ithaca and London: Cornell University Press, 1990), 37–67, 214–16, and Buckley, "To the Opera House," 147, 294–409.

16. David Montgomery, "Labor in the Industrial Era," in Richard B. Morris, ed., *A History of the American Worker* (1976; rpt. Princeton: Princeton University Press, 1983), 94; Buckley, "To the Opera House," 346–53, 370–76; Stott, *Workers in the Metropolis,* 222–29, 247–76.

Erik Olin Wright's *Classes* is to date the best theoretical discussion of class. Wright makes a distinction between class structure and class formation. "Class structure refers to the structure of social relations into which individuals (or, in some cases, families) enter which determine their class interests" (9). "Class formation, on the other hand, refers to the formation of organized collectivities within that class structure on the basis of the interests shaped by that class structure" (10). "Classes," then, "have a structural existence which is irreducible to the kinds of collective organizations which develop historically (class formations), the class ideologies held by individuals and organizations (class consciousness) or the forms of conflict engaged in by individuals as class members or by class organizations (class struggle), and . . . such class structures impose basic constraints on these other elements in the concept of class" (28).

My concern is minstrelsy's role in antebellum class formation. I am assuming that structurally the minstrel show was at all times part of a class-inflected culture that began to emerge after 1830 and that underwent an increasing separation from the dominant culture; and that while the people who made up minstrelsy's audiences often employed a populist language of the "industrious" or "producing" classes to describe themselves, they nevertheless had a sense of belonging to this class-inflected culture. By "class formation," then, I mean the ways minstrelsy and other "raced" forms participated in or redirected class conflict, or contributed shifting languages of race for such conflict.

17. Roediger, *The Wages of Whiteness*, 97–100.

18. F. C. Wemyss, *Theatrical Biography; or, The Life of An Actor and Manager* (Glasgow: Griffin, 1848), 178–79.

19. *Journal of Music* (September 17, 1853), 191.

20. For a similar point, see Roediger, *The Wages of Whiteness*, 110, 116.

21. Northall, *Before and Behind the Curtain*, 152–53; *Spirit of the Times*, February 6, 1847; Stedman Jones, *Languages of Class*, 9–10.

22. Burton Bledstein, *The Culture of Professionalism: The Middle Class and the Development of Higher Education in America* (New York: Norton, 1976), ix; Karen Halttunen, *Confidence Men and Painted Women: A Study of Middle-Class Culture in America, 1830–1870* (New Haven: Yale University Press, 1982), xvii; Mary P. Ryan, *Cradle of the Middle Class: The Family in Oneida County, New York, 1790–1865* (Cambridge: Cambridge University Press, 1981); Paul Boyer, *Urban Masses and Moral Order in America, 1820–1920* (Cambridge, Mass.: Harvard University Press, 1978), 61; Louis Hartz, *The Liberal Tradition in America* (1955; rpt. New York: Harcourt Brace Jovanovich, 1983), 51; Stuart M. Blumin, "The Hypothesis of Middle-Class Formation in Nineteenth-Century America: A Critique and Some Proposals," *American Historical Review* 90(2) (1985):304. It is time, one would think, to put the somnolent idea of American exceptionalism to bed; recent labor historians have certainly demonstrated striking class parallels between the American and European contexts. For a first-rate discussion of this matter, see Eric Foner, "Why Is There No Socialism in the U.S.?," *History Workshop Journal* 17 (1984):57–80.

23. Paul Johnson, *A Shopkeeper's Millennium: Society and Revivals in Rochester, New York, 1815–1837* (New York: Hill and Wang, 1978), 42 (see also the fascinating account of the origins of "boss" in Roediger, *The Wages of Whiteness*, 50–54); Stuart Blumin, "Hypothesis," 313–16.

I have drawn most on the following sources for these historical developments: Herbert Gutman, *Work, Culture, and Society in Industrializing America: Essays in American Working-Class and Social History* (New York: Vintage, 1976), 3–78; David Montgomery, "The Shuttle and the Cross: Weavers and Artisans in the Kensington Riots of 1844," *Journal of Social History* 5(4) (1972):411–46; Paul Faler, "Cultural Aspects of the Industrial Revolution: Lynn, Massachusetts Shoemakers and Industrial Morality, 1826–1860," in Milton Cantor, ed., *American Workingclass Culture: Explorations in American Labor and Social History* (Westport, Conn.: Greenwood, 1979), 121–48;

208   ERIC LOTT

Alan Dawley, *Class and Community: The Industrial Revolution in Lynn* (Cambridge, Mass.: Harvard University Press, 1976); Alan Dawley and Paul Faler, "Working-Class Culture and Politics in the Industrial Revolution: Sources of Loyalism and Rebellion," *Journal of Social History* 9(4) (1976):466–80; Johnson, *Shopkeeper's Millennium*; Susan Hirsch, *Roots of the American Working Class: The Industrialization of Crafts in Newark, 1800–1860* (Philadelphia: University of Pennsylvania Press, 1978); Bruce Laurie, "'Nothing on Compulsion': Life Styles of Philadelphia Artisans, 1800–1850," *Labor History* 15(3) (1974):337–66; Bruce Laurie, *Working People of Philadelphia, 1800–1850* (Philadelphia: Temple University Press, 1980); Bruce Laurie, *Artisans into Workers: Labor in Nineteenth-Century America* (New York: Noonday, 1989), 15–112; David Gordon, Richard Edwards, and Michael Reich, *Segmented Work, Divided Workers: The Historical Transformation of Labor in the U.S.* (New York: Cambridge University Press, 1982), 1–17, 48–99; Mary Blewett, "Work, Gender and the Artisan Tradition in New England Shoemaking, 1780–1860," *Journal of Social History* 17(2) (1983):221–48; Wilentz, *Chants Democratic*, 23–142; Steven Ross, *Workers on the Edge: Work, Leisure, and Politics in Industrializing Cincinnati, 1788–1890* (New York: Columbia University Press, 1985), 3–192; Blumin, "Hypothesis"; Amy Bridges, "Becoming American: The Working Classes in the U.S. Before the Civil War," in Ira Katznelson, ed., *Working-Class Formation: Nineteenth-Century Patterns in Western Europe and the U.S.* (Princeton: Princeton University Press, 1986), 157–96; Christine Stansell, *City of Women: Sex and Class in New York, 1789–1860* (New York: Knopf, 1986), 43–62; Elizabeth Blackmar, *Manhattan for Rent: Housing and Property Relations in New York City* (Ithaca and London: Cornell University Press, 1989); and Stott, *Workers in the Metropolis*.

24. Stuart Hall et al., *Policing the Crisis: Mugging, the State, and Law and Order* (London: Macmillan, 1978); Dan Schiller, "From Rogues to the Rights of Men: Crime News and the *Police Gazette* (1845–1847)," *Media, Culture, and Society* 2(4) (1980):377–88; Richard Slotkin, *The Fatal Environment: The Myth of the Frontier in the Age of Industrialism, 1800–1890* (Middletown, Conn.: Wesleyan University Press, 1985), 150.

25. See, among others, Bernard Mandel, *Labor: Free and Slave: Workingmen and the Anti-slavery Movement in the U.S.* (New York: Associated Authors, 1955), 65–70; Leon Litwack, *North of Slavery: The Negro in the Free States, 1790–1860* (Chicago: University of Chicago Press, 1961), 158–68; John Runcie, " 'Hunting the Nigs' in Philadelphia: The Race Riot of August 1834," *Pennsylvania History* 39(2) (1972):197, 203; Leonard Richards, *"Gentlemen of Property and Standing": Anti-Abolition Mobs in Jacksonian America* (New York: Oxford University Press, 1970), 151–55; Emma Jones Lapsansky, " 'Since They Got Those Separate Churches': Afro-Americans and Racism in Jacksonian Philadelphia," *American Quarterly* 37(1) (1980):61; Laurie, *Working People*, 63–66, 156–58; Paul Gilje, *The Road to Mobocracy: Popular Disorder in New York City, 1763–1834* (Chapel Hill: University of North Carolina Press, 1987), 165–66; and Iver Bernstein, *The New York City Draft Riots* (New York: Oxford University Press, 1990), 27–31.

26. Robert Ernst, *Immigrant Life in New York City, 1825–1863* (1949; rpt. Port Washington, N.Y.: Ira J. Friedman, 1965), 105–6; Litwack, *North of Slavery*, 162–66; Slotkin, *Fatal Environment*, 149; Dale T. Knobel, *Paddy and the Republic: Ethnicity and*

Nationality in Antebellum America (Middletown, Conn.: Wesleyan University Press, 1986), 88–103; Roediger, *Wages of Whiteness*, 133–163.

Minstrel skits portrayed the Irish in terms identical to those in which it portrayed blacks; see, for example, "Paddy Conner's College," in *Billy Birch's Ethiopian Melodist* (New York: Dick and Fitzgerald, 1862), 11.

27. Slotkin, *Fatal Environment*, 150.

28. In *The Politics and Poetics of Transgression* (London: Methuen, 1986), Peter Stallybrass and Allon White insist that discourses and discursive hierarchies owe much to the specific social locations or ideological topography in which they are produced (194–95).

29. Northall, *Before and Behind*, 7; Buckley, "To the Opera House," 141; Theodore Schank, "The Bowery Theatre, 1826–1836," Ph.D. dissertation, Stanford University, 1956, 282; Elliott Gorn, *The Manly Art: Bare-Knuckle Prize Fighting in America* (Ithaca: Cornell University Press, 1986), 133–34; Neil Harris, *Humbug: The Art of P. T. Barnum* (Chicago: University of Chicago Press, 1973), 40–41; Stott, *Workers in the Metropolis*, 212–35, 242–46.

30. Buckley, "To the Opera House," 383; Charles Haywood, "Negro Minstrelsy and Shakespearean Burlesque," in Bruce Jackson, ed., *Folklore and Society* (Hatboro, Pa.: Folklore Associates, 1966), 86; Levine, *Highbrow/Lowbrow*, 11–82; Ray B. Browne, "Shakespeare in American Vaudeville and Negro Minstrelsy," *American Quarterly* 12(3) (1960):382; Ray B. Browne, "Shakespeare in the Nineteenth-Century Songsters," *Shakespeare Quarterly* 8(2) (1957):215–18; Tilden G. Edelstein, "Othello in America: The Drama of Racial Intermarriage," in J. Morgan Kousser and James M. McPherson, eds., *Region, Race, and Reconstruction* (New York: Oxford University Press, 1982), 187–88; William Mahar, "Ethiopian Skits and Sketches: Contents and Contexts of Blackface Minstrelsy, 1840–1890," *Prospects* 16 (1991):248–54; Gary Engle, ed., *This Grotesque Essence: Plays from the American Minstrel Stage* (Baton Rouge: Louisiana State University Press, 1978).

In addition to Buckley, "To the Opera House," 3–409, Robert Allen, *Horrible Prettiness: Burlesque and American Culture* (Chapel Hill: University of North Carolina Press, 1991), 51–76 offers a fine account of antebellum theatrical culture.

31. Buckley, "To the Opera House," 390; Cornelius Mathews, *A Pen-and-Ink Panorama of New York City* (New York: Taylor, 1853), 89.

32. Wilentz, *Chants Democratic*, 53; Johnson, *Shopkeeper's Millennium*, 55; E. P. Thompson, "Time, Work-Discipline, and Industrial Capitalism," *Past and Present* 38 (1967):73; Gutman, *Work, Culture*, 33–39; Laurie, *Working People*, 55. See also Roy Rosenzweig, *Eight Hours for What We Will: Workers and Leisure in an Industrial City, 1870–1920* (Cambridge: Cambridge University Press, 1983), 35–64; Gorn, *Manly Art*, 133–36; and Stott, *Workers in the Metropolis*, 217–22.

33. Robert Ernst, "The One and Only Mike Walsh," *New-York Historical Society Quarterly* 36(1) (1952):43–65; Wilentz, *Chants Democratic*, 326–35; Saxton, *Rise and Fall of the White Republic*, 205–22; Roediger, *Wages of Whiteness*, 75–77; Laurie, " 'Nothing on Compulsion,' " 100; Frederick Douglass, *Life and Times of Frederick Douglass* (1892; rpt. New York: Collier, 1962), 339; J. B. Harrison, *Certain Dangerous Tendencies in American Life* (Boston, 1880), 178–88.

34. Harris, *Humbug*, 33 (for Tappan's remark); the dime museum as a decline from

earlier incarnations is implied in Constance Rourke's essay on Barnum in *Trumpets of Jubilee* (New York: Harcourt, Brace, and World, 1927), 276–319; for earlier museums see Thomas Bender, *New York Intellect: A History of Intellectual Life in New York City* (New York: Knopf, 1987), 47, 83–87; Buckley, "To the Opera House," 489.

35. Henry James, *A Small Boy and Others* (London: Macmillan, 1913), 162; P. T. Barnum, *Struggles and Triumphs: or, Forty Years' Recollections of P. T. Barnum* (Hartford, Conn.: J. B. Burr, 1869), 90, 74–75; M. R. Werner, *Barnum* (New York: Harcourt, Brace, 1923), 31.

36. Werner, *Barnum*, 204; Barnum, *Struggles and Triumphs*, 90. For the mulatto figure as a fictional device of racial mediation, see Hazel V. Carby, *Reconstructing Womanhood: The Emergence of the Afro-American Woman Novelist* (New York: Oxford University Press, 1987), 88–91, 171–73.

37. *De Susannah, and Thick Lip, Melodist* (New York: Strong, 1850), 80, 83–84.

38. Alexander Saxton, "Problems of Class and Race in the Origins of the Mass Circulation Press," *American Quarterly* 36(2) (1984):232–33.

39. Walt Whitman, *Uncollected Poetry and Prose*, ed. Emory Holloway (New York: P. Smith, 1932), I:236. For the 1858 remark, and for more on Whitman and race, see Daniel Aaron, *The Unwritten War: American Writers and the Civil War* (New York: Knopf, 1973), 59–62.

40. William Austin, *"Susannah," "Jeanie," and "The Old Folks at Home": The Songs of Stephen C. Foster from His Time to Ours* (New York: Macmillan, 1975), 61; Whitman, *Uncollected Poetry and Prose*, I:236; Eric Foner, *Politics and Ideology in the Age of the Civil War* (New York: Oxford University Press, 1980), 92.

41. Michael Denning, *Mechanic Accents: Dime Novels and Working-Class Culture in America* (London: Verso, 1987), 116.

42. *New York Mirror*, December 29, 1832; Buckley, "To the Opera House," 156–57.

43. Washington Irving, *Letters of Jonathan Oldstyle, Gentleman* (1812; rpt. Boston: Twayne, 1980), 12; here as elsewhere, Peter Buckley's "To the Opera House" has been indispensable, esp. 139–61.

44. Richard Dorson, "Mose the Far-Famed and World-Renowned," *American Literature* 15(3) (1943):288.

45. Quoted in Buckley, "To the Opera House," 316.

46. T. Allston Brown, *History of the New York Stage*, 2 vols. (1903; rpt. New York: Benjamin Blom, 1969), I:284.

47. Benjamin Baker, *A Glance at New York in 1848* (New York, 1848), 15.

48. Antebellum volunteer fire companies approximated gangs or fraternal organizations as much as fire-fighting units. Sporting names like Lady Washington and Old Maid, they not only involved themselves in party politics but engaged in intense intercompany enmity, often neglecting a raging fire to combat or sabotage a rival company in the street. For the fire companies see Harlow, *Old Bowery Days*, 201–15 and Stott, *Workers in the Metropolis*, 229–31.

49. Baker, *Glance at New York*, 20. For accounts of Mose and the Bowery milieu generally, see George Foster, *New York in Slices: By An Experienced Carver* (New York: Graham, 1849), 43–47; Harlow, *Old Bowery Days*, 190–215; Dorson, "Mose the Far-Famed"; John B. Jentz, "Artisans, Evangelicals, and the City: A Social History of Abo-

lition and Labor Reform in Jacksonian New York," Ph.D. dissertation, City University of New York, 1977, 238–55; Buckley, "To the Opera House," 294–409; Wilentz, *Chants Democratic*, 257–71; Stansell, *City of Women*, 89–100; Gorn, *Manly Art*, 129–36; David Reynolds, *Beneath the American Renaissance: The Subversive Imagination in the Age of Emerson and Melville* (New York: Knopf, 1988), 463–66; and Stott, *Workers in the Metropolis*, 222–29.

50. Walt Whitman, "The Old Bowery" (1885), in *The Collected Writings of Walt Whitman*, 2 vols., ed. Floyd Stovall (New York: New York University Press, 1964), II:595; *Spirit of the Times*, February 6, 1847.

51. Baker, *Glance at New York*, 22.

52. Alexander Saxton also notes the overlapping of class and racial concerns in the blackface version of Mose; see "Blackface Minstrelsy," 9–11.

53. "Wake Up, Mose!," in M. Campbell, *Wood's Minstrels' Songs* (New York: Dick and Fitzgerald, 1855), 25; *White's New Illustrated Melodeon Songbook* (Philadelphia: Peterson, 1848), 72; *White's New Book of Plantation Melodies* (Philadelphia: Peterson, 1849), 24. See also "The Fireman's Boy," in *Beadles Dime Song Book #3* (New York: Beadle, 1860), 34. A daguerreotype of blackface performers T. Prendergast and Dan Bryant (c. 1850–56) shows the two in full blackface *b'hoyisme*—cocked stogeys, canes, stovepipe hats (Harvard Theatre Collection).

54. "Letter from A. W. T.," *Journal of Music* 1(22) (1852):170.

55. George Foster, *New York By Gas-Light: With Here and There a Streak of Sunshine* (New York: DeWitt and Davenport, 1850), 73, 74.

56. *Home Journal*, May 12, 1849; *New York Herald*, May 12, 1849.

57. William Davidge, *Footlight Flashes* (New York: American News Co., 1866), 202.

III CLASS AND LITERARY ANALYSIS

6 HAWTHORNE AND THE MAKING OF THE MIDDLE CLASS

Michael T. Gilmore

I

The currently fashionable triad of American literary studies, race, gender, and class, a triad born of the egalitarian dethroning of the white, male, largely Anglo-Saxon canon, contains its own tacit hierarchy and rests on its own unenunciated principles of exclusion and privileging. Disagreements abound over whether race or gender should occupy the top tier in the new cultural ranking, but about the subordination, even the effacement, of class, there can be no doubt. Few working-class authors have been recuperated—George Lippard, author of *The Quaker City* (1845), is a notable exception from the antebellum period—and no programs in class and its multifarious manifestations have entered college curricula to compete for students with women's studies and African-American studies. Class as a thematic or formal consideration, once the obligatory nod has been made, usually recedes to the background, if it does not vanish altogether, while the critic goes about the business of interpreting *Uncle Tom's Cabin* (1852), *Clotel* (1853), or *Pierre* (1852) in the light of racial and feminist concerns.

One might speculate about the reasons for this omission. It could be argued that the assimilation of the children of working-class parents into the white-collar professoriate has dulled academic sensitivity to the reality of socioeconomic difference. Or it might be claimed that the historic dominance of the middle class in the United States has produced a relatively homogeneous society in which class conflicts have been muted to the point of unimportance. Or if one balks at the notion of an ideological monolith, a related hypothesis offers itself. One might still hold that the United States, in contrast to the stratified nations of Europe where social and economic alterity erupted into armed combat in 1848, subsumes its class divisions under the sign of gender and/or race. What we find in nineteenth-century American writing, goes a version of this argument, is not economic struggle but a clash of gender styles, not a confrontation between social groups but the displacement of a patrician ideal of masculinity by an entrepreneurial or marketplace model.[1]

This paper takes issue with the critical consensus that relegates class to the margins of antebellum American literature. It does so not by examining the novels of a certified labor activist like Lippard, but rather by turning to a familiar and much-analyzed classic of the American Renaissance, *The Scarlet Letter* (1850). Nathaniel Hawthorne, perhaps our most "canonical" nineteenth-century novelist, the writer, indeed, in whom the canon is given birth, maps the emergence of middle-class identity and simultaneously reveals the self-contradictory and unsettled nature of the new configuration. Behind this claim lies the work of historians and students of gender and the family who have shown, convincingly to my mind, that the period when Hawthorne was writing saw the appearance of the middle class in its recognizably modern form. These scholars dispute the idea of an unbroken ideological or class hegemony in the United States. They recount the development of a social formation that declared itself, in part, through gender arrangements, the separation of public and private spheres, and the substitution of naturalism for historical contingency. Their work suggests not so much that class was submerged in gender but rather that gender and the family were imbued with the determinants of class.[2]

Yet Hawthorne's text complicates the findings of these scholars. *The Scarlet Letter* points not simply to the development of an American middle class but also to the highly ambiguous character of that construction. It makes clear that the category of class, at least as the category arises in the Age of Jackson, does not march under the banner of essentialism. Hawthorne's masterpiece amounts to a warning that, in rescuing class from erasure, we must dispel any notion of its being a self-consistent entity.

The social indeterminacies of *The Scarlet Letter* problematize the current view of Hawthorne as an important figure in the formulation of a conservative brand of liberal individualism. According to the interpretation put forward most forcefully by Sacvan Bercovitch, Hawthorne contributed to the building of an ideological consensus that complemented the middle class's coalescence.[3] But the class loyalties knitted into *The Scarlet Letter* seem altogether too unstable to authorize so unambiguous a cultural function for the narrative. And recognizing the textual vacillations fosters a certain skepticism about the critical method of reasoning by analogy or homology. The case for Hawthorne's "liberalism" often seems to rest on structural resemblances between literary and social states of affairs, a mode of demonstration that commonly suppresses evidence of dissimilarity.[4] The resemblances are undeniably there in *The Scarlet Letter*, but the differences are no less real, and Hawthorne's text can be usefully studied to bring out the historical and gender oppositions concealed within literary-social congruity.

It remains true that *The Scarlet Letter* participates in the project of shaping middle-class identity. The novel registers the exfoliation of a socially specific way of life. It encodes the deep structures of the middle class within its discursive patternings and to some degree labors to win consent to that class's dominance by validating its claims to universal legitimacy. But at the same time *The Scarlet Letter* obscures the boundary lines it seems to posit as impermeable. The book undoes its own synchronizations of gender roles, private and public spaces, and socioeconomic categories. Hawthorne's notion of what constitutes middle-class personhood turns out to be internally beleaguered. Patterns of male and female behavior, as pictured in the novel, slide into inversions of themselves, and the tale's image of the present is disrupted by pressure from the past and foreshadowings of the future. To borrow the terminology of Raymond Williams, we might say that Hawthorne's middle class incorporates both residual and proleptically oppositional elements,[5] but because gender is so integral to middle-class character as it crystallizes in the text, sexual ambiguation necessarily accompanies ideological and vocational exchange. The middle-class mother assumes a relation to the social like that of a free-market individualist, while the middle-class father embraces feminized sentiment. Hawthorne's new class threatens to come apart even as it comes into being.

Doubtless these inconsistencies can be traced in part to Hawthorne's own anomalous class position, a matter to which I will return at the end of this paper. But insofar as Hawthorne can be taken as an influential maker and articulator of nineteenth-century American culture, it is possible to generalize from the inconstant allegiances of his greatest work. The reversals and impasses of *The Scarlet Letter* betoken not merely his own unsettled status as an impoverished patrician trying to earn a livelihood by literature. They attest to the instability, the persistent vulnerability, of the ideological closure of the antebellum middle class.

II

Like the word *adultery*, the name of the middle class is never mentioned in *The Scarlet Letter*. The only socioeconomic groupings Hawthorne refers to are the rich and the poor, or, in the antiquated vocabulary the novel sometimes adopts, the high and the low. Hester Prynne is said to receive abuse equally from the poor on whom she bestows her charity and from the "[d]ames of elevated rank" for whom she plies her needle.[6] The mass of Puritans are distinguished from their rulers only by being designated "the people," with little detail provided about their material condition.

Yet like the act of adultery, the middle class occupies a crucial position in Hawthorne's narrative. Following Roland Barthes—who defined the bourgeoisie as the class "*which does not want to be named*"—one might see the avoidance of nomination as the proof of textual centrality.[7] Hawthorne's labeling of those who are presumably neither rich nor poor as "the people" would be in keeping with this universalizing or self-excising impulse. Fortunately, there is more to go on than deletion. Hawthorne writes that the Puritan order supplanted the "system of ancient prejudice" associated with "nobles and kings" (164). He invites us to view the inhabitants of seventeenth-century Boston as the precursors of post-feudal—that is, bourgeois—civilization. But historical commonplace dissolves into anachronism, and anticipation gets conflated with actuality as the Puritan past merges into the American present. For Hawthorne presents colonial Boston as a preindustrial settlement sheltering a contemporaneous middle class, and he inscribes his major characters, above all Hester, with attitudes and modes of behavior that did not become normative until the entrenchment of commercial and industrial capitalism in the nineteenth century.

It might be useful to summarize some of the salient features of that emergent social and economic organization. Perhaps most important for *The Scarlet Letter* is the increasingly rigid segregation of work from the household, a divorce accelerated by the decline of domestic production and by the rise of factories and offices. Along with this change came a revaluation of female personality. Excluded from the public and male preserve of "productive" labor, women began to be identified with, and supposedly to derive their nature from, the private space of the home. They shed their traditional image as lustful and socially disruptive and were now believed to find fulfillment in moral purity, self-sacrifice, and caring for others. This revision, it should be emphasized, centered on middle-class women, who have been pictured—by, among others, Mary Ryan in history, and Nancy Armstrong in literature[8]—as the principal makers of middle-class lifestyle. The dominant values obviously penetrated working-class culture as well, but many laboring people retained residual or eighteenth-century perspectives on work and the family. Working-class women, for instance, were slower to assimilate domestic ideology because they typically sought employment in manufactories or carried paid work into the home.

The Puritan commonwealth depicted in Hawthorne's early chapters, and at various subsequent moments throughout the text, looks decidedly premodern in its emphasis on hierarchy and patriarchy and in its blurring of the boundaries between public and private. It is a community of rulers and ruled, of ministers, magistrates, and soldiers exercising authority over a deferential and largely undifferentiated people. Hawthorne says that seventeenth-century Boston takes its character from "the stern and tempered energies of manhood, and the sombre sagacity of age" (64). He distances its customs from his own time by observing that the Puritan elders regularly intervene in the most intimate details of moral and family existence. This patriarchal world antedates the Victorian model of domesticity and assumes the primacy of fathers in governing the family. Governor Bellingham, the Reverend Mr. Wilson, and other civil authorities contemplate removing Pearl from Hester's care because they assume the public's right to oversee the socialization of children. And just as the public intrudes into what came to be seen as a private and female enclave, so Puritan women in the novel think nothing of "stepping forth into the public ways" and loudly proclaiming their opinions of Hester's misdeed. For these New England matrons, writes Hawthorne, "the man-like Elizabeth"—not, one might add, the modest and sentimental Victoria—"had been the not altogether unsuitable representative of the sex" (50).

Although Hester emerges out of the seventeenth-century past, her Elizabethan qualities belong mainly to the narrative's prehistory. Hester the sexually sinful female, exemplar of traditional womanhood, seems outdated when the action commences. Her refusal to identify her lover in the marketplace reveals the heroine as someone who is already in transition toward a post-Puritan order that guards the private from public exposure. Dimmesdale is also revealed in this opening scene as a Janus-like figure with one eye on a future respectful of the separate spheres. He tells the Reverend Mr. Wilson, much to the older man's bewilderment, "that it were wronging the very nature of woman to force her to lay open her heart's secret in such broad daylight, and in the presence of so great a multitude" (65).

The later pages on Hester's psychological metamorphosis are read too narrowly if we make out in them only the account of one unhappy woman's accommodation to repression. The celebrated descriptions of Hester's change "from passion and feeling, to thought," of her once sensual but now forbidding aspect "that Passion would never dream of clasping in its embrace" (163–64), condense into the span of a few years and a single chapter the reconstruction of feminine nature that required roughly a century to complete. Hawthorne dissolves the transgressive, appetitive Eve into her sexless opposite, replacing concupiscence with the condition that Nancy Cott has accurately labeled "passionlessness" and that underwrites the age's ascendent ideal of self-negating motherhood.[9] He historicizes, as it were, the dark lady/fair lady split in classic American literature by portraying Hester as a dangerous adulteress recasting herself into a model Victorian saint. In the course of the story, she assumes all those mother-related callings available to nineteenth-century middle-class women, winning the people's reverence for her selflessness as a volunteer nurse and self-ordained "Sister of Mercy." The townspeople forget the "original signification" (161) of Hester's letter because that original meaning—of woman as fallen Eve—has been eclipsed historically by middle-class woman's role as self-sacrificing dispenser of nurturance.

Just as Hester is a woman in transition, so *The Scarlet Letter* itself can be understood as a text mutating from one generic category to a second, historically posterior, literary form. The tale, like the heroine, appears anachronistic at first, an eighteenth-century seduction story that has somehow strayed into the age of *Uncle Tom's Cabin* and *The Wide, Wide World* (1850). But Hawthorne's narrative quickly shows its hybrid character as a contemporaneous sentimental novel superimposed upon that obsolete seduction plot. It is remarkable how much of the book approximates the fiction of the "scribbling women" Hawthorne famously disparaged in his correspondence. The structure of the antebellum middle-class family is replicated, or rather disfigured, in the novel's central human reality, the mother and daughter who spend all their time together while the father absents himself at work. The many scenes involving Hester and Pearl parallel the sometimes affectionate, sometimes troubled, mother-daughter relationships familiar to readers of domestic literature. Hawthorne admits that the wearer of the letter behaves more like a mother from the permissive present than from the rigid Puritan past. Loving her daughter "with the intensity of a sole affection," she lacks the resolve to discipline Pearl severely and expects little return for her tenderness other "than the waywardness of an April breeze" (179). This domestic Hester almost lives up to Hawthorne's description of her as "the image of Divine Maternity" (56).

But Hester, even in her maternal avatar, is not, or not merely, the Victorian angel in the house, the woman Dimmesdale hails as his "better angel" (205). The proto-feminism into which her alienation modulates is, in Hawthorne's treatment, the corollary to her solitary mothering and doing of good. Thrust into a modernized family arrangement by her infraction, Hester experiences as compressed personal history the gradual sundering of realms—public disjoined from private, male separated from female—that by the mid-nineteenth century constituted middle-class existence. One need only contrast the gawking, vociferous matrons who surround the scaffold in the early chapters with the mother and daughter who retire into the background while Dimmesdale delivers his election sermon. The now fully modern heroine, clinging to the margins of the marketplace, feels overwhelmed by a sense of her lover's remoteness "from her own sphere." Despite their private interview in the forest, Dimmesdale seems to have no connection to her; in his public, professional capacity, he is "utterly beyond her reach" (239). Such stark compartmentalizing underlines the rigid genderization against which antebellum feminism rebels but that simultaneously empowers feminist protest by making women cognizant of themselves as a separate human category and interest group. Hester is a female reformer two hundred years before her time because alone among the Puritans she is able to conceptualize "the whole race of womanhood" (165) as a branch of the human race apart from men.[10]

Dimmesdale is Hester's male counterpart as middle-class father and "new man" emancipated from the paradigms of an earlier cultural system. Unlike the Puritan patriarchs, he expresses admiration for Hester's unwillingness to speak in public: what for them is a failure of religious and civil duty is for him the mark of true womanhood. The split between public and private defines masculine identity for Dimmesdale, too. He internalizes the fundamental rupture of modern social life as a division between his inner and outer selves. The self he displays in public to his parishioners is sharply differentiated from—it is the contradiction of—the private self that the reader knows to be Pearl's unacknowledged father and Hester's soulmate. The minister is tortured by "the contrast between what I seem and what I am" (191) and struggles to take his place beside his "wife" and child before the public gaze. But every attempt to confess, to overcome the breach between family and workplace, founders on his fear of the consequences of exposure. As we shall see, Dimmesdale does succeed in mediating between the private and the public, but he does so in ways that controvert his characterization as middle-class male.

Dimmesdale is further set apart from Boston's ruling elders by his having risen in the community through ambition and ability. "It was an age," Hawthorne writes, "when what we call talent had far less consideration than now, but the massive materials which produce stability and dignity of character a great deal more" (237). Dimmesdale has acted the part of a Jacksonian man on the make and pushed ahead of his seniors through assiduous cultivation of crowd-pleasing verbal skills. The homology to Hawthorne's own situation as a professional author trying to win fame and affluence through his linguistic gifts is evident enough.

Indeed, Dimmesdale's curious dwelling arrangements both highlight his post-Puritan professionalism and epitomize the text's enforcement of gender sequestration. The minister lives not with his "family" but with Hester's former husband, Roger Chillingworth, a man who, like himself, has a university education and practices an intellectual calling. Their lodgings resemble a workspace or office building more than a home. In one half is Dimmesdale's library, crammed with "parchment-bound folios" and writing materials, in the other the physician has installed his "study and laboratory," and the "two learned persons" daily settle down to their specialized vocations, at the same time "bestowing a mutual and not incurious inspection into one another's business" (126). Hawthorne has written into the narrative a graphic image of male professionals "married" to their work in the era after family production, when mental and manual forms of labor were segregated almost as sharply as men and women. Or better yet, he has given us a picture of the intensifying rivalry between the two great healing professions of the nineteenth century, the clerical attendants of the soul and the medical doctors of the body. Only Hester, in her gendered and unpaid role as charity worker, is entitled to treat spiritual as well as physical ailments.

Hawthorne is able to render the world of middle-class professionalism so vividly because he endeavors to enter it. His ambition to write for a livelihood, to become that invention of modernity, an independent author, gives him sympathetic understanding of his two male characters even as it figuratively places him in competition with them for status and income. As a young man about to matriculate at Bowdoin College, Hawthorne already pictured himself as a professional; in a well-known letter to his mother, he weighed the pros and cons of a career in law, medicine, and the ministry, ending with the question, "What would you think of my becoming an Author, and relying for support upon my pen?" As a writer who specialized in character analysis, Hawthorne did not flinch from rivalry with the other professions but positively cultivated it, as he ventured into territory traditionally reserved for clergymen and doctors. Reviewers, repelled or amazed by his psychological penetration, regularly compared him to a preacher, a Puritan, or an anatomist. "[H]e shows the skillful touches of a physician in probing the depths of human sorrow," exclaimed an admirer of the tales, and a reader of *The Scarlet Letter* was uttering a commonplace when he remarked that "of all laymen he [Hawthorne] will preach to you the closest sermons."[11]

Just as Hawthorne the novelist would lay claim to professional standing, so his novel apes the mores of the white-collar paradigm. *The Scarlet Letter* is formed by the same structural divisions that beset Hawthorne's principal characters. The book reproduces the separation of spheres most palpably in the line isolating "The Custom House—Introductory" from the ensuing narrative. The preface encloses the reader in the public and male domain of the Salem customhouse, "Uncle Sam's brick edifice" (15) symbolizing government and commerce. Here Hawthorne introduces us to his fellow workers, all of them men, describes his duties as Surveyor of the Revenue, and sets forth a kind of professional primer for writers, a detailed account of the genesis and composition of his romance. This sketch abuts but does not encroach upon the family romance of Hester, Pearl, and Arthur. Affective life quarantines itself in the tale of frustrated love, with its copious notation of female domesticity and private suffering. Holding in tension the oppositions endemic to nineteenth-century capitalism, the text as an entirety organizes itself as an instantiation of middle-class experience.

A similar splitting operates on a smaller scale within the romance proper, once the opening scene of Hester's punishment on the scaffold has run its course. Thereafter, imperceptible lines of gender division radiate throughout the plot and give the tale its exemplary character as a kind of microcosm of the divergent forms of antebellum American storytelling. Chapters track Hester and/or Pearl on the one side, and Dimmesdale and/or Chillingworth on the other; mother and daughter inhabit one fictional space, the two males work and reside in another. When gender intersections occur, they do so outside society or in highly privatized settings that do not disturb the developing barrier between the familial and the public— places such as a jail cell, the scaffold at midnight, the seashore, or the forest. *The Scarlet Letter*'s spatial demarcations point to its double character as feminized domestic tale and canonical "drama of beset manhood."[12] The novel's divisions miniaturize respectable— that is, middle-class—literary culture's bifurcation into the two subgenres of sentimental fiction and the fiction of male bonding and competition.

III

Thus far we have been concerned with the parallels or homologies between Hawthorne's fictional universe and the historical details of middle-class formation. *The Scarlet Letter*, according to the argument, reinscribes the spatial and gender divisions constitutive of middle-class identity in the era of its rise. A change of focus is now in order, for it will bring to light some of the dark spots that concentration on similarity has ignored. The "dark spots" are complications and contradictions whose effect is to destabilize the particular alignments posited between textual and historical patterns. A first step toward correcting these occlusions would be to note that the gendered locus of class membership wavers in the novel and that Hester and Dimmesdale change places by donning the other sex's social characteristics.

The Scarlet Letter, for example, contains an American Adam figure who bears comparison to other Adamic heroes of nineteenth-century male sagas, heroes like Natty Bumppo, Ishmael, and Henry David Thoreau. This character, writes Hawthorne, "roamed as freely as the wild Indian in the woods" and criticizes the institutions of Puritan Boston "with hardly more reverence than the Indian would feel for the clerical band, the judicial robe, the pillory, the gallows, the fireside, or the church" (199). The character conceptualizes freedom and autonomy as qualities existing apart from the social order. For Hawthorne's Adam figure, the individual is defined not as a member of some larger unit but primarily in opposition to community; he is self-made and owes allegiance only to his own values and interests.

The character, of course, is Hester, but Hawthorne's account of her fierce independence suggests less Victorian womanhood than the Jacksonian individualist. It is appropriate to use the pronoun "he" in describing such a person because to Hawthorne's contemporaries, the solitary subject was necessarily a man. Ralph Waldo Emerson's representations stand as typical. In that most famous of treatises on the midcentury summons to autonomy, "Self-Reliance" (1841), the seeker after independence is always gendered as male. The iterated nouns and pronouns do not mask but instead proclaim the cultural exclusions. "The nonchalance of boys who are sure of a dinner, and would disdain as much as a lord to do or say aught to conciliate one, is the healthy attitude of human nature." Emerson's masculine insistences implicitly invert the clauses in his declaration, "Whoso would be a man, must be a nonconformist."[13]

In actuality, this virile nonconformist conformed to the social practices of his time. He was more entrepreneur than Transcendentalist or sourceless Adam. Karl Marx's comments in *The Grundrisse* on Robinson Crusoe, a literary avatar for the Adam myth, are illuminating not just about Hawthorne's tale but about the disjunction between the individual and civil society generally, a separation that provides so recurrent a feature of American masculine writing. Marx explains that the presence in eighteenth- and nineteenth-century literature of the isolated, apparently presocial individual—a figure he himself likens to Adam or Prometheus—entails a massive forgetting or ignorance. Entering the novel "[n]ot as a historic result but as history's point of departure," the Robinson Crusoe character reverses the actual circumstances of his appearance. He belongs to, and can only arise in, a "society of free competition" where "the individual appears detached from the natural bonds etc. which in earlier historical periods make him the accessory of a definite and limited human conglomerate."[14] Some of the bonds Marx has in mind, like clans or feudal hierarchies, never existed in America, but Hawthorne's rendering of the Puritan commonwealth reminds us that on this continent, too, the human community involved a dense network of responsibilities and connections. The autonomous individual who dominates antebellum narratives of male rivalry and maturation is a corollary to the acceleration of market capitalism in the Age of Jackson, not a reflection of humanity unencumbered by history but a product of the breakdown of republican commitment to the common welfare and its displacement over the century by laissez-faire ideology. The bearer of this historical change was Jackson's man-on-the-make, vocal opponent of customary restrictions on economic development and building block of the new middle class. But in *The Scarlet Letter*, paradoxically enough, this quintessential individualist and free-thinking pioneer in regions forbidden to women is herself a woman and otherwise the antithesis of Jacksonian man.

Hester's dissident side, as noted earlier, associates her with antebellum feminism. Recent critics have construed Hawthorne's strictures on his heroine as a repudiation of the movement for women's rights that was gathering force while he composed his romance, less than two years after the Seneca Falls Convention of 1848.[15] While this may be an accurate appraisal of Hawthorne's conscious purpose, it slights the historical volatility of his characterization of Hester. The heroine's assumption of masculine traits—which Hawthorne obviously intends as a disparagement—encodes a shadowy hint of future developments in female reformism. For a brief moment at the end of the story, Hester appears to overshoot, as it were, the domestic feminism of Hawthorne's own day and to verge on the androgynous "New Woman" of the post–Civil War period.

As Carol Smith-Rosenberg has pointed out,[16] the feminism of the late nineteenth and early twentieth centuries thrived outside conventional social arrangements. It broke with the ideology of domesticity. The "New Woman" differentiated herself from her mother's generation by rejecting marriage and opting for a career. She braved the charge of "mannishness" by choosing a life not in the traditional family but in female institutions like women's colleges and social settlements, the best-known example of which was Hull House in Chicago, and she strove to cultivate autonomy in a nondomestic environment.

Hester's denial of her (hetero)sexuality can thus be viewed not simply as a de-eroticizing but as a prefigurement of the Gilded Age woman reformer. Such a reading would be patently anachronistic, but my point is that Hawthorne's portrait of Hester as self-reliant individualist converts her, in the novel's "Conclusion," into a prophecy of supercession. She never remarries after Arthur's death and, upon returning to New England from Europe, assembles around her a community of women who console and advise each other in the face of masculine oppression. In this liminal, nonfamilial setting, Hester creates an alternative institution to patriarchal structures. Her stated message, in which she assures her followers of a "brighter period" when "the whole relation between man and woman" will be established "on a surer ground of mutual happiness" (263), is far less radical and less meaningful than her example. Hester endures as an independent being who separates herself from the prevailing social order—her cottage lies on the distant periphery of the Puritan settlement—and who finds fulfillment in the company of other females. The image of her in the book's final pages seems as much a historical postscript as a textual coda to the action.[17]

Just as Hester undergoes a series of social and sexual mutations, so Dimmesdale, exemplar of midcentury manhood, alchemizes into a communal being who looks remarkably like a sentimental novelist. The minister, according to Hawthorne, could never join Hester—or the Deerslayer, or the hermit of Walden Pond—in "the hardships of a forest life." His "culture, and his entire development" as a man of the cloth forbid it (215). Standing at "the head of the social system," Dimmesdale derives his very identity from its framework; he internalizes the community's "regulations, its principles, and even its prejudices" (200). Whereas Hester discovers her authentic self in isolation from the Puritan colony, Dimmesdale—to revert to Marx's formulation—knows himself to be "the accessory to a definite and limited human conglomerate." He is a residual presence in the commercial and industrial middle class, a product as much of the eighteenth or seventeenth century as of the Age of Jackson and Hawthorne. The minister can be seen as demonstrating the accuracy of Hawthorne's historical imagination—he is supposed to be a Puritan, after all—but more interestingly, his portrayal underscores the persistence in the text of loyalties and assumptions about individuality that clash with the ideology of liberalism. As a man, Dimmesdale is an anachronism from the past, as Hester as a woman is a potential anachronism from the future.

But Dimmesdale is not just a man; he also completes

Hawthorne's fictionalization of middle-class womanhood. From the outset, he is delineated in terms that typify nineteenth-century femininity more than conventional maleness. First beheld on the balcony during Hester's punishment, he has "large, brown, melancholy eyes," a "tremulous" mouth, and a "nervous sensibility." His diffidence ill suits public office and causes him to feel most at ease in "shadowy by-paths." Dimmesdale is said to keep himself "simple and child-like" and to retain "a freshness, and fragrance, and dewy purity of thought" that affect many people as the manner of "an angel" (66). It would appear from his description that the angel is domestic, the pure and retiring homemaker of Victorian ideology.

Besides physically resembling a woman—much as Hawthorne does in surviving daguerreotypes—Dimmesdale is identified with the female realm of the emotions. His feminine qualities tally with his (residual) immersion in the social; he and Hester swap positions dramatically in this respect. Hawthorne, speaking in his most naturalizing mode, observes that her years of isolation have stripped Hester of the capacity for affection and passion, the preservation "of which had been essential to keep her a woman" (163). But what Hester has temporarily forsaken, Dimmesdale, nominally a man, has possessed all along. The feeling evident in his voice when he addresses the Puritan populace works so powerfully on the hearts of his auditors, that the minister's words weld them "into one accord of sympathy" (67).

Dimmesdale's skill at deploying and manipulating sentiment enables him, like the popular women novelists of the 1850s, to bridge the gap between private affect and public occupation. The young preacher is conscious of the rift between the two realms, an awareness that certifies his modernity and places him apart from the Puritan patriarchs, who act as though the closet and the marketplace are synonymous. Dimmesdale's attempt to surmount the division rhetorically, through the mediation of language appealing to the emotions, inflects his nineteenth-century contemporaneousness toward the feminine and allies him, as an artist figure, with Stowe or Warner rather than Cooper or Melville. For the minister's sermons, delivered "in a tongue native to the human heart" (243), constitute a sentimental literature; they validate and make public—they publish—the inner feelings that the text denominates as female or domestic. Hawthorne tropes the heart as a chamber or residence, a space that only a woman can humanize and make inhabitable. He has Chillingworth observe to Hester, "My heart was a habitation large enough for many guests, but lonely and chill, and without a household fire" (74). Dimmesdale's "Tongue of Flame" suffuses the public world with affectivity; he feminizes culture by lighting a hearth fire in the popular heart.

Dimmesdale's volte-face, from rising male professional to domestic novelist reaching out from the private sphere to engage "the whole human brotherhood" in the language of sentiment (130), alerts us to the fact that the neat structural divisions of Hawthorne's own novel tend to lose their resolution upon closer scrutiny. Hawthorne himself is a male fiction writer redoing the seduction formula as a domestic love story of mother, daughter, and missing father. Moreover, the partition between public and private, male and female, encapsulated in the break between "The Custom-House" and the romance proper, inverts itself with a slight alteration of perspective. Hawthorne terms the preface an indiscreet surrender to the "autobiographical impulse" (3). Not only does he lay out his theory of romance, he divulges intimate details about his struggles with a writer's block. He gives an account of his personal affairs, including his resentment at being dismissed from office—the kind of washing one's laundry in public that Hawthorne well knew would create a stir. He even conducts the reader into a chamber of his home, with its "little domestic scenery" of doll, child's shoe, and hobby-horse (35). The tale that follows, on the other hand, is an impersonal commodity contrived for sale on the literary marketplace. Hawthorne, who addressed his readers as "I" in the introduction, now extinguishes the private self and assumes the mask of omniscience as a third-person narrator. The pigeonholing on which the text seemed to rest its articulation of social life under expanding capitalism proves impossible to maintain. *The Scarlet Letter*'s formal separation into preface and narrative operates to exhibit *and* to dissolve the structures of middle-class existence.

These migrations demonstrate the lability of structural parallels between text and history. They testify to the overflow or supplement that class brings to gender. Hester is a female denizen of the private sphere, but she is also an isolated individualist whose stance toward the social mimics laissez-faire doctrine rather than the cult of domesticity. Dimmesdale is an absent father and male co-worker, but he is also a domestic author. Both characters, in both their avatars, inhabit positions in the middle class—positions that did not emerge as ubiquitous until that class jelled in the Jacksonian era. Yet the two characters hold those places as occupational and ideological transvestites.

Class refuses to be permanently absorbed into gender in Hawthorne's text. For while gender style is always tethered to class, class exceeds the capacity of gender to contain it. The refusal of fixed gender roles returns upon class, as it were, to advertise a problem in Hawthorne's attitude toward middle-class identity. The midcentury middle class proscribed the very gender ambiguity he sponsors in his novel. To be a "masculine" woman was to veer toward the attributes of the working class; to be a feminized male was to ape the manner of the social aristocracy. Hawthorne's sense of occupational and gender mutability connotes a refusal to abide by the dominant class's sexual and spatial requirements. The novel's constant shifting of boundaries betrays authorial doubts about the middle-class ethos. The shifts intimate, not Hawthorne's collusion in the liberal consensus, but rather his indecision about a historical emergence that his art commemorates but simultaneously chafes at as stultifying.

IV

The ending of Hawthorne's novel precipitates a last effort to confront the compartmentalizations of market culture. The ending can be read in either of two ways, as an undoing of middle-class conventions or as their apotheosis. The final tableau on the scaffold, with Dimmesdale joining Hester and Pearl as he had failed to do at the beginning, reconstitutes the intimate nuclear family. T. Walter Herbert, in an influential article on gender in Hawthorne, calls this scene a recreation of "essential manhood and essential womanhood."[18] And there is no doubt that the last chapters contain some of the narrative's most ideologically sanitized pronouncements. A consolidating of gender stereotypes and cultural boundaries appears to signal Hawthorne's complete capitulation to middle-class ideals. He projects the fissures of his time into the afterlife. Not Hester and

Dimmesdale, he suggests, but Dimmesdale and his male rival, "the old physician," will find themselves reunited in the "spiritual world," their "antipathy transmuted into golden love" (260–61). Pearl's shedding of tears at her father's dying kiss is construed, in the best sentimental fashion, as "the pledge" that she will cease to "do battle with the world, but be a woman in it" (256). The reader learns that Hester's hope of reforming gender relations will have to wait upon an "angel" of unblemished character, "a woman indeed, but lofty, pure, and beautiful"; and capable of "showing how sacred love should make us happy, by the truest test of a life successful to such an end!" (263). Though Hester delivers this prophecy to a community of women, Hawthorne's words imply that his heroine's feminist longings are to find fulfillment in the dream of a perfect marriage.

If at moments the ending strives to naturalize the doctrine of pure womanhood, however, it never does so without equivocation. Pearl's defection to Europe, where she reenters the gentry from which her mother's family descended, hints at a persistent and unmastered distaste for the confinements of middle-class life. The same impatience hovers behind Hawthorne's disclosure, in the tale's final paragraph, that on the tombstone of his ill-starred lovers "there appeared the semblance of an engraved escutcheon" bearing a heraldic device (264)—feudal and aristocratic residues that affront middle-class closure. Moreover, Hester's insistence on reassuming the scarlet letter, on advertising her youthful sinfulness, acts as a reminder of the premodern understanding of woman's character. The letter reminds us that nineteenth-century female essentialism is a temporally bounded, post-Puritan construct, not an eternally existing ideal. Contemporaneous gender roles can be thought of as universally desirable only by repressing the historical differences that the tale itself has documented.

To put this more positively, Hawthorne seems as intent on rending the barriers of Jacksonian culture as he is on legitimating its norms. The scaffold scene, with its reuniting of the middle-class family unit, illustrates the point. The apparent essentialism of this episode is qualified, not to say undermined, by the physical setting of its occurrence. Hawthorne brings together the Victorian trinity of mother, father, and child in the very site where domestic ideology proscribes it: before the stares of the multitude in the marketplace or public stage. Understood in this way, the building of the entire narrative toward the climactic reconstruction of the family indicates a wish on Hawthorne's part, not to uphold, but to challenge nineteenth-century binary logic. The scaffold scene marks a trespassing of the industrial order's boundaries, a reversion to older patterns of behavior and an anticipation of future struggles to insert familial or domestic issues into the political sphere.

A glance at Hawthorne's own circumstances, and another look at Hester's standing in the community, may help to elucidate his oscillations. The author of *The Scarlet Letter* occupied a highly irregular class position. As he impresses upon us in "The Custom-House," he was descended from one of New England's most distinguished families. The Hathornes (spelled without the "w") were long-standing members of the Massachusetts elite and perhaps the closest thing the non-slave-holding states boasted to an aristocracy. The novelist's ancestors journeyed to the New World with the first wave of Puritan immigrants. They were prominent jurists and magistrates whose deeds—or rather, misdeeds—were recorded in histories of the country's earliest settlement. But like Poe's mythical Ushers, the line's fortunes have declined precipitously. When the future novelist was a child of three, his own father, a merchant, died at sea, and he was raised on the charity of relatives. As an author, he has not escaped dependency. He has continued to receive hand-outs to support his family; indeed, as we know from the preface, he has failed so miserably as a writer that he has had to accept employment as a government functionary. Little wonder that he imagines his forefathers dismissing him as a mere "writer of story-books! . . . Why the degenerate fellow might as well have been a fiddler!" (10).

Like his fictional minister, Hawthorne the dependent patrician seemed to have an equivocal sexual identity that inclined toward the female. Many contemporaries commented on his extraordinary good looks, Elizabeth Peabody (the sister of his wife) pronouncing him "handsomer than Lord Byron"—another aristocratic figure renowned for almost feminine beauty. Reviewers detected "a large proportion of feminine elements" in the work—to quote Henry Wadsworth Longfellow—and heaped up adjectives like quiet, passive, pure, arch, delicate, lovely, and sensitive. They called the novelist "Gentle Hawthorne" in recognition both of his genteel roots and demeanor and of his womanly tenderness. Hawthorne's celebrated reclusiveness reinforced these impressions. The description of Dimmesdale as lingering in "shadowy by-paths" can be applied to the notoriously shy and aloof creator who withdrew into his mother's home for a decade after graduating from college. And of course Hawthorne's lack of financial independence cast him in a feminized position. Like women throughout history, he had to rely on others to provide the money for his family's maintenance.[19]

Compounding the feminizing of aristocracy, Hawthorne's pauperism highlights the mutability of his location in the social order. He represents a notable instance of antebellum declassing: he is an impoverished scion of the American patriciate, an aristocrat driven to subsist on public charity. But he is also, precisely as the author of the text we are reading, on the verge of redefining his social position as a member of the rising professional class. He aspires to, and with this fiction finally attains, the economic independence that comes from appeal to the marketplace and not to a patron. He belongs to the first generation of self-supporting writers in the nation's history, the men and women of the 1850s who proved it possible to live by the pen. Hawthorne is at once a professional male, an erstwhile aristocrat, and a failed laborer at literature reeling from the loss of his government sinecure. Ideological uncertainty and ambivalence toward the new middle class seem hardly surprising in his case. He stands within the emergent social formation, but he stands above it and below it as well.

And Hester shares his categorical instability as *déclassé* aristocrat. When first forced to mount the scaffold, she thinks back to her paternal English home, "a poverty-stricken" dwelling over the portal of which hangs "a half-obliterated shield of arms, . . . in token of ancient gentility" (58). Convicted of adultery, required to wear the badge of shame, Hester's regal bearing nevertheless invests her with an aristocratic air. The servant who admits the heroine to Governor Bellingham's mansion is so struck by her manner, and by "the glittering symbol on her bosom," that he imagines she must be "a great lady in the land" (104). But in fact Hester's sexual transgression only completes her family's social collapse, arguably into the laboring class. She ekes out a subsistence for herself and Pearl with her needlework, a Puritan forerunner of the nineteenth century's favorite emblem of downtrodden womanhood, the seamstress.

Seen from a different angle, Hester evokes the middle class in the making, but, like her creator, she stands outside as well as within the nascent configuration. Her ties to the working class are particularly significant in this regard. For the Jacksonian working class was both residual and sexually problematic in its behavior; its female members were mannish and unfeminine, as well as old-fashioned, by bourgeois standards. They departed the family for workshops or toiled in the home for wages at the very moment when the middle-class dwelling was becoming equated with leisure and with exemption from the rapacity of the marketplace. Female laborers approximated women of the past or men of the present more than the wives of antebellum lawyers, retailers, and manufacturers. Hester's erasure of her femininity and adoption of free-market attitudes may thus stem as much from the ambiguities of her class status as from the sliding of her gender position and historical specificity.

But these ambiguities do not negate the evidence linking Hester and Arthur to middle-class formation. As much as the overt allegiances, the instabilities in their respective characterizations announce the entrance into American literature of a new historical phenomenon. For the slippages are not unique but were in actuality common to the antebellum middle class. It is hardly a coincidence that the novel's version of that class materializes as a consequence of sin. To Hawthorne, middle-class emergence is a fraught difficulty, not a matter for congratulation. His two principal actors reflect his own, and presumably many other people's, incomplete incorporation into, and continuing uneasiness with, the social revolution of his time. Hawthorne's lovers proclaim the circumstance that at a time of profound sociological dislocation, Americans who were acquiring middle-class values and lifestyle were by no means unanimous about the process. Some retained older loyalties and patterns of behavior that could generate internal disaffection; others developed commitments that could lead to open resistance. Hester and Arthur's permutations bespeak the still fluid nature of an ideological ascendancy that hardened into dominance only after the Civil War—and did so, moreover, in relation to an increasingly restive and militant working class.

Gender and race have been rightly reinstated at the center of American literary history. We have learned, thanks to the insights of feminists and African-Americanists, to revise our thinking about the supposedly essential qualities that determine those two rubrics. It is now accepted that gender and race are social constructions with indeterminate boundaries that fluctuate over time and are shaped by historical circumstances rather than by anything innate. In the case of class, the situation in the United States has traditionally been the reverse. Americans have long taken for granted the proposition that there was no such thing as class in the country's past; unlike gender and race, it simply didn't exist. If this reading of *The Scarlet Letter* accomplishes nothing else, it is meant to suggest that here, too, change is necessary. Class, no less a social construction than gender and race, has been just as fluid and difficult to ascertain exactly. But its existence has been just as real, and it is time that we admitted its importance in the making of our cultural inheritance.

NOTES

1. I refer here specifically to the formulation of David Leverenz. See his book, *Manhood and the American Renaissance* (Ithaca: Cornell University Press, 1989). The elision of class, usually in favor of gender or race, is so pervasive in criticism on antebellum literature that to illustrate the practice, one could simply call the role of leading Americanists: Jane Tompkins, Philip Fisher, Lawrence Buell, etc. Some "second generation" New Historicists have argued for greater attention to class, although their own writing tends to marginalize it. See, for instance, Gillian Brown, *Domestic Individualism: Imagining Self in Nineteenth-Century America* (Berkeley and Los Angeles: University of California Press, 1990). A recent article that attempts to recuperate class more centrally in relation to several Hawthorne short stories is Nicholas K. Bromell, "'The Bloody Hand' of Labor: Work, Class, and Gender in Three Stories by Hawthorne," *American Quarterly* 42 (1990):542–64.

2. Of the many writers who could be mentioned here, I would single out Stuart Blumin, *The Emergence of the Middle Class: Social Experience in the American City, 1760–1900* (New York: Cambridge University Press, 1989); Bruce Laurie, *Artisans into Workers: Labor in Nineteenth-Century America* (New York: Noonday Press, 1989); Mary P. Ryan, *The Cradle of the Middle Class: The Family in Oneida County, New York, 1790–1865* (New York: Cambridge University Press, 1981); and Eli Zaretsky, *Capitalism, The Family, and Personal Life*, rev. ed. (New York: Harper and Row, 1986). On the English side, see Leonore Davidoff and Catherine Hall, *Family Fortunes: Men and Women of the English Middle Class 1750–1850* (Chicago: University of Chicago Press, 1987).

3. Bercovitch has developed his position in essays published over a number of years and drawn together in *The Office of "The Scarlet Letter"* (Baltimore: Johns Hopkins University Press, 1991). A somewhat similar interpretation of Hawthorne's novel as a document of ideological compromise has been advanced by Jonathan Arac in "The Politics of *The Scarlet Letter*," which appears in Bercovitch and Myra Jehlen, eds., *Ideology and Classic American Literature* (New York: Cambridge University Press, 1986), 247–66.

4. This form of argumentation has become identified with the New Historicism and is illustrated, in criticism on Hawthorne, by Walter Benn Michaels's essay "Romance and Real Estate," reprinted in his *The Gold Standard and the Logic of Naturalism: American Literature at the Turn of the Century* (Berkeley and Los Angeles: University of California Press, 1987), 85–112. On the totalizing character of Michaels's book, see Brook Thomas, *The New Historicism and Other Old-Fashioned Topics* (Princeton: Princeton University Press, 1991), 117–50.

5. See Williams, *Marxism and Literature* (Oxford: Oxford University Press, 1977), esp. 108–27.

6. *The Scarlet Letter*, volume 1 of *The Centenary Edition of the Works of Nathaniel Hawthorne* (Columbus: Ohio State University Press, 1962–), 84. Subsequent page numbers given in the text refer to this edition.

7. See Barthes, *Mythologies*, trans. Annette Lavers (New York: Hill and Wang, 1972), 138.

8. I refer to Ryan's *Cradle of the Middle Class* and to Nancy Armstrong, *Desire and Domestic Fiction: A Political History of the Novel* (New York: Oxford University Press, 1987).

9. See Cott's essay, "Passionlessness: An Interpretation of Victorian Sexual Ideology, 1790–1850," in Nancy Cott and Elizabeth H. Pleck, eds., *A Heritage of Her Own* (New York: Simon and Schuster, 1979), 162–81.

10. I should perhaps qualify this statement by noting the conspicuous seventeenth-century exception (that proves the nineteenth-century rule?) of Anne Hutchinson. On the continuities between Hutchinson and Hester, see Amy Lang, *Prophetic Woman: Anne Hutchinson and the Problem of Dissent in the Literature of New England* (Berkeley and Los Angeles: University of California Press, 1987).

11. Nathaniel Hawthorne to Elizabeth C. Hawthorne, letter of March 13, 1821, in *The Letters, 1813–1843*, volume 15 of *The Centenary Edition*, 139; see the reviews collected in J. Donald Crowley, ed., *Hawthorne: The Critical Heritage* (New York: Barnes and Noble, 1970). Quotations are from 78, 193.

12. I am paraphrasing the title of Nina Baym's article, "Melodramas of Beset Manhood: How Theories of American Fiction Exclude Women Authors," *American Quarterly* 33 (1981):123–39. *The Scarlet Letter* is fairly unique among the classics of the American Renaissance in encompassing both male and female domains.

13. The quotations are from *Essays: First Series*, volume 2 of *The Collected Works of Ralph Waldo Emerson* (Cambridge, Mass.: Harvard University Press, 1971–), 29.

14. References are to the selection from *The Grundrisse* reprinted in Robert C. Tucker, ed., *The Marx-Engels Reader*, 2d ed. (New York: W. W. Norton, 1978), 222.

15. See Bercovitch, *The Office of "The Scarlet Letter"*, 106.

16. See particularly the essay "The New Woman as Androgyne: Social Disorder and

238 MICHAEL T. GILMORE

the Gender Crisis, 1870–1936," in her *Disorderly Conduct: Visions of Gender in Victorian America* (New York: Oxford University Press, 1985), 245–96.

17. This is not to suggest that the argument for a nondomestic feminism wasn't made in Hawthorne's day; Margaret Fuller's *Woman in the Nineteenth Century* (1845) is a case in point. But as a widespread cultural movement, the phenomenon belongs to the latter third of the century.

18. Herbert, "Nathaniel Hawthorne, Una Hawthorne, and *The Scarlet Letter*: Interactive Selfhoods and the Cultural Construction of Gender," *Proceedings of the Modern Language Association* 103 (1988):285–97; quotation from 289.

19. Peabody is quoted in James R. Mellow, *Nathaniel Hawthorne in His Times* (Boston: Houghton Mifflin, 1980), 6; the Longfellow review appears in Crowley, ed., *Hawthorne: The Critical Heritage*, 80–83 (quotation from 81). Although I invert his emphases, I wish to acknowledge here the work of David Leverenz on types of antebellum masculinity. See *Manhood and the American Renaissance*.

7 CLASS AND LITERATURE

THE CASE OF
ROMANTIC CHARTISM

Anne Janowitz

I want to introduce a discussion of the poetic the-
ory and some of the poetic practice of Chartist orators and laborer-
poets by making some sense of our contemporary literary criticism's
curious version of the analytical category of class. As Michael
Gilmore points out, within the triad of race, class, and gender that
has been fueling some very interesting recent critical explorations,
class appears to be given the shortest shrift.[1] And it is, I believe,
equally true that often the category *is* analytically invoked primarily
for the sake of describing the triumphant universalizing of the bourgeois ideology.[2] This tendency is accompanied by a virtually tauto-
logical version of such universalizing, as if the success of the bourgeoisie was not the outcome of struggles but the unfolding of a
process whose purpose had been all along to make the lamentable
bourgeois subject slave to its own apparently parentless domination.

This quite recent way of using the category of class within contemporary literary discussion arises from, on the one hand, a structuralist rather than a dynamic model of social shaping and, on the
other hand, from an insufficiently considered sense of the central

difference between class as a category and those of race and gender. These two issues, moreover, are themselves interconnected, for recent discussions of gender and race have been aided by structural-ist framing, while discussion of class has, to my mind, been disem-powered by it.

The criticism of essentialist thought, which is crucial to structur-al understandings of social formations, has allowed us to interpret the meanings of gender and race as socially constructed and not inarguably deriving their meanings from biological features. But class is meaningful only *as* a social category, and so to approach it as analogous with the anti-essentialist, structuralist-derived projects of race and gender studies amounts to an analytical confusion.

Class is most illuminating as an analytical category when it is con-ceived of as *dynamic*. The usefulness of class analysis is not primari-ly in taxonomizing its internal constituents but watching its move-ment, particularly the dynamic of the relations between classes. When literary critics make class, race, and gender all interchangeable tokens along an axis of substitution, the subsequent pathologies of capitalism become racism, sexism, and classism. Understood as a set of subjectively experienced *attitudes* (socially constructed though they be), racism, sexism, and classism then appear to be contestable through struggles of representation, ideology, even "structures of feeling."[3]

But the spuriousness of the relatively informal category of "clas-sism" reveals itself immediately, since the analytical scope of class is not that of demystifying the social construction of apparently "nat-ural" or ineluctable features, nor a matter of curing pathological atti-tudes. Rather, the problem is that bourgeois ideology, insofar as it successfully universalizes itself, has an interest in denying the cate-gory of class altogether. It is, on the other hand, the study of the dynamic amongst classes that yields up to view the reality of class society and renders it potentially responsive to *revisions* of that dynamic. It is the study of this dynamic that allows the evidence to surface of the incomplete or contradictory character of the bourgeois project.

In our immediate context, there is a dangerous possibility that the "end of history" narrative, which poses the end of Stalinism as the end of an alternative vision to capitalism, will collaborate with the discussion of bourgeois ideology as inexorable. Many critics and intellectuals who had consistently opposed to Stalinism the possibility of socialism have given way to the pressures of "end-of-history-ism," and have abandoned the idea of a nonrecuperable opposition.

The discussion that follows depends upon a dynamic model of class. Such a dynamic is crucial for the study of two themes of great interest to Romantic studies: tradition and nationhood. Moreover, it allows us to see that literary forms that we now tautologically identify with bourgeois, universalized ideology, are themselves the outcome of conflicts, most properly called conflicts of *intervention* rather than of *representation*. We disable ourselves aesthetically when we describe lyric forms as bourgeois ones, or as exhaustively determined ones. These forms, and the concepts of the aesthetic associated with them, need to be conceived of and read as factors within a struggle whose outcome was determined, not only by the forces of ideology, but by the dynamic and experience of historical class agents, attempting to universalize their class-specific interests.

Chartism—the first self-organized working class movement in Britain—is the politico-social movement that is most often invoked to describe the dynamic of class relations in the nineteenth century in Britain. In terms of literary studies, the most significant recent attempt to describe and analyze the language of Chartism was made by Gareth Stedman Jones in the early 1980s, in his powerful discussion, "Rethinking Chartism."[4] As an innovative labor historian, Stedman Jones was concerned with the application of *literary* and *linguistic* analytical techniques to Chartist political rhetoric. The following discussion of poetry engages with a rather different aspect of Chartist production: I am investigating the politics of literary rhetoric. It is, however, appropriate here to make a few remarks about the controversy that Stedman Jones's argument provoked. The central contention in "Rethinking Chartism" is that it was the antiquated rhetoric of the Radical-Reform movement, from Wilkes through the Reform Bill of 1832, that lay at the heart of the defeat of the Chartist movement as a force: this anachronistic rhetoric both expressed and constructed the demands of the movement.[5] Linked to this contention, and to Stedman Jones' own political project, is the criticism of subsequent Marxists who have, he argues, read the infant voice of class consciousness and class struggle backward from the character of the more coherent working class of later in the century.[6]

Stedman Jones grounded his debunking work in the premise that there was *one* consistent rhetoric to this political and social movement; namely, the rhetoric of its orators and leaders. But insofar as the languages of class are constitutive of class agents, we can look at the variety of levels of languages and their contradictions: how they are transformed and appropriated by the variety of speakers within the movement, and by the variety of rhetorical forms available. To be fair, Stedman Jones does add a note that says that he is not exhausting the languages of the movement in his analysis, but he implies that the pivot of the movement was its national language, the language that he discusses in his essay. "I am not arguing that this is the only language Chartism employed. What is examined here is only the public political language of the movement."[7]

But even in national formulations, the language of Chartism was comprised of different voices and layers. One of the idiolects of the national language of Chartism—its lyric-poetical language—was, like its political discourse, linked to the forms of an earlier moment. But if we examine Chartist poetic rhetoric in terms of what Raymond Williams would call a "residual structure" available to a counterhegemonic group, these apparently hegemonic poetic structures reveal themselves to be quite pointedly and successfully appropriated by the movement as a tool of poetico-political intervention, seriously modulated by claims proper to the agents using these forms.[8] In her important critique of Gareth Stedman Jones's analysis of Chartism, Ellen Meiksins Wood gives an accounting similar to this on the larger scale of Chartism as a whole. In pointing out how the Radical political cast to public Chartist rhetoric coexisted with the economic underpinnings of a social movement, Meiksins Woods writes, "In a sense, the weakness of Chartism, with it anachronistic political focus, has also been it strength; and while it is certainly true that the realities of capitalism demanded struggle 'on the economic plane,' it is also true that the labor movement lost a great deal when the focus of its struggles shifted to the 'economic' sphere."[9] Meiksins Woods goes on to point out that Stedman Jones's version of Chartism is tied to a program for the contemporary Labour Party in

Britain—namely, "socialist politics must be constructed out of an alliance between right-minded people and a working class that abandons its divisive class-consciousness and learns from its betters."[10]

Gareth Stedman Jones's work on Chartism, then, is of interest to literary history and theory not only because of its significance as an attempt to look at the problem of language in a political-social context, but also because it provides a good example of the affinities between a critic's analysis of the rhetoric of the past and his or her conception of a political practice in the present. Stedman Jones's discussion in the early 1980s sits comfortably with more recent literary analyses that, also having eschewed class analysis as an explanatory motor of ideological formations, articulate the problem of class as another extrusion of ideology, structurally akin to the problems of racism and sexism.

One of the effects of the study of pathologies of capitalism, on the one hand, and the social construction of subjectivity, on the other, has been, within American literary history, to dismissively conflate the beautiful with the ideological, thereby handing over the aesthetic to the right wing. In order to recover the possibility of a progressive aesthetic beauty, we need an informed return to a model that analyzes literary language within a contentious dynamic of agents. The success of such a model depends as well on a return to a view of social movements that goes beyond a focus on localism, a focus that has been closely linked to the new social movements. In our contemporary scene, the most influential version of this position, and one deeply in debt to literary history, is the discussion by Ernesto Laclau and Chantal Mouffe in *Hegemony and Socialist Strategy*, where they make the case for "the autonomization of the spheres of struggle and the multiplication of political spaces."[11] Interestingly, Stedman Jones initiated his own polemic against the localism of Chartism studies in the 1970s: "Too much attention to local or occupational peculiarities can obscure the extent to which Chartism was a national movement. Yet this more surprising phenomenon— the extent of unity in the early Chartist movement and the enduring loyalty of a sizable minority over more than a decade to the remedies of the Charter, despite all disagreement and difference—has been left in the realm of commonsense assumption."[12] In this essay, I am similarly concerned with the national character of the movement, and the extent to which the very category of "nation" was itself inflected by the dialectic between competing Chartist and middle-class conceptions of what the nation might be.

The proper name of the dynamic within literature that I wish to investigate is the familiar one of *Romanticism*: its constituent conceptual elements are the forces of individualism and communitarianism. That is, I propose that Romanticism ought no longer to be considered as solely 1) a set of literary functions or 2) a set of ideological mystifications (the Althusserian-derived method), but rather as the literary form of a contest taking place on many levels of society between individualist and communitarian versions of identity formation (individual and collective). The point is to open up the category of the Romantic from being an object of study to a dynamic of forces liable to investigation. This will enable us as well to recover from the terrain of Burkean reaction the progressive and utopian aspects of tradition and community.

What is extraordinary about the life of poetic forms within Chartism is the extent to which they participated in the building of the politico-social aims of movement as a whole. This poetic material, which has been largely unstudied by either literary critics or social historians raises interesting questions about nationalism and poetry, as well as illuminating issues within the history of Romanticism, which itself provides the larger literary category through which this dialectic can be understood. For literary historians, Chartist poetry offers a surprising stage on which to watch the fortunes of Romanticism, and to consider a way of reinterpreting primary Romantic poetic texts. While important social historians such as Eileen Yeo have studied the popular cultural institutions of Chartism—clubs, reading groups, recreational activities, etc.—they have ignored Chartist poetry, I think, because it appears to be too emulative of middle-class culture.[13] This is, as we will see, a mistaken valuation of the potential purposes of lyric forms.

To measure from the outset the dynamic of class as productive of competing conceptions of the Chartist movement, we can begin with the literary evidence we have of the Chartist movement from the representation of Chartists painted by Carlyle, Mrs. Gaskell, or Disraeli, in the period after the defeat of the movement. To read these authors, even in their more sympathetic displays, one would think that Chartists were unkempt, ignorant animals. Since literary scholars and critics are more likely to have read Carlyle's essay on Chartism than Chartist texts themselves, they may themselves be influenced by his description of Chartists as "wild inarticulate souls" whose voices are an "inarticulate uproar." The persistent nineteenth-century literary depiction of Chartism as a movement of the subliterate, almost subhuman, is, however, a good index of the dialectic of anxiety provoked in the British middle class by this autonomous working-class movement.

And the middle-class version of the Chartists as brutes is a particularly *telling* misrepresentation of the movement, since Chartism placed literature and literary practice near the heart of its political agenda. When we look at the actual literary culture that was produced *within* the Chartist movement, we are offered a glimpse into a culture that continually asserted the importance of literature, and poetry in particular, to political intervention and to the making of a collective identity based on the universalizing of the working class.

The poetry column in the central Chartist newspaper, Feargus O'Connor's *Northern Star*, offers an immense array of poetic forms. Running from the late 1830s until 1850, the paper ran a weekly poetry column throughout its life. In 1839 weekly circulation ran as high as 36,000 copies paid per week, and given an illiteracy rate of about one-third of the working class, the estimate is that each copy served between fifty and eighty readers/listeners in radical coffee houses, working-class taverns and reading rooms, and working people's clubs.[14] Poetic texts ranged from lyrics based on popular ballad measure ("The Slaves Address to British Females," "The Factory Girl's Last Hour") to great stretches of dramatic iambic pentameter ("Prologue to a new Drama, spoken by a Druid, on John Frost and the Insurrection at Newport"), as well as poems that belonged to a more meditative mode ("A Fragment for the Laborer" "Sonnets Devoted to Chartism" and many others). Throughout Britain, Chartist political leaders used poems as political interventions, not just to represent political situations. William Sankey, a spokesperson for Scottish operatives, built upon Shelley's "Men of England" stanzas in a public address recorded in the *Northern Star*, revising them to make the lines even more topical. As Stedman Jones recognizes, crucial to the political power of Chartism was its centralizing social function, and one national use of Chartist poetry may be exemplified by a set of "poetical enigmas" printed in the *Northern Star*, in which rank-and-file Chartists exchanged political riddles and replies. Henry Dunn from South Molton in Devon wrote a riddle poem printed by the *Northern Star* (in Leeds) in the first week of July 1840. On July 13 the *Northern Star* printed a reply, written by a Chartist from Newcastle with the answer, "Justice": "Chartists, unite to haste the happy hour / When Justice shall again resume her power— / Unite, unite in one vast patriot band / To gain our Charter and to free our land." The poem is here a vehicle for communicating and linking together Chartists from north and south. Some poets even produced texts with collective authors, such as a "Song for the People" by "Two Ultra-Radical Ladies."[15]

Given how easily we accept the marginality of poetry to our contemporary Anglo-American political world, what is striking and exciting about Chartist culture is not only the huge number of poems printed in Chartist publications, but also the importance assigned to poetry as an instrument of social change. An 1839 article in the *Chartist Circular* warns: "Statesmen would do well to feel the throb thus swelling [from poetry] from the pent-up breast of society. Like the feather [poetry] tells which way the wind blows. It points the dial-hand of time with unerring certainty to a coming period, when a deep and sweeping change must take place in all our institutions."[16]

What is of interest to literary historians attempting to trace the class dynamic within poetic forms is that activist Chartist poets and poetical theorists were *particularly* interested in, even preoccupied with, their inheritance from Romantic poetry. While there has been a significant amount of recent work done on the contribution of Romantic poetry to the formation of hegemonic ideology in Britain, there has been a falling off of discussion of how Romantic poetry cooperated with the progressive struggles of the period, a tradition we can associate with E. P. Thompson and the British writers and critics who rethought Romanticism in the 1960s.[17] This falling off has resulted from the double pressure of the work of ideology criticism and of the criticism inspired by the new social movements themselves. For instance, the work of Jerome McGann and Marjorie

Levinson on the ideology of romanticism has been heavily influenced by Althusser's theory, while the recent work of Louis Crompton, Donna Landry, and others has been influenced by the practices of gay and feminist politics.[18] And there is an intelligible dialectic between ideology theory and identity politics. After the ideology critic has analyzed the apparently ineluctable determinations through which literary subjects are formed, and cultural institutions created, for regulative ends, she may have just enough strength left to listen for and then begin to hear the voices of those who refused to obey the cultural hegemony, and so hear in those voices the more authentic or liberating sound of the period in question. At the same time, the critic who has been influenced by the claims and possibilities that come from the new social movements has a particular interest in analyzing the ways in which those claims are retarded or appropriated by the culture at large. This dialectic is what makes the term *agency* so charged and self-divided for us at the moment, as we investigate whose agents we are. A corollary movement has been the dialectic between ideology theory and the more agency-oriented theory of cultural materialism, as theorized particularly by Raymond Williams in *Marxism and Literature*, which itself responded to Terry Eagleton's mid-1970s Althusserian formulations. For some scholars, a return to a Williams who had himself traveled far since the days of *Culture and Society*, has offered a way out of the radical skepticism that awaits the post-Althusserian.

The larger part of this work in Romantic studies belongs to critical discussion of poetic representation. And one of the more important strands of work on poetic representation has been the enunciation, description, and critique of what we broadly call "aesthetic ideology." Within the history of poetic structure, the lyric mode, and its shift into the central position in poetic hierarchy has been variously linked to the explicit separating out of poetical and political intentions at the end of the eighteenth and the beginning of the nineteenth centuries, and has been characterized as the cultural vehicle of the Romantic ideology as a *fact* of bourgeois ideology. Yet if this aesthetic, "Tintern Abbey" ideology marks a moment when politics and poetry appear to be separating out their explicit spheres of influence, Chartist poetry refuses such a separation and asserts itself *as* action, while explicitly claiming and analytically revealing an equally Romantic inheritance. Thus, an anonymous poem tells us that "The Voice of the People" "rushes on, like the torrent's loud roar; / And it bears on its surges the wrongs of the poor. / It's shock, like the earthquake shall fill with dismay, / The hearts of the tyrants and sweep them away."[19]

In refusing the separation between the aesthetic and the political, however, Chartist poetry does not abandon the Romantic poetry of meditation, even when it eschews the notion of a solitary consciousness. In fact, Chartist poetry exhibits a double commitment to both lyric forms and to political intervention, offering a utopian counterstatement to the notion of lyric as the terrain of landscaped solitude and secular transcendence through the extension of the unencumbered self, and whose conventional representations are modeled on the Romantic poets.

The obviously Romantic cast to much Chartist poetry reminds us, however, that quite as much as an official Romanticism was invented and incorporated into British nationalist and imperialist culture, so did Chartist poets and poetry theorists theorize an *unof-ficial* Romanticism to ground a counterculture that was not yet a marginal culture. Against the example of Palgrave's 1861 anthology, *The Golden Treasury*, which was designed to conveniently export poetic superiority "wherever the dominant language of the world is spoken" and which labels its most recent age "The Age of Wordsworth," we can set that of the Chartist John Watkins, author of two poems commemorating the Chartist Newport Uprising of 1839, who writes a sonnet exhorting, "Chartists! What strive ye for? For liberty! / 'Twas liberty inspir'd the British Bard / Who surnam'd our Britannia—"The Free!" / Byron, chiefest of poets! yes, 'Twas he."[20]

The Romantic character of this quotation may begin to suggest the ways in which an attention to Chartist literature may in turn inflect a reading of more familiar Romantic texts and unsettle an Althusserian-based idea of a seamless Romantic ideology, for the subject of the relationship between Romanticism and Chartism intersects with the subject of middle-class and Chartist conceptions of literary culture right at the spot where British Romanticism is itself self-divided. That is, Romantic poetry offers at times a poetic of transcendence, lyric solitude, and private meditation—

performing the ideology of aesthetic autonomy; while, at other times, Romantic texts polemically invite political activism and poetic militancy.

Some Romantic poems stumble back into the picturesque landscape from the urban and industrial fray, and from the increasingly hectic pressure of other consciousness. These poems, like "Tintern Abbey," provide aesthetic spas. Others, however (you need think only of "The Mask of Anarchy"), call on individuals to bind themselves into active communities, and to take up collective, or communitarian, resistance, not only to "mind-forged manacles," but also to the State and its military excrescences.

There is a double intention then, within Romantic poetics, which can be discriminated as its individualist and its communitarian perspectives on identity formation. That is, we can link the poetry of solitude and meditation to individualism—that conception of the individual as an "unencumbered" self formed before, and voluntarily engaging *in* social groups—and link the poetry of intervention and political activism to communitarianism, which describes identity as built through and in relation to social goals and aims. This notion of a communitarian self is one in which, as the philosopher Alasdair MacIntyre puts it, "The story of my life is always embedded in the story of those communities from which I derive my identity."[21] An obvious example of the distinction with respect to Romantic poems might be Wordsworth's two versions of "Animal Tranquillity and Decay": the first version, which describes the old man's trek to the military hospital to see his dying son, suggesting quite explicitly the social determination of the old man's consciousness, while the second truncated version gives an *extreme* example of an unencumbered, virtually asocial self.

What is of interest then within Chartist poetry is that kind of lyric that can be characterized by its presentation of a voice that is neither marginally solitary (as in modernist avant-garde forms of oppositional art) *nor* representatively solitary (the Wordsworthian model in the 1805 *Prelude*). Rather, this voice is intended to embody a manifold rather than a singular poetic voice and a manifold of social determination. As Samuel Laycock, a late Victorian socialist poet, analogized, perhaps sentimentally, in a poem part of and adverting to the collective work of a Northern poets' club, "The pipes of an organ all vary in tone; / Their sound must be several, their music is one."[22]

Because the struggle was decided in favor of bourgeois capitalism and the accompanying ideology of individualism, we have lost the full power of the communitarian poetic tradition. Its origins are found, of course, in the oral traditions of folk culture, in ballads and broadsheets, and in the radicalism that oppositionally attends the growth and the crisis of the absolutist monarchy into the seventeenth century. It flourishes, in contest with individualism, in the great crisis of the mid-eighteenth through mid-nineteenth centuries, as the poetics of Romanticism. After 1848, the tradition narrows considerably. The communitarian elements of Romanticism are washed away through the critical pronouncements of Arnold and the anthologizing of Palgrave, among others. It turns up again most interestingly in the Socialist movement at the end of the nineteenth century, again in the Anglo-Communist poetry of the 1930s, and then amongst the new social movements of the second half of the twentieth century in Britain and the United States: the Black Arts movement, feminism, Chicano poetics, and also in the poetry written by the Women Against Pit Closures in the 1984–85 British miners' strike.

That the communitarian voice of Chartist poetry can be as deeply Romantic as it is a claim I make despite those made by Soviet literary critics in the middle 1950s that Chartist poetics represented an early flowering of socialist realism. V. Y. Kovalev's 1956 strict social realist norms were only slightly modified by Phyllis Ashraf in her vast 1978 work on English working-class literature, by her methodological steeping in New Critical terms to produce what she calls "aesthetic realism."[23]

My sense (after the sometimes numbing experience of reading hundreds of Chartist poems in the *Northern Star*) is that Chartist poetry at times foregrounds individualist and at times communitarian poetic ends, but that by the end of the 1840s, individualism came to dominate the Chartist aesthetic. That domination accompanied the demise of Chartism itself as a political force—individualist ideology finally transformed the collective and visionary notion of a revolutionary people's culture into the ameliorist models of reformism and laborism. At the same time, and this is one example of how Chartist literature carries residual cultural meanings from *before* the emergence of a homogeneous working class, visionary communitarianism, with its imagined community of working-class national identity, often drew upon anachronistic utopian models, those visions of community that had been central to radicalism in the seventeenth century and that persisted in circles of artisans. We hear this, of course, also in the peculiar lexicon of Blake's poetry. Chartism's own mix of artisans and industrial workers, who then engaged with textile outworkers and refugees from middle-class radicalism—all this was the uneven ground on which images of community were built that referred back to agrarian utopias (the Chartist land scheme being one disastrous example) and forward to a revolutionary working-class movement. And a central aspect of this mix of residual cultural materials was the familiar and Romantic poetic elaboration of the landscape as the site of personal meditation, which became for Chartist poets the site of a potentially transformed collective identity.

The rhetorical scaffolding within which the Chartist poetic intervention was built was the notion of a repressed "people's" national literary heritage, which Chartist poets and poetic theorists both *excavated* and *invented*. For Chartist poetry is centrally a contestation of the received shape of literary tradition, within the larger context of the class struggle over the questions, "Whose nation? What people?" in which the issue of the nation was often congruent with, because figured as, the landscape. That class struggle over the proprietorship of the nation was clear to William Benbow, who first called for a general strike as soon as the betrayal of the 1832 Reform Bill had become apparent, and who speaks on behalf of the working class: the middle class and aristocracy are, he writes, "the *jugglers* of society, the pick-*pockets* of society, the *plunderers*, the pitiless *Burkers*." The working classes, on the other hand, "do everything and enjoy nothing. The people are nothing for themselves and everything for the few. When they will fight for *themselves* then they will be the people."[24] On the other hand, Henry Brougham, Whig reformer and founder of the Society for the Diffusion of Useful Knowledge, is equally confident: "By the people, I mean the middleclasses, the wealth and intelligence of the country, the glory of the British name."[25] In other words, in the period of the late 1830s and early 1840s, the definition of the nation was up for grabs, just as the two classes making their competitive claims for that "imagined community" were in the process of dynamically defining themselves, of dialectically discovering and developing their class consciousness.[26]

In *Literature and Revolution*, Trotsky argues that there can be no proletarian culture within bourgeois society.[27] But in an important sense, there was *not* in the late 1830s a confident national bourgeois culture in the sense that there would be by the middle of the century, and Chartist poetry quite interestingly exhibits the strains of a struggle to literarily define itself in a context in which the working class also was just coming into being as a coherent force. Chartist poetry and literary culture took on the task of wresting away the middle class's own *new* claim to universality and to nationality, by providing its own alternate, though equally purposive genealogy. For the Chartist movement, the building of the working-class movement and the naming of a national culture were identified. And, importantly, popular sovereignty would define the nation and the nation would be born, not from Painite and rationalist first principles but out of and in relation to an inherited tradition, a tradition linked to the land. The nationalism of Chartism awkwardly but affectively intertwined the nationalism that we associate with the French revolutionary-democratic movement that invented the nation-state in its modern form, and the earlier radical patriotism of community.[28] And this intertwining of older with contemporary ideas of the nation is itself linked both to the importance of the landscape as the site of community *and* to the jostling of human elements within Chartism itself: a movement made up of artisans, with their local traditions and customary practices, radical reformers, and new industrial workers, naming themselves as something new—the working class—but just as eager to give themselves a historical ground. Chartist poets and literary theorists tried to define working-class identity by yoking it to a national poetic tradition in which, they asserted, the history of the laboring poor had always been woven into poetic purpose. In aid of that intention, the *Chartist Circular* ran a year-long series of articles in 1839 on "Politics of Poets." Of course as Chartist poetry claims a past as well as a future, it finds that past only partially, fitfully, and with a necessary reliance upon the texts and poets from the culture from which it was seeking to distinguish itself, insisting that Shakespeare, Milton, and Marvell were the ancestors of the contemporary Chartist poetic aesthetic. So, for example, the *Northern Star* ran a series in the spring of 1840 of what it called "Chartism from Shakespeare," culling passages from the plays with which to exemplify Chartist principles and issues. One such column is titled "Frost and Physical Force," referring to John Frost, the leader of the Newport Uprising of 1839, and to the debate within the Chartist movement on "physical" versus "moral" force. The title "Frost and Physical Force" heads a set of quotations from *Henry the Fourth Part II.*[29] That the dramatic sequence that culminates in the presentation of Henry V as the embodiment of absolutist coherence should be appropriated by the politically just-awakening working class to describe their own will to national power is a good measure of the contestability and inextricability of both national and poetic claims in the early nineteenth century.

Once we invite our attention to settle on the place of poetry and its importance to the definition of the nation it becomes clear that Kitson-Clark was wrong when he defined the Romantic element in the literature of 1830–1850 to insist that what he called "Romantic nationalism" was irrelevant to Chartism; he was, I think, as wrong as Engels was when he asserted that "all feelings of patriotism have been crushed in the heart of the worker."[30] The internationalism Engels desired was in actuality cohabiting within Chartism with a domestic nationalism—though the Britain to which the Chartist felt patriotic duty was less Peel's than Blake's sleeping Albion and Shelley's "Own indignant Earth / Which gave the sons of England birth." The importance of traditions of the past for the formation of progressive collective identity ought not to be underestimated. From the revolutionary agrarians of the nineteenth century through the Red/Green networks of today, these claims must be rescued from the Burkean as well as distinguished from the Painite traditions.

And Chartists did often cite as their closest forbears the previous generation's apparent martyrs to liberty, Shelley and Byron. It is certain that Chartist poets felt a complex sense of debt to Byron and Shelley, who they continually quoted and alluded to in the pages of their periodicals. As a radical aristocrat, whose effectively marginal class position made him liable to produce a critique of the politics and culture of the bourgeoisie, Byron's poetic prestige was as high as

Shelley's within the movement, and his influence is felt chiefly in the satirical verse of the *Northern Star*. Byron the individual is presented as an icon of the conjuncture of national and poetic aspiration: "The poet and the patriot met in Byron," one article declares, and another tells us that as he "had mixed extensively among mankind" he was able to trace "through its ramified complications the development of the democratic principle."[31]

We hear something very close in imagery and intention to Blakean Romanticism in an anonymous poem in *Notes to the People*, a late Chartist paper that compares the poisonous Javanese upas tree to the poison tree at home in England:

> Fixed firmly in the British soil,
> Though old, yet undecayed,
> Its baneful vapours stunt the growth
> Of life within its shade.
>
> Oh Heaven! may yet thy lightnings strike
> And cleave it to its root:
> While Man shall rear fair Freedom's tree,
> And all partake its fruit.[32]

In this poem, we hear an echo of Blake's poetic analysis of the Tree of Mystery as a deformed version of the Liberty Tree. We might notice also some poets who were thought of as ones who ought to be dumped from the national canon.

Wordsworth was the object of some debate. One critic in 1839 produces an apologia for Wordsworth's poetry that corroborates one strain of the Radical rhetoric that Stedman Jones analyzes in "Rethinking Chartism": "Look at his poems altogether" and they are Radical—deeply essentially, entirely Radical."[33] But another idiolect of Chartism declares, even in its latter moments: "In announcing [Wordsworth's] death, we must acknowledge that we are not impressed with any heavy sense of sorrow. . . . Unlike those Great Spirits [Burns, Byron, and Shelley], Wordsworth passes from amongst us unregretted by the great body of his country-men, who have no tears for the slave of Aristocracy and the pensioned parasite of Monarchy."[34]

Part of the radicalizing power of Romantic influence on the interventionist goal of Chartist poetry can be measured by comparison with the purely autodidactical poets, whose roots were in the laboring classes, but whose thematically more acceptable literary accomplishments gave them entry into the culture of higher social ranks. In his essay, "Our Uneducated Poets," Robert Southey, about ten years before the foundations of Chartism, was able to theorize poetry as social control. Writing of the servant-poet John Jones, Southey remarks: "This exercise of the mind [i.e., writing poetry], instead of rendering the individual discontented with his station, had conduced greatly to his happiness."[35] By midcentury, however, Charles Kingsley in his ameliorative Christian Socialism was quick to point to the social dangers of poetry, and he blames Shelley, as one who had done Chartist poets "most harm . . . and one can imagine how seducing [such a] model must be, to men struggling to utter their own complaints."[36] Kingsley anxiously responds as well to the powerful rebelliousness encoded in the nonchalance of Shelley as the radical aristocrat.

Queen Mab and "The Masque of Anarchy" were the poems most frequently reprinted and excerpted in Chartist poetry columns. But Shelley was also an important influence by way of his more meditative poetry. The point here is that it was not simply the communitarian and interventionist side of Romanticism that influenced Chartist poetics. Most obviously, much Chartist linking of intervention and poetry derives from and makes explicit Shelley's assertion in the *Defense of Poetry* that "the most unfailing herald, companion and follower of the awakening of a great people to work a beneficial change in opinion or institution, is Poetry." But Ernest Jones, Chartist poet and leader, also commented that "Shelley had the happy power of never swerving from a practical aim even in his most ideal productions."[37]

And many Chartist poems do in practice attempt to link meditative idealism to the interventionist goals of the movement, by transforming the individualist into a communitarian intention, within a poetic discourse that draws on the landscape poetic built in the period of sensibility and Romanticism, rather than the more public languages of antiquity, republicanism, or satire. W. J. Linton, for example, borrows the sweep of the "Ode to the West Wind" and the

imagery of Mont Blanc to produce a sublime language of the communitarian movement:

> Roll, roll, world-whelmingly! . . .
> It is accomplished!
> Melt us away!
> Gather ye silently!
> Even as the snow
> Buildeth the avalanche
> Gather ye, Now.[38]

Land, poetry, and nationhood are continually identified in the nineteenth-century arguments of class consciousness. We might recall
once again here the imperialist mandate of Palgrave's *Golden Treasury* and think also of Matthew Arnold's assertion that the glory of
British nationhood was best measured by its poetry.[39] Though
Arnold and Palgrave are in one sense collusive in the explicit separation of politics and poetry, they are nonetheless eager to have aesthetics serve politics. Chartist poetic theorists think quite differently: the glory of British poetry lies in the tradition of popular sovereignty that, they argue, has always been the central purpose of
English poetry. This assertion allows the Chartist poet to appropriate the landscape of personal meditation for the uses of the class, and
such a poetic claim simultaneously reaches back before Romantic
landscape atemporality to the tradition of topographical poetry that
used the visible remains of history in the landscape as a set of general moral markers, a tradition that had been virtually overgrown by
the detemporalizing and individualizing picturesque sensibility of
meditative poetry.[40] This is a counterhegemonic activity in that it
rolls back the bourgeois, picturesque dehistoricizing of landscape,
while preserving the metaphorical power of such naturalizations.
The Chartist poetic landscape is revisioned from the perspective of
the working class imagined as "the people": " 'Tis the voice of the
people I hear it on high, / It peals o'er the mountains—it soars to the
sky; / Through the wide fields of heather."[41] The links amongst pictured rurality, a people's tradition, and a poetry associated with that
tradition is articulated by the Chartist poet and orator Gerald
Massey in his "Our Land," with its refrain, "For our rare old land,
and our dear old land! / With it's memories bright and brave! . . .

Sing O! for the hour its sons shall band,—To free it of Despot and Slave." The forward movement of a democratic impulse is linked to the antiquity of the soil, which is in turn linked to the poetry inspired by that land, where (and I cite the same poem) "Freedom's faith fierce splendors caught, / From our grand old Milton's love."[42] In the face of the economic hardships accompanying industrialization, it was an easy poetic move to draw upon an idealized picture of rurality to build up the utopian vision of a possible future, and to modify that idealization by repeopling the landscape with a history of labor.

In some cases, Chartist poems invoke the landscape in order to disengage it from the proprietorship of the ruling class: "earth, its mines, its thousand streams, the mountain-cleaning waterfall,—God gave, not to a few, but all, / As common property." In others, the land is figured more brutally as the sanguinary battle site of class struggle: "There is blood on the earth, all wild and red / It cries to our God from the freeman's bed! / It will not fade or be washed away."[43]

Up to this point, I have been giving examples of the use of lyric forms by the Chartist movement that we are rather more used to considering as bourgeois forms. These examples provide some evidence for the claim that the double intention within the Romantic poetic—its individualism and its communitarian ends—was available to interventionist appropriation by Chartist poets. This evidence suggests the dialectical life of lyric forms with the dynamic of class relations.

There is, nonetheless, an evident problem within the retrospective perspective embedded in the use of the landscape as a central motif. For in communitarianism lay a contradictory model: the dream of a revolutionary working-class movement *and* the obstruction built into its very antiquated character since the categories of the "people's tradition," on the one hand, and the working class under capitalism, on the other, are not congruent. This does not mean, however, that Chartist literary activity was doomed by its anachronistic forms and motifs. Rather, it suggests that the contradictions within Chartism were produced in the context of class dynamics, whose outcomes were not enclosed in rhetoric, but through agency. Nonetheless, the often stubborn attachment to nativism within Chartist poetry does act as a political *encumbrance,* a mood that George Meredith captures ironically in "The Old Chartist" in the 1860s: "Whate'er I be, Old England is my dam! . . . I'm for the nation! / That's why you see me by the wayside here, / Returning home from transportation."[44]

And certainly from the perspective of those Chartists penally exiled from Britain because of their activities, the contours of the vanished landscape appeared attractive, generating a Chartist poetic linked to a geographical rather than temporal nostalgia. I want to push a bit further at the mobility of poetic form by focusing on one example of the romantically inflected Chartist poetic, examining a few poems written in the wake of the defeated Newport Uprising of November 4, 1839. For the transportation of its leader John Frost to Tasmania, or as it was then called, van Dieman's Land, was a rich source for topical Chartist poetry.[45]

In the aftermath of the unsuccessful insurrectionary event, once the Queen's Troops had occupied Newport and arrested the putative leaders William Jones, Zephaniah Williams, and John Frost, there was a national campaign to save these men from being hanged and quartered, the result of which was that they were shipped to the newly opened penal colony near Port Arthur, Tasmania.

A large number of John Frost transportation-exile poems appear in the national Chartist press, next to another popular topic of poems on the uprising, the death of a child-martyr, George Shell. A series of meditative sonnets, "Sonnets Devoted to Chartism," published throughout 1840 in the *Northern Star* by one of the Newport Chartists under the pseudonym of "Iota," linked the two heroes together in a sequence of landscape meditations, beginning "Once more I visit thee, sweet rural walk."[46]

The anecdote of George Shell was widely disseminated. This young Chartist had written a poignant letter to his parents the night before the attack, ending, "I shall see you soon; but if not, grieve not for me. I shall fall in a noble cause. My tools are at Mr. Cecil's, and likewise my clothes. Yours truly, George Shell."[47] The romanticized pathos of the Shell story has remained literarily affective into the twentieth century and is echoed in a 1934 Anglo-Communist boys' book, *Comrades for the Charter*, in which the certainty of defeat is juxtaposed to Chartist idealism, as the dying boy, with tears in his eyes, gasps, "We *are* winning, aren't we?"[48]

In Iota's sonnet beginning " 'Tis long since last I came this pleasant way"(Sonnet 1), Shell is given a elegiac context amidst a set of poems chiefly concerned with the landscape within which the Newport Uprising took place. "Iota" participates in the association of the continuity of land and poetic glory: "Some future bard shall sing thy triumph, Shell. . . . Thy patriot spirit hovering o'er the land / that gave thee birth" (Sonnet 2). The sequence of eight poems as a whole belong to the landscape meditative mode, presenting that vague ahistorical antiquity that picturesque landscape imparts to the rougher facts of historical confrontations. Iota excuses the "Patriot" Frost from insurrectionary intentions. No, he was searching for justice, "[Frost] wandered o'er this pleasant way, / With heart-felt ardor for his country's weal"(Sonnet 3). "His country" is the nation figured as a sweet rurality, and is meant to be sharply juxtaposed to the terrifying sublimity of the penal landscape in Australia where Frost serves his time even as Iota writes his sonnets.

John Watkins, a Chartist poet who wrote "Lines on Shell," also wrote a play about Frost, extracts of which were published in 1841 in the *Northern Star*.[49] Watkins's poetic version of Frost utters a soliloquy filled with the agony of separation from that land that, however needful of change, remains the natural possibility for futurity. In this Chartist vision of Tasmania, art asserts instead the descent of the human into a terrifying and unfathomable nature, a sublime of terror: "In such an irresponsive wilderness," Watkins writes, "Man is authoriz'd to torture man, / And so exults in his most savage power." Watkins implies that the British soil acts as a human break upon cruelty because it is, in accordance with a Romantic conception of the dialectic of nature and mind, *responsive*, and hence responsible.

To those in penal servitude in Australia and Tasmania, the picturing of British landscape *was* particularly sweet. In *The Fatal Shore*, Robert Hughes cites an early convict ballad of exile and rural loss. "It's oft-time when I slumber I have a pleasant dream: / With my pretty girl I've been roving down by a sparkling stream; / In England I've been roving, with her at my command, / But I wake broken-hearted upon Van Dieman's land."[50]

The Chartist inheritance from Romanticism sometimes takes the form of the inspiration of Romantic communitarianism, an image of which is, for example, Blake's fantasy of the multiple-personed

Giant Man Albion. At other times, Chartist poetry takes the form of Romanticism's meditative individualism, and it also at times super-imposes the two. An anonymous poem on Frost's transportation very literally occupies one of Moore's *Irish Melodies*,

He [Frost] recalls the scenes of his dear native land,
The hearts who to life had entwined him;
And the tears fall uncheck'd by one friendly hand
For the joys he has left behind him.[51]

This Chartist occupation of Moore's text foregrounds the political content of the relationship between the exiled class leader and the beauties of his native land by linking Frost's individual sorrow to a collective potentiality of transformation: "Nor soon shall the tears of his country be dried, / Nor for long shall its efforts desist." In Moore's earlier version, we are given rather a solitary female mourn-er who will soon join her Irish patriot lover in death and her song will be lost in the grave.[52]

The history of the image of Britain as it was appropriated by con-victs and settlers in Australia provides an interesting mirror to the domestic politics of the Romantic landscape. The reality of Tasmania offered a landscape of agonizing sublimity to the political convict that contrasted with a picturesque calmness of the dream of home; but for the military and the apparatus of the ruling class, the prison sublime was planted over with cuttings from the British Romantic picturesque.

George Thomas Blaney Boyes, a nineteenth-century colonial auditor and artist in Tasmania, attempted to cultivate both local gar-dening and painting, hoping thereby to "raise the standards of pub-lic taste" and stave off what he considered to be the encroaching bar-barity from the influence of convicts on the children of settlers in Tasmania. One result of that attempt is captured in L. A. Meredith's memoir: "The scenery around Newtown in the most beautiful I have seen on this side of the world—very much resembling that of the Cumberland Lakes. But the most English, and therefore the most beautiful things I saw here, were the hawthorn hedges. . . . It seemed like being on the right side of the earth again."[53] For the mil-itary settler family, this aesthetic was a mode of linkage back to Britain as well as a method of obscuring the presence of the penal world.

For the Chartist prisoner, on the other hand, the imagination of a picturesque Britain was an appropriative reply to the terror of prison life. The sublime of servitude was foregrounded by John Frost himself when he returned to Britain in the 1850s. He lectured throughout the United States and Britain on the topic "The Horrors of Convict Life," calling work in the Tasmanian mines the "hardest kind of labor that any man could endure" in an alien environment.[54] What is striking in Frost's lectures is that he draws no parallel between working-class servitude in Welsh mines and penal servitude in Tasmania. One senses that for the Chartist exile (and Frost remained a committed Chartist until his death), the affective power of a poetic picturesque landscape had displaced the realities of the southern coalfield of Wales. Oscillating between different intentions and interests, the poetic convention reveals its plasticity as we examine its life within class dynamics.

This example shows, from some varying points of view, the contradictory appropriation of a Romantic topic by activist-poets within a counterhegemonic group: the use of the landscape poetic was helpful to Chartist poets insofar as it, however marginally, linked the contemporary struggle to a communitarian past located in the countryside. It was helpful when it intersected with a vision of the future built on the premises of popular sovereignty, and when it was given poetic shape in images of the nation as belonging to a people defined as the universalizing of the working class. But the landscape poetic was a hindrance to the extent that it mystified the relationship between a rural past and a proletarianized present. And the irony of that rural myth becomes acutely palpable to us when we see it used to assuage homesickness among the transportees. The reality of the mines in Wales was not much less oppressive than those in Tasmania, though the nativist language offered a poetic terrain belonging not to the coalfield but to a generalized British Romantic landscape.

The foregoing examples give some presence to what we might call complementary contradictions within Romanticism and Chartism, which participate in the larger engagements between communitarian and individualist values in the early to mid-nineteenth century. Attending to this engagement within Chartism may help explain the liability of the movement to an assimilation into reformist trade unionism and the laborist ideology associated with it, and of its relation to what will become, in the imperialist period, working-class national chauvinism. For the repercussions of what I earlier described as a "nativist" hindrance are historically marked, since Chartism as a movement was dead by the 1850s. From the success of the ruling class came a thorough campaign of ruining the autonomous institutions of working-class culture, and of extending the Nation universalized as middle-class and imperialist. And from within the movement, the ideals of laborism came to replace those of Chartism. John Saville, the historian of British labor history, describes the ideology of laborism in this way: "Labourism was a theory and practice which recognized the possibilities of social change within existing society and which had no vision beyond existing society."[55]

The vision within the communitarian impulse, however, and the idea of poetry as a social intervention imbued with a collective visionary purpose, continues to inhabit less massive social movements and is beginning to have its history written. It finds its next significant chapters in the Socialist movement in the last decades of the nineteenth century. A look through the nineteenth and early twentieth centuries from the early political poems of Coleridge through the Romantic Anglo-Communism of W. H. Auden will continue the compelling story of the interweaving of Romantic and socialist, individualist and communitarian, purposes in British poetry. The newly recovered resources of forgotten poetry in ephemeral publications will enrich the materials that comprise the communitarian poetic tradition.

The outcome of this moment of the class struggle resulted in the defeat of Chartism and the emergence of laborism. Its repercussion in cultural life can be felt in the defeat of the communitarian impulse within Romantic lyric poetry. The poetry of individualism won that struggle, which is why our syllabi for nineteenth- and twentieth-century literature cherish meditative over interventionist poems. We continue to see communitarian poetics only in the poetic practice that emerges from culturally marginal political movements, developed in struggle in the United States, for example, by African-American, feminist, and Chicano activists. But when we return to the first half of the nineteenth century, we find a compelling presence of the idea of poetry as intervention instead of meditation.

Once we look at the history of poetry again in a dynamic way, in relation to its class interests, familiar terrain looks different to us. Learning to read Chartist poetry invites us to read the Romantics in a new way, to reexamine their theory and practice, looking for ways in which they present the constituents of identity in relation to community. For example, the making of the self as it appears in "On First Looking into Chapman's Homer," expands beyond a purely textual sense of identity when read through the matrix of the communitarian and individualist identity formation. Similarly, by paying closer attention to Coleridge's pantisocratic conception of community and his use of the Indic elements that generate the notion of "The One Life," we can recover those elements within his Romanticism that engage with a far more social self than we have thought before.

Finally, if we attend to and explore the counterhegemonic forces that attempt to seize and intervene in the apparently coherent ideology of aesthetic autonomy, we may be able to recover those aesthetic categories so lately demystified, and then often, and to my mind unfortunately, abandoned as so much ideological detritus. We will be better able then to recover a past culture and contribute to the making of a contemporary culture that is both interventionist and beautiful.

NOTES

1. See Gilmore's discussion in this volume.

2. This is the legacy of both the Althusserian and the Foucauldian strains in ideology theory.

3. See Raymond Williams, *Marxism and Literature* (Oxford: Oxford University Press, 1976). The rather naive use of "classism," ought to be distinguished from, though it is paradoxically empowered by, that theorized by Ernesto Laclau and Chantal Mouffe in *Hegemony and Socialist Strategy: Towards a Radical Democratic Politics* (London: Verso, 1985), 177: "Classism . . . is the idea that the working class represents the privileged agent in which the fundamental impulse of social change resides."

4.Gareth Stedman Jones, "Rethinking Chartism," in his *The Languages of Class: Studies in English Working Class History* (Cambridge: Cambridge University Press), 1983.

5. Ibid., 110.

6. Ibid., 92.

7. Ibid., 95.

8. Williams, *Marxism and Literature*, 121–27.

9. Ellen Meiksins Woods, *The Retreat from Class: A New "True" Socialism* (London: Verso, 1986), 111–12.

10. Ibid., 114.

11. Laclau and Mouffe, *Hegemony and Socialist Strategy*, 178.

12. Stedman Jones, "Rethinking Chartism," 99.

13. See, for example, Eileen Yeo and Stephen Yeo, eds., *Popular Culture and Class Conflict 1590–1914: Explorations in the History of Labour and Leisure* (Sussex: Harvester Press, 1981); Trygve R. Tholfsen, *Working Class Radicalism in Mid-Victorian England* (London: Croom Helm, 1976).

14. J. A. Epstein, "Feargus O'Connor and *The Northern Star*," *International Review of Social History* 21 (1976):69–80, 97.

15. *Northern Star*, July 13, 1839.

16. *Chartist Circular* no. 57, October 24, 1840.

17. For the debates of the 1960s, see *New Left Review*, nos. 16–18, with articles by Gabriel Pearson, David Craig, and Stanley Mitchell.

18. Jerome McGann, *The Romantic Ideology* (Chicago: University of Chicago Press, 1980); Marjorie Levinson, *Wordsworth's Great Period Poems* (Cambridge: Cambridge University Press, 1986); Louis Crompton, *Byron and Greek Love: Homphobia in Nineteenth-Century England* (London: Faber, 1985); Donna Landry, *The Muses of Resistance: Laboring-Class Women's Poetry in Britain, 1739–1796* (Cambridge: Cambridge University Press, 1990).

19. *Northern Star*, December 4, 1841.

20. John Watkins, *Northern Star*, April 29, 1842.

21. Alaistair MacIntyre, *After Virtue*, 2d ed. (South Bend, Ind.: Notre Dame University Press, 1982), 221.

22. Samuel Laycock, *Collected Works* (Oldham, 1900), 224–25.

23. See Y. V. Kovalev, "Introduction," in Y. V. Kovalev, ed., *An Anthology of Chartist Writing* (Moscow, 1956), and Phyllis Mary Ashraf, *Lehrmatieral zur Ausbildung von Diplomlehrern Englisch*, 2 vols. (East Berlin, 1978, 1979). Martha Vicinus, in *The Industrial Muse* (New York: Barnes and Noble, 1974), has an interesting chapter on Chartist poetry and fiction. In the different context of American poetry, Michael T. Gilmore has produced an important discussion of communal issues and poetry in a chapter of his forthcoming section in the *Cambridge History of American Literature*.

24. William Benbow, *Grand National Holiday and Congress of the Productive Classes etc.* (London, 1832), 4.

25. See Eileen Yeo, "Culture and Constraint in Working-Class Movements, 1830–1855," in Yeo and Yeo, eds., *Popular Culture and Class Conflict*, 155–86.

26. I borrow the phrase from Benedict Anderson, *Imagined Communities* (London: Verso, 1983).

27. Leon Trotsky, *Literature and Revolution* (Ann Arbor: University of Michigan Press, 1960), 186.

28. See E. J. Hobsbawm, *Nations and Nationalism Since 1790* (Cambridge: Cambridge University Press, 1990) for discussion of meeting up of traditional and revolutionary democratic nationalisms; Ralphael Samuel, ed., *Patriotism: The Making and Unmaking of British National Identity* (London: Routledge, 1989), 3 vols., for the domestic tradition of patriotism; and especially Hugh Cunningham, "The Language of Patriotism, 1750–1914," *History Workshop Journal* 12 (1981):8–33.

29. *Northern Star*, May 23, 1840.

30. G. S. R. Kitson-Clark, "The Romantic Element, 1830–1850," in J. H. Plumb, ed., *Studies in Social History: A Tribute to G. M. Trevelyan* (London: Longman's, 1955), 234; F. Engels, *The Condition of the Working Class in England* (New York: Macmillan, 1958), 242.

31. *Chartist Circular* no. 64, December 19, 1840.

32. Cited in Kovalev, ed., *Anthology of Chartist Writing*, 42.

33. *Chartist Circular* no. 45, August 1, 1840.

34. *Democratic Review*, May, 1850, 473.

35. Robert Southey, *Lives of Uneducated Poets* (London, 1836), 12.

36. Cited in Brian Maidment, *The Poorhouse Fugitives: Self-Taught Poets and Poetry in Victorian Britain* (Manchester: Carcanet Press, 1987), 305.

37. Cited in Paul Foot, *Red Shelley* (London: Bookmarks, 1984), 241.

38. W.J. Linton, "The Gathering of the People," *The English Republic* (1851):136–37, cited in Maidment, *The Poorhouse Fugitives*, 40.

39. Matthew Arnold, *English Writers and Irish Politics*, ed. R. H. Super (Ann Arbor: University of Michigan Press, 1973), 55.

40. See my *England's Ruins: Poetic Purpose and the National Landscape* (Oxford: Blackwell, 1990) for a fuller discussion of this issue.

41. *Northern Star*, December 4, 1841.

42. *Friend of the People*, December 21, 1850.

43. "The Patriot's Grave," *Northern Star*, September 9, 1843.

44. George Meredith, *The Poetical Works* (London: Constable, 1912), 117.

45. My main historical sources are: Ivor Wilks, *South Wales and the Rising of 1839: Class Struggle as Armed Struggle* (London: Croom Helm, 1984); David Williams, *John Frost: A Study in Chartism* (Cardiff: University of Wales Press, 1939); David J. V. Jones, *The Last Rising: The Newport Insurrrection of 1839* (Oxford: Clarendon Press, 1985).

46. Iota, "Sonnets Devoted to Chartism," *Northern Star*, May 9, June 27, August 1, August 15, 1840.

47. Shell letter reprinted in *Welsh Labour History* 1 (1970):8.

48. Robert Geoffrey Trease, *Comrades for the Charter* (London: Martin Lawrence, 1934), 142.

49. *Northern Star*, November 30, 1840; January 2, 1841.

50. Robert Hughes, *The Fatal Shore: A History of the Transportation of Convicts to Australia, 1787–1868* (London: Collins Harvill, 1987), 368.

51. J. H., "Frost," *Northern Star*, May 2, 1840.

52. Thomas Moore, *Irish Melodies* (London: Muse's Library, 1908), 104–5.

53. L. A. Meredith, *My Home in Tasmania during a Residence of Nine Years* (London, 1852); quoted in Bernard Smith, *European Vision and the South Pacific,*

1768–1850: A Study in the History of Art and Ideas (Oxford: Clarendon Press, 1960), 220.

54. John Frost, *The Horrors of Convict Life* (1857; rpt. Hobart: Sullivan's Cove, 1973), 27.

55. John Saville, *The Labour Movement in Britain: A Commentary* (London: Faber and Faber, 1988), 14.

8 THE SYNTAX OF CLASS IN ELIZABETH STUART PHELPS'S *THE SILENT PARTNER*

Amy Schrager Lang

When literature was a thing apart and organic wholeness the sign of its value, the task of the literary critic was, if not simple, at least clear. As we begin to restore literature to history, however, we confront the problem not only of the discursive complexity of texts and of scholarly colloquy but the problem of coherence itself. Even as we acknowledge the contingency of texts, the impulse toward unity has been displaced onto the critical endeavor. The system of homologies that characterize much of the new historical criticism in this sense restores the working conditions of the New Criticism: in lieu of organic unity within the literary text, a new coherence founded on a structural likeness between cultural and textual moments measures the complicity of the literary work in the culture of its production or, alternatively, its subversive potential.

But if the historical is to enter our considerations of literature—if, more particularly, ideologies of race, gender, and class are to be taken as organic to the problem of literary form—then we must acknowledge the ways in which the limits of literary language are exposed by history. These ideologies may be organic to literary form but they are not, by dint of that fact, able to be controlled by it. On the contrary, more often than not as we trace their effects we uncover the ways in which reigning assumptions about the operation of race, class, and gender compose mutually constitutive systems of associations that are both enabling and constraining. At these moments, the failure of literary form to produce coherence is of greatest formal interest for it is precisely here that the relationship between the historical and the literary becomes most visible. Likewise, it is here that the critics' desire to impose coherence becomes most problematic.

For in fiction, as in life, the constitution of social identity is accomplished by the conjunction of traits variously ascribed to nature or circumstance. Class, race, and gender appear not as self-sufficient categories, much less independent ones, but as vocabularies from which the language of identity is drawn. But these social vocabularies are not commensurate. The emphasis in recent criticism on the construction of gender and race has highlighted the fabrications of social description, unpacking from these categories the qualities that purportedly inhere in them by nature and leaving in its wake the ambiguities of essentialism. But differentials of wealth, power, and prestige are less readily accounted for. The very contingency of class, while it would seem to encourage such deconstruction, seems instead to foster its elision from considerations of nineteenth-century American fiction. This elision results at least in part from the essentialist claims made by the language of class in this period, claims that are necessarily strategic in nature and that depend upon ideologies of race and gender for their expression. This is not to say that gender and race stand as metaphors for class. On the contrary, imbued with the determinants of class, they both displace the vocabulary of class and provide the currency in which to negotiate class identity. In this sense, then, patterns of displacement are central to an investigation of the construction of social identity in the nineteenth-century novel and return us necessarily to history.

Some texts more than others, however, resist historical framing. I would like to offer as a case in point Elizabeth Stuart Phelps's *The Silent Partner*. Written in 1871 by the author of the enormously popular *The Gates Ajar*, *The Silent Partner* is a novel in which the politics of representation, the imperatives of the novel form, and the reformist intent of the author require radically different interpretive frames. Like a series of polarizing lenses, each of which reveals a different pattern in the same spectrum of light, no one historical frame is wholly adequate to the task of interpretation, for each obscures the pattern revealed by the one before. My intent in this essay is twofold. On the one hand, I want to explore the difficulty experienced by American writers of the mid-nineteenth century in writing about social class by way of an exemplary text and, more particularly, to examine the expression of this difficulty in the displacement of the language of class by that of gender. On the other hand, I want to suggest the difficulty of bringing history to bear on the representation of class in the novel.

The first of these tasks would seem to be a straightforward one. *The Silent Partner* is, after all, a novel about class written at a moment when, by almost any measure, class was the absorbing question of the day.[1] Its plot centers on the evolving relationship between Perley Kelso, a pampered millowner's daughter, and a ragged factory girl named Sip Garth. Following a brief and entirely accidental encounter in Boston, Perley and Sip meet again, three weeks later, in the milltown of Five Falls to which Perley has repaired after her father's sudden death in an industrial accident. Awakened from the moral and emotional stupor in which she has heretofore subsisted by Sip's appalling account of the conditions in the mill to which she has fallen heir, Perley informs her fiancé, the junior partner in the firm, of her decision to take an active role in the running of the mill. As her father's sole heir, she assumes that the position of partner is hers by right, only to learn that she commands nothing more than "a certain share of interest." Relegated to the position of silent partner, Perley devotes her time to improving the lot of the mill operatives.

The revelation of her powerlessness in the firm, however, pushes Perley to a realization of her larger powerlessness as a woman—a powerlessness mirrored in Sip, the conditions of whose life are dictated by the men who run the mills—and, thence, to a repudiation of marriage, which even when founded on love, appears to her as yet another silent partnership. Refused a partnership in the mill and rejecting the partnership of marriage, Perley enters into a partnership of another kind with Sip, who likewise rejects her male suitor. Their alliance, founded on sexual identity and reinforced by their common orphanhood, is characterized by an interdependence in which Sip lends Perley access to the tenements while Perley introduces Sip to the parlor. The partnership that liberates Perley from marriage and enables her benevolent activity on behalf of the working poor likewise gives Sip a voice. Forgoing her early aspirations to the music hall stage, Sip takes her place instead as a street preacher at the end of the novel.

Episodic in its construction, *The Silent Partner* moves the reader through a series of views of the life of labor as Perley learns how the other half lives. The working-class family is revealed in all its dysfunction. The blacklisted trade unionist, the factory operative turned partner, the striking mob and the heartless millowner "fil[ing] handcuffs . . . against the day when [his] 'hands' shall have gone hungry long enough"[2] all make their appearances, as do representatives of the oblivious upper class who profit by the labor of unseen workers.

Like the social reform fiction to which it alludes—Harriet Beecher Stowe's *Uncle Tom's Cabin* (1851) and Rebecca Harding Davis's *Life in the Iron Mills* (1861)—the mission of *The Silent Partner* is clear: the novel is designed to prompt "intelligent manufacturers" to expend their "Christian ingenuity" to ameliorate the lot of their employees. The origins of Phelps's fiction in the factual is, as it is in *Uncle Tom's Cabin*, crucial to the novel's purpose. "Every alarming sign and every painful statement," we are assured, is attested to by the reports of the Massachusetts Bureau of Statistics of Labor and by eyewitnesses to the conditions in the textile mills. Explicitly the story of an encounter between capital and labor, *The Silent Partner* sets "ease and toil . . . millions and mills" in sharp contrast. Viewed in this way, the argument of *The Silent Partner* is structured by the public debates of the 1870s over the relationship between capital and labor.

At the center of those debates was the doctrine of the harmony of interests of the classes that I have elsewhere argued found its literary analogue in antebellum domestic fiction.[3] Despite the hard realities of increased class segregation, the emergence of a class of permanent wage laborers, and spreading labor unrest after the Civil War, the proponents of this view—followers of the prominent political economist Henry C. Carey—insisted that labor and capital were joined in "partnership" by an "indissoluble bond." The impression of conflicting interests, they maintained, belied an underlying and wholly natural harmony. For how could the "true interests" of capital and labor be other than "identical" when, in a free market, the capitalist was only an avatar of the independent laborer. As one advocate of this view, Albert S. Bolles, author of *The Conflict Between Labor and Capital* (1876), pointed out, the gradations of society "shade off almost imperceptibly" one into the other. What is more, free individuals move freely between these imprecise categories. Economic mobility, which confounded the social taxonomer, proved the impossibility of opposed interests; the very categories on which such an interpretation of class relations depended had neither real nor rhetorical stability. Labor and capital, rightly regarded, were indistinguishable.

The doctrine of harmony and the ideology of free labor that characterized antebellum political theory still dominated the thinking of political economists after the Civil War. But by the 1870s an alternative model for the relation between capital and labor—what one historian has called "the heresy of opposed interests"[4]—was gaining force. The proponents of harmony exploited the distinction between free labor and chattel slavery in order to establish the ground for the identification of the independent worker with capital. They were answered by those who saw the spread of wage slavery, the aggression of a capitalist class, and the deprivations suffered by workers as the harbingers of "irrepressible conflict," as William H. Sylvis, president of the National Trade Unions, put it.

Adopting William Seward's ominous description of the impending Civil War, heretics like Sylvis asserted an analogy between wage slavery and chattel slavery wholly unassimilable to the harmony-of-interests model offered by the political theorists. The more radical of the trade unionists accused their opponents of ignoring the demands of justice and anticipated what they saw as the inevitable violent collision of classes by taking to the rhetorical field to demand recognition of the dire condition of labor and legislation to end the enslavement of the industrial worker. Other, more moderate, unionists were willing to concede an "identity," if not a harmony, of interests between employer and employed. But even they insisted that the "one dividing line" in American society fell between "the class that labors" and "the class that lives by others' labor."[5] However interdependent, capital and labor were not "partners in the same concern": one, after all, owned shares in the firm while the other did not.

Likewise Perley and Sip. *The Silent Partner* begins by directing our attention to the material circumstances that separate Phelps's female representatives of capital and labor. As she does elsewhere in her fiction, Phelps draws these distinctions with devastating specificity. Perley, "swathed to the brain" in comfort, is introduced on a rainy afternoon sitting in her father's library before a "cannel blaze" contemplating an evening at the opera (11). Her idleness is matched only by her familiarity. Beautiful, wealthy, indulged, and unconscious, Perley is scarcely in need of "the ceremony of an introduction" (9). She is, it seems, the very type of her class and sex: "twenty-three . . . the daughter of a gentleman manufacturer . . . a resident of Boston" (9), and engaged to marry her father's junior partner. An "indexical" person who never does "anything that is not worth watching," she nonetheless does almost nothing, though she is much observed. She exerts herself only to order her dinner and choose, with impeccable taste, the scent for her carriage. Despite the "passions of superfluous life" from which she intermittently suffers, Perley is as devoid of mental and emotional life as she is of physical occupation. Throughout the rainy afternoon, she has "found no occasion to dampen the sole of her delicate sandals" nor "found herself to be the possessor of . . . [a] thought since dinner" (11). Admired for her taste and beauty, Perley is engulfed to the point of drowning in luxury.

Perley, her beringed hands "folded . . . like sheets of rice paper" (13), stands at the greatest possible distance from the millhand Sip who is threatened by a deluge of a different kind. While Perley traces the "chromatic run" of the raindrops on her window with her idle hands, Sip does battle with the storm out on the street. En route to the opera, Perley follows with interest and amusement Sip's "manful struggles" with the wind, as she strikes "out with her hands as a boxer would" and pommels the wind "with her elbows and knees like a desperate prize-fighter" (17). Dressed in a dingy plaid dress, Sip is ragged and bitter and, as Perley discovers when, on a whim, she invites Sip to shelter in her newly scented carriage, smelly. She is also, and most importantly, unfeminine.

The distance across which Sip and Perley meet is marked, on one side, by Perley's decorative, genteel femininity and, on the other, by Sip's manful struggle. While rarely deployed in the context of an explicit consideration of the relations between labor and capital, these are nonetheless conventional representations. Perley is modeled on the wealthy and self-indulgent belle of antebellum domestic fiction who serves as the foil for the middle-class protagonist. So familiar is this model that we not only already know her, but we know from the moment of her introduction that we are to condemn her idleness and excess. Likewise, Sip conforms, morally if not physically, to an existing model of the honest working girl in whom the problems of industrial life were distilled for the stage. A "good girl," burdened with family obligations, entirely without resources, cast upon a heartless (male) world, she is the stock heroine of midcentury melodrama—"Bertha, the Sewing Machine Girl," "The Seamstress of New York," "Katy, the Hot Corn Girl," "The Beautiful Shoe Binder of Lynn," "Vanna, the Girl of the Factory."[6]

Class estrangement is, then, rendered from the start of *The Silent Partner* in a standing vocabulary of gender. But that vocabulary, deployed to distinguish the circumstances of millions and mills, functions to a different end in Phelps's novel. The excesses of the belle of domestic fiction serve to highlight the genteel virtues of the protagonist with whom she is paired while these same virtues in the honest working girl magically summon the economic resources that will allow for their full expression. At the outset of *The Silent Partner*, however, no such virtuous woman exists, and gender ideologies are deconstructed as an aspect of class. By this I mean not only that gender is expounded as a marker of class difference but that it is offered as the product of class position. Gender ideologies are presented as an intrinsic feature of class.

Forced to struggle "manfully" to earn her keep in a weaving room that pits the dehumanized "hand" against an all-too-human machine that "rage[s] . . . throws its arms about . . . shakes at the elbows and knees . . . writhes and roars (76)," Sip suffers under the arbitrary impositions of an industrial workplace where gender differences are routinely abrogated. In fact, one of the crimes of capital lies precisely in its willingness to sacrifice gender difference to the goals of production. Sip is dehumanized exactly to the extent that she is masculinized; what the mills take from her is her femininity.

Similarly, Perley's highly ornamental and utterly idle femininity—a femininity that leads men to relegate her to the position of a "lay figure"—is equally dehumanizing. Swaddled in luxury, lulled by admiration, she at first neither thinks nor feels, much less acts. Perley's membership in the capitalist class depends on her idle femininity as surely as Sip's identity as wage slave rests on her "masculinity." Phelps exposes the class origins of gender formations. And having thus deconstructed gender, she can represent Sip's struggles and Perley's indolence as equally unnatural, equally as signs of the distorting effects of industrial capitalism.

But the associative chain that defines social identity does not end with gender. Phelps's use of the vocabulary of gender to indicate the distance between Perley and Sip is reiterated in the vocabulary of race. Again and again, the reader's attention is drawn to Sip's "little brown face" (48, 54, 189, 294, 295, 300). She is one of a "great many muddy people" (17), people whom the sleet does not "wash . . . as fast as the mud splatter[s] them" (17). Accosting Perley at the opera house, with the elegant crowd breaking in "billows about her," Sip is as "black and warning as a hidden reef" (29). Lest we miss the point, Sip herself expounds her relation to blackness in the course of explaining why she will never marry: "I'll never bring children into this world to be factory children . . . never. I've heard tell of slaves before the war that wouldn't be fathers and mothers of children to be slaves like them. That's the way I feel . . . I'll never marry anybody" (287–88). Sip, of course, is white, not black—a "Yankee," like Perley with her Pilgrim forebears. Employed in the mills and not the fields, there is no natural explanation for her brown skin—in fact, the other weavers are identifiable by their bleached skin—but the historical explanation is not hard to find.

The sign of her enslavement, Sip's dark skin is made explicable by the debate over class harmony. The ideology of free labor obviates class conflict by imputing mobility to the wage laborer; the harmony of class interests is guaranteed, that is, by individual change over time. Conversely, the representation of the wage laborer as chattel fixes the class location of the individual; only social revolution or benevolent intervention on the part of the powerful can alter the condition of the wage slave. In *The Silent Partner*, economic mobility is rendered next to impossible. Even the novel's exemplary man,

Stephen Garrick, who has miraculously moved from a life of poverty in the mills to the partnership Perley covets, insists that his economic rise is anything but the common lot: "The odds are twenty to one when a poor man makes a throw in the world's play. . . . Twenty to one against poverty, always"(145).

As the blackening of Sip suggests, when a poor woman rolls the dice, the odds are even worse. Urged by Perley to find a new and less onerous form of employment, Sip resists, claiming that it is "too late" for her to leave the mills. "It's in the blood," she insists, pointing to the factory folk of England: "From father to child, from children to children's children,—a whole race of 'em at the looms"(198). Nonetheless, to indulge Perley, she tries the experiment. She goes out as a cook and burns the bread, attempts nursemaiding but is afraid she'll "shake" the baby when it cries. Before Perley will admit defeat, Sip has waited tables in a hotel, tried to market her sewing skill, clerked at a dry-goods counter, and attempted the printing trade—all with equal lack of success. Naturalized in her brown face, Sip's condition as mill operative is unalterable.

Yet Phelps's association of Sip with the newly freed slaves of the South does more than indicate her economic doom and, by extension, the necessity of her liberation. It also accentuates her difference from Perley and enables the novel to borrow moral force from the arguments against chattel slavery. Sip's renunciation of marriage and maternity—a form of liberation in the genteel Perley—recalls us to the tragic fates of the slave mothers in *Uncle Tom's Cabin*. But as it must be, the analogy between wage and chattel slavery is both tragic and threatening. The blackening of Sip carries with it the danger of irrepressible conflict: should the "intelligent manufacturers" fail to cede the justice of labor's demands, the "hand," the narrator assures us, will become the clenched fist of labor, striking "foolishly . . . madly . . . and desperately" (245). The ship of industry, Phelps threatens, will founder on the black reef that hides just below the surface of the "radiant sea" of society. The tragedy of the slave mother who refuses to bequeath her condition to her children is paired with the threat of slave rebellion, the rising of the drunken, mud-spattered mob of strikers among whom Perley, living up to her name, stands "so white and still" (251).

The representational scheme of *The Silent Partner* continually reinscribes the asymmetry of class. Sip's darkness, like Perley's pallor—her "rice paper" hands that have never worked and her white face—is one of a set of tightly associated terms that together constitute a socially recognizable identity. To be poor, to struggle "manfully," to be ragged and dirty, to have a brown face, to be dangerous—to be all of these things is to be a millgirl, is to be a slave, is to be black. And that, in turn, is to be poor, and so on. There is, as the narrator observes late in *The Silent Partner*, "a syntax in Sip's brown face and bent hands and poor dress and awkward motions" (295)—an orderly arrangement of parts without which Sip loses meaning. To parse the sentence, to account for the conjunction of attributes that lend Sip identity, would be to render that identity contingent. If the distinction between ease and toil, millions and mills, is to be sustained, the representational syntax that defines Sip's class position must be rendered so intrinsic as to elude explanation. Each element in the chain of associated terms can be deconstructed but not their conjunction, which, if the novel is to measure accurately the "fixed gulf of an irreparable lot" that divides Perley and Sip, must stand as inevitable.

Turning as it does on a series of dualities—black/white, masculine/feminine, slave/free, dirty/clean, poor/rich—the representational scheme of *The Silent Partner* would seem to bring us to an impasse. On the one hand, the requirements of realistic representation demand that the portraits of Perley and Sip mirror the estrangement of classes, measure the width of the gulf across which they meet. On the other hand, however, the imperatives of the novel form and the politics of reform alike require change over time. Perley and Sip cannot simply be left eyeing one another across the gulf. Something, to put it bluntly, has to happen. The problem is what: at one extreme, individual economic mobility is disallowed both by Phelps's representational scheme and by her commitment to what might be called moral realism. The responsibility of the artist is "to tell the truth about the world he lives in"[7] —both the truth according to the Massachusetts Bureau of Statistics of Labor and the truth of life as the artist sees it. In the case of *The Silent Partner* the "truth" is that the fate of the wage slave is sealed. But if realism precludes social mobility as an avenue of change, morality—the "personal equation," as Phelps would have it—equally precludes social revolution, envisaged in the novel as reckless, fruitless destruction. The representational scheme of *The Silent Partner*, in other words, exhausts the terms of the public discourse of class. Having measured unflinchingly the gulf that separates millions from mills, Phelps turns from the public to the private, from capital and labor to women and the middle class. This turn does not constitute a repudiation of class as the subject of *The Silent Partner* but rather its representation in a form more consonant with the requirements of the novel, the middle-class origins of which are disclosed by its emphasis on individual change.

To regard *The Silent Partner* as a novel about capital and labor, as the preface encourages us to do, forces us to see the limits of the historical frame with which we began. Like the sensational antebellum sketches of the urban rich and poor,[8] the picture drawn by political economists and labor unionists rendered a world split in two, divided between those who labor and those who live on the labor of others. What goes unacknowledged in such a model is the emerging middle class, whose sensibility nonetheless governs these representations. Unlike capital and labor—relations of production—the emerging middle class took its definition from a set of cultural preferences, values, and family strategies shaped by the canon of domesticity. As Stuart M. Blumin has argued, the American middle class is both pervasive and elusive—in fact, "elusive precisely because it is pervasive."[9] *As a class*, that is, the middle class eludes us because it identifies not a bounded position between a plebian working class and an aristocratic upper class but a pervasive cultural norm. That norm emerged as those domestic ideals taken to be resident in the private home and embodied in genteel white women translated themselves into a dominant set of values and styles of living. In this sense, as Blumin goes on, "middle-class formation was women's work."[10] Cutting across the bipartite division that purportedly rent American society, the middle class manifested itself in new styles and manners, in the forms of daily life, in the parlor and in the novel.

It is precisely in the parlor scene—in the account of an evening entertainment at Perley's "lofty, luxurious" Five Falls house—that we become conscious of the middle-class sensibility that shapes *The Silent Partner*. The purpose of the evening is to bring labor and capital face to face. Thirty mill workers, all "in decent clothes," are invited to join a cluster of Perley's well-heeled Boston friends for an evening of music, ice cream, and dramatic reading. The Scottish novelist Margaret Oliphant, reviewing *The Silent Partner* in 1871 for *Blackwood's Magazine*, commented acidly on Perley's "little tea parties": "A most truly American and young-lady-like way of making the spinners happy," she observed. The happiness of the spinners is not, however, the point of the scene, nor even its most American attribute. Rather, Perley's soiree is intended as a lesson in democratic equality. Take the spinners out of the mills; dress them in the "best suits" all Americans, regardless of station, manage to have; put them in a parlor, and they do not, Phelps claims, "leave a very different impression" from that left by any thirty people who might gather at a Boston musicale.

This claim is as remarkable in the context of Phelps's novel as it is commonplace in the culture of midcentury. It would seem not only to undo the work of representation, directed as that is toward elaborating class difference, but to suggest that class conflict can be averted by interclass sociability. "Going into Society," the chapter's title, seems at first glance to refer to the workers' attendance at the soiree, but this assumption is misguided. The title refers, instead, to leaving the precincts of wealth and privilege and going out into the world: going into society, not Society, as Perley makes clear. But this last meaning is undermined by the account of the soiree. While the condition of labor remains a nominal subject of discussion—Sip tells the assembled about the summer heat in the weaving room and ridicules a newspaper account of life in the Lorenzo mills, Bijah Mudge rants about the ten-hour day—the working-class characters are clearly admitted into the parlor on the condition that they mimic the dress and manners of their social betters. "Society" does not accomodate them; they conform to its requirements, thus enabling the successful encounter between rich and poor. Finding their better selves mirrored in the mill workers, the wealthy are recalled to virtue, their dominance intact. They need not confront the difference between themselves and the workers, much less the ugliness of the life of labor but only a new and improved version of themselves. For the common humanity of capital and labor is demonstrated by labor's appreciation of the things of capital—most especially their appreciation of the "superior" art produced by a leisured class of which they are not a part. The norms of dress and behavior to which the workers at the soiree conform, like the art that is applauded there by millions and mills alike, belongs to a class whose universality goes unquestioned in the novel.

Perley's soiree makes us acutely conscious of the middle-class narrator whose voice directs our responses in *The Silent Partner*. The bitterly ironic tone of the descriptions of the self-indulgent rich and the earnest sympathy expressed for the embattled poor serve to locate the narrator outside the very dualities of class that define Perley and Sip. Claiming the high moral ground of the disinterested observer, the narrator advances a set of ideals typically inscribed in the middle-class household—from simplicity of dress to a well-ordered domesticity to sincere Christian feeling and benevolent activity on behalf of the poor.

But if the voice and values of the narrator immediately identify her as middle class, they no less immediately identify her as female. And it is by means of the narrator's governing consciousness that change becomes possible in *The Silent Partner*. The gulf between labor and capital can be bridged after all, it seems, by universalizing middle-classness and naturalizing gender. Abandoning the divisive dualities that constitute social identity, Phelps finds the ground for a common identity in the femaleness—and by extension, the shared middle-class ethos—of her characters. From Phelps's point of view, this shift moves the problem of class out of history and into nature; the answer to the arbitrary impositions of class lies in the true nature of woman, a nature that seeks expression even in the face of the distortions of class. From our point of view, however, the novel moves out of the historical frame provided by the debate over capital and labor and into a different frame, this one shaped by the history of the elusive, pervasive, and feminized middle class.

Even as the portraits of Perley and Sip open the prospect of class conflict, the plot of *The Silent Partner*, governed as it is by the middle-class narrator, moves irresistably toward harmonizing the differences that separate them by rendering these differences inessential—or anyway inconsequential by comparison to their identity in nature. Economic enemies, Sip and Perley are nonetheless offered as natural allies; their friendship figures a harmony of interests more natural by virtue of its origin in gender and more transcendent in its moral claims than any founded on economic interest. Both are orphans, both refuse marriage, both struggle with the bequests of their fathers, however different. They are, moreover, allied in their efforts to improve the condition of labor, in their devotion to Sip's deformed sister Catty,[11] in their exclusion from power, in their disinterested Christianity. The gulf that separates Perley and Sip is to be bridged, then, by gender—which, I would propose, turns out to be an alternative rendering of class. Not simply as women, but as versions of the middle-class Christian woman, Perley and Sip are proposed as sisters. If the impossiblity of economic mobility precludes a harmony of interests in the workplace, gender stability can nonetheless assure a more perfect harmony in the "home," in the parlor and the heart alike.

In a clear effort to find in gender the answer to class inequality, Phelps reconfigures the opposition between capital and labor as an opposition between men and women. The oppression of labor is accomplished by men like Maverick Hayle, the junior partner, who blink at the violation of child-labor laws, ignore the condition of the tenements for which their employees pay them rent, "cannot afford . . . experiments in philanthropy" (135), and believe that "master and man meet on business grounds, and business grounds alone" (136). Motivated solely by profit, men control a world that silences Perley and Sip alike. Both the oppression of labor and the oppression of women are the doing of men. Women, on the contrary, insofar as they allow themselves (or are permitted) to feel, feel right. Moreover, the disinterested demands of conscience urged by feeling propel them out of the home and into the world to right the wrongs they find there. Unable by virtue of their sex to fully inhabit the positions to which they are remanded by the language of capital and labor, Perley and Sip are relocated in a position marked by sexual identity.

What I mean to suggest is that, faced with the recalcitrance of class, Phelps, like Stowe in *Uncle Tom's Cabin*, turns to a vision of women empowered by a disinterested morality to bring harmony to a world rent apart by the selfishness of men. Her feminist critique of woman's place in the scheme of production leads to the assertion of sexual identity as the basis for a new social order. Thus awakened to the condition of labor, Perley suffers an internal revolution that supplants the need for a social one. "I cannot tell you how the world has altered to me," she explains to her puzzled but, as always, admiring fiancé, "nor how I have altered to myself . . . these people seem to have been thrust upon my hands—as empty, idle, foolish hands, God knows, as ever he filled with an unsought gift" (139). Assuming her God-given responsibility for the mill workers, Perley renounces her life of leisure. Giving up her house in town, her place on "the best pew list in Five Falls," and her "duty to Society," she dedicates herself to building model tenements, establishing libraries for the edification of the working class, nursing the sick, and converting the wicked. She becomes, as she puts it, "not a reformer" but a "feeler"; she becomes, that is, a true woman.

This shift in the frame governing the novel is reflected in its structure. While the first half of the novel is taken up with vignettes exposing the injustices of wage slavery—Bub Mell's death in the machinery, the blacklisting of Bijah Mudge, the wickedness of Dib Docket, the temptation of Nynee Mell—the second half is replete with images of reconciliation and redemption. In an episode that the narrator, in one of her few intrusions into her story, insists she was "urged . . . to find a place for . . . although it is fragmentary and incomplete" (243), the workers at the Hayle and Kelso mill threaten to strike after their wages are reduced. "Uneasy like the rest" of the owners, Perley urges that the partners send the newly risen partner, Stephen Garrick, to the millyard to "tell them *why* we must reduce their wages" (248). This expedient proves unsuccessful and, at the workers' demand, Perley herself goes out to speak to them. With her, we are told, comes "a sudden tide of respectability": oaths, brickbats, and rum disappear, and silence falls on the crowd standing in the rain and mud. Reiterating Garrick's claims about the necessity of lowering wages, Perley arrests the strike before it has properly begun. "It's not that they so much disbelieved Mr. Garrick," we learn later from Sip, "but when *she* said she couldn't afford to pay 'em, they believed *that*" (252).

Standing "so quiet," "so white and still," with "a shining to her," Perley's mere presence apparently shames the workers into renouncing their decision to strike. The response of Reuben Mell is typical: "It's very perplexing to me. It doesn't mean a dollar's worth less of horses and carriages, and grand parties to the Company, such a trouble as this don't seem to. And it means *we* go without our breakfast so's the children sha'n't be hungry. . . . That's what reduction o' wages means to *us*. I don't understand the matter myself, but . . . I'll take the young leddy's word for it, this time" (253). Remarkably, given its beginning, the novel offers no answer to Mell's dilemma, nor does the narrator suggest that it in any way represents a challenge to Perley's anti-labor position. Instead, the "flood-tide" that had threatened Hayle and Kelso simply ebbs away, leaving behind its flotsam and jetsam, a "few small boys" and a drunk.

Marked off by the narrator's initial disclaimers and offered primarily as "indicative" of Perley's character, this incident is not, in the last analysis, about the strike at all but rather about the spiritual power to restore harmony invested in the true woman. Paradoxically, at the one moment in the novel when Perley speaks publicly—the only moment in which the silent partner genuinely gains a voice—we are told almost nothing of what she says. Moreover, what we are told we feel to be compromised. For despite Sip's admiration for her efforts, Perley's alliance with Sip is, we feel, betrayed by her efforts to put down the strike despite the apparent legitimacy of labor's position. Class interest, it would seem, outweighs gender solidarity. But then what Perley says is not the point, which lies, instead, in the power of her altogether female presence, as the title of the chapter suggests: "Maple Leaves" refers not to the strike at all but to the romantic scene that follows it in which Perley refuses to become Stephen Garrick's silent partner.

The problem of *The Silent Partner* is set by the rigid distinction of capital and labor, but the solution we are offered lies in the ethos of a middle class whose boundaries are permeable, whose ideals are universal, and whose representatives are female. Ultimately, the effort to displace class with gender and thus generate a solution to the problem of class fails. Not only is maternity, the conventional source of a female social ethos, complicated by the determined singleness of Phelps's characters,[12] but the changed and heightened social consciousness that enables the identification of women across class lines emerges as itself a prerogative of class.

Perley's character is defined by change—change of heart, of circumstances, of residence, of taste, of behavior—but Sip's fate remains sealed. In fact, while Perley's change of heart is enabled by her identification with Sip, who provides both motive and means for her benevolent activity, that same change of heart reinscribes the distance between the lady and the factory girl. For it is not, finally, her femaleness but her class status that frees Perley to reinvent herself—and to redirect the resources she commands by virtue of that status. Representing Perley's powerlessness as the result of her passive but voluntary acquiescence to the false demands made upon women by social position, Phelps can at least in part remedy Perley's largely spiritual predicament. Perley can, in other words, be turned from feminine to womanly just as her money can be turned from the purchase of sandalwood scent for her carriage to the purchase of beefsteak for starving workers.

But not so Sip. She is doomed to remain a factory worker by the very "syntax" that defines her. Despite Phelps's efforts to indicate that Sip, too, is a woman—and a woman like Perley—by invoking her self-sacrificing affection for her sister, her sensitive appreciation of the arts, her sexual continence and her Christian faith, Sip cannot be saved from the mills. As long as her "manful" struggle remains an economic necessity and remains, moreover, an essential feature of the novel's realism, her nature as woman must remain potential only. Just as Maverick's language of class—of masters and men—writes the working-class woman out of existence, so the language of middle-class feminism cannot render the particularity of life as a mill girl.[13]

Thus, at the novel's close when Sip is given her opportunity to speak publicly, we are recalled to the inevitability of her position, to her exclusion from the middle-class luxury that supports Perley's philanthropy and allows her to fulfill her sexual identity. Inspired by the mute Catty's "words"—words that turn out to be God's—Sip takes up street preaching and, like Perley in the strike scene, she discourages social action and urges instead reliance on Christ. But the importance of the final scene lies less in Sip's conventional resort to a feminine faith of the heart in the face of economic injustice than in Phelps's return to the original representational scheme of the novel.

Whereas Perley has become "healthy" and "happy," her "womanly, wonderful face . . . beg[ging] for nothing" but "opulent and warm" with "life brimming over at it" (302), Sip remains, for all her faith, poor and dark: "a little rough, brown girl," with "nothing saintly" about her (294); even in the throes of inspiration, her face is a "lighted, dark" one (300). Perley attends Sip's sermon, held "in a little court, a miserable place, breaking out like wart from one of the foulest alleys in Five Falls" (293), with Fly, the new Mrs. Maverick Hayle and the same companion who accompanies her to the opera in the opening scene of the novel. Sip is wholly unconscious of Perley's presence; in fact, the only person of whom we know her to be aware is Nynee Mell, now the wife of her one-time suitor. A weaver to the end, Sip addresses the mill operatives in a sermon founded on the conceit of weaving: the "tangle" of class in which "the great and the small . . . are all snarled" requires Christ for its "unwinding"; "Kings and congresses . . . [g]overnments and churches," Sip declaims, may "finger us over," but "we'll only snarl the more" (299).[14]

Class divisions, it would seem, are irremediable except by supernatural intervention, and class affiliation inescapable. No words pass between Sip and Perley in this final scene. Their partnership is effectively at an end: "I undertook to help her at the first," Perley explains to Fly, "but I was only *among* them at best; Sip is *of* them . . . so I left her to her work, and I keep to my own" (293). Leaving "the little preacher still speaking God's words" in the foul alley between shifts at the mill, the redeemed Perley, whose spiritual renovation turns out to be the raison d'être of the novel, returns to a life outside of class. Separated from the wage slave Sip by the "fixed gulf of an irreparable lot," Perley is likewise conscious of the "impassable gulf" that yawns between herself and "a pretty, good-natured little lady" like the wealthy and fashionable Fly. Just as she can be, at most, among the workers but not of them, so, too, she is now only among the rich. No longer the embodiment of idle capital and excluded from the life of labor, Perley exploits the resources of the first in the interest of the last. She marks the place of an ideal middle class.

NOTES

1. Stuart M. Blumin, among others, has argued that class was not only an absorbing question in this period but "[t]he most clearly defined social structure in American

history," and that "the deepest awareness among Americans of the classes that divided them, emerged in the years following the Civil War" (*The Emergence of the Middle Class* [New York: Cambridge University Press, 1989], 258).

2. Elizabeth Stuart Phelps, *The Silent Partner* (Old Westbury, N.Y.: Feminist Press, 1983), 245 (hereafter cited in the text by page number).

3. See my "Class and the Strategies of Sympathy" in Shirley Samuels, ed., *The Culture of Sentiment* (New York: Oxford University Press, 1992).

4. For a discussion of the public debate over class, see Martin J. Burke, "The Conundrum of Class: Public Discourse on the Social Order in America," Ph.D. dissertation, University of Michigan, 1987.

5. Quoted in ibid., 307.

6. For discussions of the working-girl melodrama as a popular literary form in this period, see Dorothy S. Pam, "Exploitation, Independence, and Solidarity: The Changing Role of American Working Women as Reflected in the Working-Girl Melodrama, 1870–1910," Ph.D. dissertation, New York University, 1980; Mary Noel, *Villains Galore: The Heyday of the Popular Story Weekly* (New York: Macmillan, 1954); Michael Denning, *Mechanic Accents: Dime Novels and Working-Class Culture in America* (New York: Verso, 1987).

7. Elizabeth Stuart Phelps, *Chapters from a Life* (Boston, 1896; rpt. New York: Arno, 1980), 259.

8. I have in mind here works like George G. Foster's *New York by Gas-Light*, James Dabney McCabe Jr.'s, *The Secrets of the Great City*, or Matthew Hale Smith's, *Sunshine and Shadow in New York.*

9. Blumin, *The Emergence of the Middle Class*, 2.

10. Ibid., 191.

11. For a discussion of the figure of Catty and the role of the disabled woman in mid-nineteenth-century reform fiction, see Rosemarie Thompson, "Aberrant Bodies: Cultural and Textual Representations of Physical Disability in Nineteenth- and Twentieth-Century America," Ph.D. dissertation, Brandeis University, 1992.

12. It is worth noting that, in her vulnerability and dependence, the deaf, dumb, and blind Catty occupies the space conventionally inhabited by the child in domestic fiction. The maternal impulses that prove womanhood and provide the ground for larger social engagement in that fiction find their place in an analogy that reflects relative social "ability": Perley, that is, "mothers" Sip, and Sip, in turn, "mothers" Catty.

13. Along similar lines, Christine Stansell observes that "the language of feminism subsumed working-class women's experience into categories of victimization, and the language of class struggle blurred the particularities of their lives into the unified interests of the working-class family" (*City of Women* [Chicago: University of Illinois Press, 1987], 220).

14. Given Phelps's fears of the "hand" that "strikes," it is impossible not to see that "snarl" as a double entendre—the "snarl" of the oppressed worker as well as the "snarl"—or tangle—of class.